Activating Your Ambition

Activating Your Ambition

A Guide to Coaching the Best Out
of Yourself and Others

Mike Hawkins

Brown Books Publishing Group
Dallas, Texas

Activating Your Ambition
A Guide to Coaching the Best Out of Yourself and Others
© 2009 Mike Hawkins

Manufactured in the United States of America.

For information, please contact:
Brown Books Publishing Group
16200 North Dallas Parkway, Suite 170
Dallas, Texas 75248
www.brownbooks.com
972-381-0009

A New Era in Publishing™

Hardbound ISBN-13: 978-1-934812-41-9
Hardbound ISBN-10: 1-934812-41-2
Paperback ISBN-13: 978-1-934812-42-6
Paperback ISBN-10: 1-934812-42-0

LCCN: 2009927176
1 2 3 4 5 6 7 8 9 10

Contents

Acknowledgments

I dedicate this book to my partners and clients—past, current, and future. I owe a great deal to the wonderful people I've worked with while coaching, training, and consulting. Through you, I learned many things about myself and about how to be a successful coach, trainer, and consultant.

I also dedicate this book to other coaches, trainers, and consultants who share the vision that we should take the greatest advantage of every learning opportunity. Many great seminars, books, workshops, and training programs are capable of delivering incredible results when the participants apply what they learn. We will not be satisfied until we have delivered a method that ensures that every participant benefits from the content to the fullest extent possible.

I thank my wife, Elizabeth, and children—Allison, Angela, Emily, Corbin, and Mitchell—for being patient with my limited availability for the better part of two years while I put this book together. I could not have written this book without your support, encouragement, and understanding.

I thank my editor, Latham Shinder, who had not only the ability, but also the courage to rework my manuscript. You personify the phrase *take action*. Your efforts made this book readable. I also thank Dr. Janet Harris, senior editor, and the rest of the staff at Brown Brooks Publishing Group for their help in making this book possible.

To you, the reader, I hope and pray that this book not only imparts knowledge but enables your self-development and sustained success.

Preface

Business leaders insist that commitment and hard work are the keys to moving up the corporate ladder. Motivational speakers maintain that the road to success depends on a positive attitude and a desire to succeed. Respected psychologists state that accepting yourself and having a healthy self-esteem are at the core of a satisfying life. Tenured professors assert that the key to success lies in embracing knowledge and following proven research. So who am I—a consultant, trainer, and executive coach—to teach anything about reaching peak performance, much less methods different from those of contemporary thought leaders? The answer lies in my experience, particularly with adversity and overcoming obstacles.

For over twenty-five years, I've worked to help organizations, individuals, and myself overcome difficulties and raise the bar of achievement. I've had a long tour of duty in the trenches of business-performance combat, and I've been in the field of self-improvement battling the competition of bad habits for many years. Rather than watching from the spectator stands or the comforts of the corner office, I've been engaged in the conflict. I've consistently taken on the assignments no one wanted, accepted the most complex projects, put myself at risk of probable failure, and engaged in the seemingly impossible. Now, after being part of many turnarounds, helping others achieve their goals and, to be sure, experiencing many disappointments, I've learned firsthand what it takes for people and organizations to succeed. *Activating Your Ambition* is the result of what I've learned in the process of failing and succeeding in helping people and organizations raise their level of performance.

I've learned that the people and groups of people who are most successful are action oriented. In particular, they continuously look for opportunities to improve. They have an "I can do better" attitude. But this attitude isn't the reason that everything they touch seems to turn to gold. The root of their success lies in what gives them this attitude—the confidence that comes with the abilities to develop and improve and to overcome hardship. Ability and confidence, combined with desire, are the primary drivers of success. Knowledge, hard work, and many other elements are important, but at the practical level where people turn what they want to do into how to do it, these qualities are insufficient. Success takes confidence and ability.

Many business initiatives, strategic plans, and training programs fail to deliver their potential. They are implemented as impersonal programs that ignore the people's ability to execute. Impersonal might work for installing a new piece of equipment, but where behavioral or organizational change is required, it's ineffective. Change happens best when it is made personal. Whether implementing a broad organizational initiative or coaching an individual, the key to success is helping people develop their own ability to overcome obstacles to change. Initiatives that are detached from enablers to behavioral change rarely achieve their intended results.

Activating Your Ambition outlines a systematic means to accomplishment. It is a mind-set and approach that helps you and those you influence to make sustainable improvements. It helps you overcome obstacles so you can reach new levels of achievement. It is a framework you can use over and over to develop new skills, stop bad habits, create new behaviors, and achieve new results. It is a set of practical principles that will give you everlasting insight into how to get out of your comfort zone and reach new levels of success that may have eluded you before.

The unique value of *Activating Your Ambition* is the how, not merely the what and the why, of self-improvement. It imparts not only the knowledge of what you need to do to make substantive and sustainable improvements in yourself and in the people around you but also how. It provides the means to seize the opportunity for improvement that lies within you, whether for work, home, pleasure, or any other area of life. The proven principles and insights packed into this book help you reach levels of performance that you might not have thought possible.

This book is for employees who want to perform better in their jobs and make more money. It is for executives who want to become better leaders. It is for parents who want to raise better children. It is for spouses who want to improve their marriages. It is for athletes who want to spend more time on the winner's podium. It is for anyone who wants to ensure that the books they read, the seminars they attend, the initiatives they conceive, the plans they create, or the coaching they receive is reliably applied and transformed into sustainable results. It is for anyone who wants to reliably turn their ambitions into realities.

Activating Your Ambition is written in three sections. Section one lays the foundation to building an ongoing self-improvement mind-set and defining the specific improvements that will best enable your life's goals and dreams. Section two covers the approach to achieving your ambitions through the application of eight proven principles. Each of the eight principles is covered in a separate chapter containing many techniques and examples, giving the how-to for each. Section three offers tools that support you in activating your ambition.

Part 1

Developing the Mind-set

1
Embrace Change

The only person who is educated is the one
who has learned how to learn and change.

–Carl Rogers

As an executive coach and management consultant, I am often
hired by organizations to help resolve people problems, operational
bottlenecks, and ineffective business practices. What executives
fundamentally want is to take themselves and their organizations to a
higher level of performance. They have implemented various business
initiatives, attended seminars, and read the latest business books, yet
remain unsatisfied. In different ways, they simply ask, "How do I take
my performance to the next level?" The answer is straightforward:
Turn your focus to enabling people. Tap into the unused potential
of your workforce. Get more out of your initiatives by giving more

attention to how people embrace and implement them. You may think you are in a product or service business, but you are actually in the people business. Until you deal with the people issues, your performance improvement is capped.

Their response is invariably something like, "What am I missing? Every initiative we pursue is supported with training and documentation. Each employee has stretch goals and performance targets against which they are measured. Everyone in the company works very hard with little downtime. Our processes are automated with new online systems. What else can I do to leverage my people resources?"

The missing component, I tell them, is a shift in mind-set. From the top to the bottom of the organization, it is an eagerness to implement your plans, strategies, training materials, and other initiatives. It is about improving execution and implementation by focusing on what enables people's determination and ability to execute. It is helping them learn new habits, unlearn old ones, and apply what they know. Fundamentally, it is using psychological enablers to change human behavior. It is a very different approach from one that focuses on the program, equipment, system, process, or facts and figures.

The missing component is the understanding of and remedy for what prevents people from sustainably changing their behavior. It is not merely a desire to achieve that people need, but also a desire and ability to improve. It is a mind-set that wants self-improvement.

Embedding a self-development approach into the fabric of the organization by connecting the initiative to the individual and focusing on the "how," not the "what," of what needs to be done reliably enables people to apply what they learn. When multiplied across the whole department or company, this approach creates an organizational capacity to embrace change and continuously improve.

Rarely do I get a call from a person confessing that he is not eager or able to improve. Even when someone admits that the problem is his, it is typically characterized as a lack of knowledge, skill, time, money, or other resource. The truth is that few individuals or organizations recognize that the root cause of their problem, and hence the core enabler to improving performance, is building the capacity to improve.

People who need to lose weight try diet after diet and remain overweight. Poor public speakers attend one presentation training program after another and still struggle with their presentation skills. Couples with marriage problems attend marriage-enrichment seminar after seminar and still struggle in their marriages. The problem with most people and organizations is not that they need to read another book, attend a different seminar, put in an additional layer of management, institute a new system, or hire more consultants to tell them what to do. They need to apply what they have learned and execute it. The help they need is in knowing how to make their desire and ambition a reality. They need an approach that reliably overcomes their self-limiting behavior and enables them to go forward. Whether trying to improve an organization, a family, a church, a government, or a single individual, the solution lies in people.

Because you are reading this book, you probably want to take your performance to a higher level. You may want to earn a higher salary. You may be looking to improve your relationships. You may need to overcome a bad habit. You may want to improve your fitness to enjoy a longer and healthier life. You may aspire to take your organization to a new level of performance. You may intend to develop a new skill that will help you earn a promotion or start your own business. You may work in an organization where the focus is exclusively on the numbers, while crippling people issues that no one wants to confront are hindering performance. The common enabler to success is overcoming the challenges to changing behavior.

This seemingly insurmountable task for some people and organizations is actually well within their reach. They just need to go about it differently from past, failed approaches. Making significant and sustainable improvements in their behaviors, attitudes, and competencies takes more than reading a book or attending a seminar. It takes the confidence and ability that come with having the right tools and the know-how to use them.

The tools of activating and sustaining self-improvement are eight timeless principles. Combined with the subject-matter expertise of a great book, seminar, colleague, or friend, they reliably enable self-development. They help people to overcome typical challenges to self-improvement confidently.

These are the eight principles that consistently lead to self-improvement:

1. Having an accurate awareness at the outset of an endeavor.
2. Securing an intrinsic motivation.
3. Confidently believing in the ability to achieve.
4. Building an actionable plan of incremental steps.
5. Freeing up the needed time and energy.
6. Initiating under the right circumstances.
7. Involving others.
8. Making new behaviors a normal routine.

You may wish that this list was shorter and simpler. Most of us want quick-fix solutions. With 24/7 online access and next-day shipping, immediate gratification is often a realistic expectation. However, reaching your peak potential isn't something someone else fulfills. Self-improvement isn't a spectator sport. To pursue self-improvement reliably requires preparation and application. It requires multiple tools. Leave any of the eight out, and you put yourself at a significant disadvantage. The Nobel Prize-winning physicist Albert Einstein once said, "Make everything as simple as possible, but not simpler." The good news is that the eight principles are simple to use and can be applied by anyone.

The principles of *Activating Your Ambition* enable the mind-set and actions you need to succeed in changing behavior, developing skill, or achieving whatever goal you have. The principles inform, motivate, and remove doubt. They break down your development into doable steps, create the time and energy needed to perform them, and optimize the timing of your development. They enlist the assistance of others. They ensure that your changed behavior becomes a normal part of who you are, not something that you do begrudgingly.

Application Readiness

Learning studies reveal that knowledge retention following a typical training seminar falls within days to between 10 percent and 90 percent of what was learned. The two primary variables impacting where in the range participants fall are what participants do before and after the seminar. If they are prepared to learn beforehand and quickly apply what they learn afterward, their retention soars. The content of the seminar matters less. In other words, what people do to get ready and how they apply their learning are more important to their success than the time and money spent during the learning event itself.

Despite this fact, individuals and organizations routinely pay large sums of money to attend a seminar with little preparation beforehand or thought given to how best to apply their learning afterward. In effect, people regularly agree to invest their time and money for as little as 10 percent of the potential return available.

University of Scranton psychology professor John Norcross conducted a study of two hundred New Year's resolution-making adults over a period of two years, which he summarized in the April 2002 *Journal of Clinical Psychology*. Those who succeeded in sticking to their resolutions employed a variety of strategies, such as avoiding temptation-laden situations and reinforcing good behavior with rewards. He also found that the single best predictor of New Year's resolution success was readiness to change—how prepared the person was to enter the action stage of behavior change.

In my own seminars, I've discovered that I can receive top scores in the evaluations completed by the participants at the day's end, but the scores have little correlation to how well they actually put their learning into practice. If the participants were not ready up front to change their behaviors, or they weren't ready to put their learning into practice immediately after the seminar, their retention and application results ended up low, even though they claimed they got a lot out of the seminar. As much effort as most trainers put into delivering a high-quality seminar, their content is not the primary predictor of participants' ability to put what they learn into practice. The participants' *application readiness* determines how well they will apply what they learn.

Application readiness means being properly prepared to put your development desires into action. It is having a plan to sustain your application until your improvement is complete. This involves what you do before, during, and after a learning event or self-improvement initiative. Being application ready is having techniques to help translate knowledge into practice and deal with what has to be unlearned as well as what has to be learned. This includes anticipating obstacles, having plans to circumvent them successfully, and understanding what you are willing and able to do differently from what you do now. It means being positioned to absorb knowledge and having the right mind-set and tools throughout your development initiative.

Application readiness is the foundation to an achievement mind-set. The mind-set and ability that come with being application ready enable you to achieve and improve with confidence. An achievement mind-set manifests in continuous striving to improve yourself. Your thoughts dwell on being better. You compete with your old self. You want to be better, and you know you can be. You don't have to set a new world record or be the best; you just have to be better than you are now. Whitney Young, a twentieth-century African-American civil rights leader, said it well: "The truth is that there is nothing noble in being superior to somebody else. The only real nobility is in being superior to your former self."

When you are not application ready, much of the learning and improvement potential available to you is left untapped. You may attend a great training seminar, read an insightful self-help book, hear wise advice, attend a useful counseling session, or participate in a valuable coaching program, yet unless you are application ready, you will retain very little of it. The enemies of self-improvement quickly move in and leave you with little return on your investment.

When people forego application readiness, they often initiate self-development with great zeal only to lose momentum quickly and eventually give up. They lack the techniques that make their self-improvement reliable and sustainable. They put too much focus on the result they want to attain and not enough on how to get that result.

If you agree that application readiness is critical to changing behavior and you were in charge of training for an organization, how would you allocate the budget? What percent would you allocate to the participant's preparation before the learning event? What percent would you allocate to the learning event? What percent would you allocate to the application of learning following the learning event? If you had two choices, would you split the budget 10-80-10 or 40-20-40?

In my experience, most people know the right answer is the latter, yet actual budgets are allocated more closely to the former. Your decision will undoubtedly vary depending on the nature of the learning, but two principles apply regardless. First, *all else being equal, invest in the foundation.* When you invest in preparation, everything that follows benefits. An investment in establishing the right mind-set pays dividends in the learning event as well as in the post-learning application. Second, *all else being equal, invest in overcoming the obstacles to retention and application.* When you overcome the obstacles that prevent the participants from applying what they learn, you effectively pave the way to their success. Having both an application mind-set and an unobstructed path to application following the learning event gives you the best return from your training budget.

It comes down to another simple principle—*you don't get results by focusing on results.* You get results by focusing on the actions that produce results. You don't hunt for a trophy deer, for instance, by setting your gun's sights on the buck's rack. Rather, you aim at the buck. You don't make your sales quota by concentrating on the quota. You hit your sales quota by getting on the phone or out of the office and spending time with customers. If you want to change your behavior, you must focus on that which enables you to change your behavior.

You don't get results by focusing on results. You get results by focusing on those actions that produce results.

It doesn't matter what result you are pursuing. Becoming application ready is success neutral, and how you define success doesn't matter. Whether your ambition is to become a chief executive officer, a Nobel Prize winner, a great parent, an outstanding chef, or a more supportive spouse doesn't matter. Being application ready positions you to apply more effectively the knowledge you learn during your development process and to stay focused on your goal until you achieve it. Application readiness is the enabler to self-development.

Change Is Not Optional

Most of you are reading this book before engaging in a self-improvement program or attending a training program. The eight principles of *Activating Your Ambition* are specifically designed to help you get the most out of your endeavor. You are embarking on a growth initiative, and this book is about preparing for growth and for change. Whenever there is growth, change will be part of it.

Change is a simple concept, but incredibly difficult to carry out. As Peter Senge, organizational learning expert and author of *The Fifth Discipline,* says, "People don't resist change. They resist being changed." Change requires that you stop doing something comfortable you may enjoy and start doing something uncomfortable that you may not enjoy, at least initially. Change requires that you make an investment in something now that won't bring a return until some point in the distant future. Change is hard, and therefore preparation is essential.

Preparing for self-improvement is no different from doing anything else that is really important. You wouldn't expect to give a good speech without preparing for it, achieve a good outcome in a negotiation without preparing for it, or have a successful party without preparing for it. You wouldn't compete in a sporting event without preparation. Changing yourself is no different.

While preparing for change gives you the best odds of effectively dealing with it, preparation is optional. Your change, however, is not. Change is inevitable. It happens whether you prepare for it or not. People who don't want to change end up changing anyway; it's just that their change is dictated by someone or something else. People who don't develop and grow in their profession fall behind the others who do. They lose their relevance. People who don't grow in their relationships become farther apart. Both are changes, albeit negative ones. Nothing stays the same. Ultimately, people who don't develop find themselves without a job, divorced, or missing out on something else. Change is unavoidable. You change either to stay ahead or to catch up.

Change is unavoidable. You change either to stay ahead or to catch up.

So if change is unavoidable, why do so many choose not to embrace it? Why do people let others dictate their change? Why don't they take charge and change on their terms, not on someone else's? The reason is that people lose their ambition. They quit focusing on the possibilities of better and get comfortable with the same. Or, more accurately, they get comfortable with the perception of being the same. As Will Rogers, the American cowboy and humorist once said, "Even if you're on the right track, you'll get run over if you just sit there." Standing still in your personal or professional life means the world will pass you by. Instead of being on the road to success, you are on the road to obsolescence.

Authors and leadership researchers John H. Zenger and Joseph Folkman conducted research on the competencies of great leaders. According to their research, one of the key skills that distinguish great leaders is their focus on continuous improvement. Mediocre leaders reach a position or stature and stop learning. They decide that learning is a chore designated to junior executives. They couldn't be more wrong. Exceptional leaders understand the importance of continuous self-improvement and seek out their untapped capabilities. They continue to change, grow, and develop.

Many people settle for mediocrity. They get in a comfortable position and put their lives on autopilot, sleepwalking through all the opportunity and excitement that surrounds them. As a result, they fall behind. Time works against them. They discover ultimately that they have no choice, and change becomes more painful than it would have been had they taken the initiative and embraced it earlier. If you don't want this to happen to you, don't wait until you have to react; live intentionally. Take charge of your destiny and be proactive. Put time on your side. Choose to improve and develop on your own terms. As retired General and U.S. Army Chief of Staff Eric Shinseki said, "If you don't like change, you're going to like irrelevance even less."

A Self-Development Mind-set

I put myself through college working as a junior engineer, and I continued working as an engineer for a year after graduating. During my five years in engineering, my primary value to my employer was my engineering-domain knowledge. I was good at engineering because I applied my college learning in real time on the job. My learning retention was very high. As a result, I garnered a reputation as an expert in my field. I took great pride in my knowledge of formulas, material properties, and other technical aspects of my work. When confronted with a complex engineering problem, I kicked into analytical mode, breaking the problem down into solvable chunks and applying my technical expertise. My engineering expertise was my source of confidence.

Following my stint as an engineer, I took a sales position with IBM. During my first five years as a salesman with IBM, my focus changed from technical expertise to sales expertise. I learned new skills. I focused on listening and on understanding how people made decisions, and I honed my ability to influence others. I developed new skills related to my new domain, which became my source of confidence and value. Following a successful period in sales, I was promoted into management. In ten years in various management positions at IBM, my focus shifted from sales skills to management skills. My source of confidence and value shifted again, but it was still rooted in my skills.

I left IBM and joined the senior management team at Scient, a fast-growing company in the dot-com era. First as managing director and then as global general manager, I again focused on developing new skills. My source of confidence and value was based on my ability to communicate, influence and manage the needs of our business. Throughout all three of my career experiences, I believed success resulted from developing the right knowledge and skills. I was partly right.

My knowledge and skills did make me valuable to my employers, but I've since realized that my knowledge and skills were the result, not the cause. The real reason for my success was my self-development mind-set. With a focus on continuous improvement, I could have been successful in the medical industry, the media industry, or just about anything I chose to pursue. The key to my success was and still is my desire and ability to learn, retain, apply, and repeat. That is what enables me to remain competent and knowledgeable, and it is the basis of the principles of *Activating Your Ambition*.

A self-development mind-set manifests itself in several ways. You gravitate toward people and activities that provide learning and self-improvement. You constantly look for opportunities to develop. When presented with an opportunity to learn, you engage it. You sign up for relevant seminars or programs. In the presence of someone wiser or older, you seek counsel. When a good nonfiction book is recommended to you, you read it. Given the choice between an easy assignment with little learning benefit and a more challenging one, you accept the harder assignment.

The root cause to success is having a self-development mind-set and the confidence that goes with knowing you are continuously improving.

The root cause to success isn't learning a skill, obtaining a certain level of knowledge, or having innate talent. It is having a self-development mind-set and the confidence that goes with knowing you are continuously improving.

Choosing to Succeed

The ability to develop and improve yourself continuously starts with choice. This sounds obvious, even simpleminded, but many people choose not to develop. They refuse to decide, which is a decision; they decide to rest on their prior accomplishments, or they decide to let an adversity overpower their better judgment. In this last case, they recognize a need to improve but decide to let their adversity thwart their plans. They have the desire, but they let their busy schedules, lack of resources, inconveniences, or whatever pre-empt taking action.

People who don't improve often blame a lack of time and resources. When they explain their lack of development, they sound as if they are not in control. They are so busy that they don't think about why they are so busy, much less do anything about it. They work in a demanding job, take part in family activities, attend social functions, spend time in a hobby, or perform volunteer work, and they already feel overwhelmed without taking on anything else. In their busyness, they don't see choosing to develop as a viable option. Yet their lack of time and resources is a self-created condition, often caused by their lack of development, that can be overcome—if they make the time to do something about it.

A lack of time or resources is a result of choice. Your circumstance may have resulted from a situation you did not directly control, but it remains there because you have not chosen to change it.

What you do, who you are, and what you plan to pursue start with your choices. You still have to know the "how-to's" of dealing with obstacles like a lack of time, but that is what this book is designed to help you with. The first step is to choose to move toward your goals rather than away from them.

Some activities don't seem like choices because they have become routines; the element of choice has faded into the back-ground. Some routines become obligatory; you do what you do because you've always done it *and* because others depend on you to keep doing it. This feeling of obligation can be strong, but it's just that—a feeling. Your actions are choices, whether you make them out of rational thinking, feeling, habit, obligation, guilt, avoidance, or whatever. You can choose to interfere with your routine, or to create new routines.

If you choose not to pursue your dreams, you'll still be part of a dream—only it will be someone else's.

Don't underestimate the importance of choice. If you choose not to pursue your dreams, you'll still be part of a dream—only it will be someone else's. You are in effect still choosing your future condition. Until you choose to pursue your own potential, you will be helping someone else achieve theirs and it will be on their terms.

Life Is a Series of Choices

In my youth, from fourteen to nineteen, I raced motorcycles. By eighteen, I consistently won races in the amateur ranks and faced a decision: move up into the professional class or let motorcycle racing fade into a hobby. I chose the latter. Instead of racing, I invested my time in my education. Was it the right decision? I'll never know for certain. I do know that my college education paid huge dividends early in my career, and I consider it one of my biggest achievements in life.

University life wasn't easy for me either. It, too, required many choices and trade-offs. I had to work while I attended school. I struggled at times to pay for tuition, books, and other fees. I borrowed money when I had to. I worked nights when needed. I turned down invitations to events and parties with my friends in order to study. I studied my coursework for long hours and got by with three or four hours of sleep on many weeknights. This was my regimen for four and a half years. In the end, the dedication paid off. Despite the schedule, I graduated with mostly As, Bs, and (to my disappointment) a couple of Cs.

So why did I choose an education? Why did I stick with it? Did I have more natural skills as a mechanical engineering student than a motorcycle racer? No. In fact, I had less. Did I have more desire to enter university life? I did not. I loved motorcycle racing with a passion. Was the path to success made easier by choosing an education? Definitely not. I had countless distractions and difficulties to overcome. So why did I pursue an education and turn my back on a career as a professional athlete? I did so because an education offered the biggest opportunity for self-improvement. A college education offered learning that I could leverage the rest of my life. Sure, the other fork in the road might have offered more enjoyment and more immediate income, but it would have come at the cost of missed learning and development. Fundamentally, I decided that the near-term investment was worth the longer-term benefits.

My choice to go to college was one of many self-development choices I've made that have created the life I currently enjoy. Your life, too, is the result of your choices. A good life comes about from living intentionally. It is the result of deciding to take action and stick with it. It is the outcome of deciding correctly when to stay the course and when to change. Good decisions are critical to your career, your life, and your well-being.

Dr. Eric Allenbaugh, author and leadership consultant, makes it very simple. He says every choice we make either moves us closer to or farther away from something. Whether we say yes or no determines which direction we go. Our choices determine whether we move toward or away from our goals. Choices have lifelong ramifications.

Self-improvement may seem like just one more of the many decisions you make. It may get added to or removed from your to-do list as easily as going to the grocery store or seeing an auto mechanic. But in reality, self-development has more lifelong consequences than almost any other decision you can make. Your future will be either a better place or a worse one depending on the self-improvement choices you make today. Life is a series of choices, and the ones related to your self-development are among the most important.

Acceptance Versus Improvement

If you want to become a better public speaker, musician, painter, athlete, parent, spouse, or leader, you can. You have the potential. It is well within your grasp. You don't have to be content with "I'm good enough." Be careful not to misinterpret the pop-psychology mantra, "Accept yourself for what you are." You can accept what you are and still aspire to be better. You don't have to follow mediocre norms; instead, you can pursue excellence. You have a unique combination of talents, capabilities, and ambitions, so why not take advantage of them?

If this sounds like positive thinking, it is. It isn't, however, foolish thinking. If you want to learn, grow, and change, you can. Of course it takes some work. You have to invest time and energy in the near term for something from which you won't see benefit for the longer term. But that is how you succeed. You are not born great at anything. As American poet Ralph Waldo Emerson said, "All great speakers were bad public speakers first." The same can be said for any skill, behavior, or attitude. All are developed. Great musicians start out as bad musicians. Great leaders start out as poor leaders. Great salespeople start out as inferior salespeople.

You may deal with special circumstances that give you more than the average challenge. You may have more than your fair share of adversity. You may be surrounded by unsupportive people or a victim of abuse. You may be bankrupt or unemployed. Whatever it is, you can overcome it. People even overcome serious physical and mental limitations to achieve their ambitions.

Motivational speaker Nick Vujicic was born without arms and legs. Nonetheless, he earned two college degrees, types forty-three words per minute with one foot, writes, and preaches to crowds of thousands all across the world. Former United States President Ronald Reagan, known as "the great communicator," grew up an introvert. British Prime Minister Winston Churchill did poorly in school and had to overcome a speech impediment. Lance Armstrong, winner of seven Tour de France cycling races, overcame life-threatening cancer.

Virtually anyone who has been successful started with a dream and pursued it despite initial self-doubt, physical limitations, and other adversities.

Evangelist Billy Graham overcame a fear of public speaking and subsequently preached in person to more people around the world than anyone. Marie Curie, physicist, chemist, and winner of two Nobel Prizes, persevered despite no funding and poor laboratory conditions. Pablo Picasso overcame severe poverty to become one of the most admired artists in the world. Ludwig van Beethoven overcame poor hearing and ultimately deafness to become one of the greatest composers in the history of music. Virtually anyone who has been successful started with a dream and pursued it despite initial self-doubt, physical limitations, and other adversities.

Most successful people look back and view their extreme hardships as a godsend that inspired them to higher levels of accomplishment. Had they lacked the hardship, they wouldn't have striven so diligently. The best public speakers are not those who have never had to work at their public speaking. The best are those who had to work diligently to develop their speaking skills. The same is true for the best athletes, musicians, salespeople, engineers, leaders, parents, and so on. Where you've been your worst, you can be your best.

All this is to say that you and I can accomplish our ambitions if we want to. You don't have to be the smartest, strongest, or most driven individual in your field to actualize your ambitions. You are a magnificent and unique blend of experiences, innate talents, knowledge, physical attributes, and values. Accept yourself for what you are at this point in your life, but accept, too, that you can improve. Acceptance and improvement are not mutually exclusive; they coexist. It's not only okay to strive to be better; it is critical to your success.

Real Change Is Possible

Some suggest that people can't change. The evidence, they say, is all around us. More people fail at diets, exercise programs, anger management, and marriage counseling than succeed. More people fail to quit smoking, stop procrastinating, and overcome disorganization than succeed. Undeniably, these changes aren't easy, especially given the way some people go about them, but they are not impossible. If change is impossible, then people who get fired for incompetence and people who go to jail do so for reasons they can't control. If change is impossible, how do those who do quit smoking and get into better physical condition do it?

We all agree that change can be difficult to make and sustain, but to suggest that people can't change simply isn't true. If people can't change, the entire education system is a sham. Why would anyone bother going to school? Why would we bother to ask for or give advice? Why is there a multibillion dollar training industry? How could average people with average grades and average abilities in their youth become such successful entrepreneurs, corporate executives, athletes, preachers, farmers, scientists, engineers, musicians, artists, doctors, psychologists, and architects?

Obviously people can change because they do.

Obviously people can change because they do. Apprentices become supervisors. Managers become CEOs. Junior salespeople become great salespeople. College graduates become professional engineers. People grow and develop, either a little or a lot, year after year, if they choose to do so.

I consider myself the embodiment of change and growth. As a matter of fact, my own self-development journey makes me uniquely qualified to write this book. I've not just read about, taught, or researched change; I've lived it. I've changed and grown so much over my lifetime that I sometimes think I've surely exceeded my potential. My family and longtime friends, too, are shocked to see just how much I have changed.

The change naysayers would say that just because I wasn't an executive coach earlier in my career doesn't mean I've changed. They would argue that I was always a coach, deep inside; it was just covered up for forty years by youthful ignorance. I don't think so. I'm an executive coach because of my ambition and ability to improve continuously.

To make my ambitions a reality, I learned to leverage the eight principles of *Activating Your Ambition* which you, too, are learning as you read this book. These eight principles don't only make ambitions realistic; they enable them within your ordinary capabilities. They make change easier. Put into practice, they enable you to overcome the obstacles that derail so many self-improvement efforts. In my case, despite a shortage of money, knowledge, and other resources, these principles enabled me to put myself through college, reinvent my career, replace a plethora of bad habits with good ones, change my character in positive ways, overcome a debilitating phobia, start up two companies, establish my faith, build my dream home, lose weight, improve my relationships, and now help others become successful. If anyone ever tells you that change isn't possible, suggest that they review the facts. It might be that they've just been going about it in the wrong way.

Strengths Versus Weaknesses

In my leadership development work, I've coached hundreds of managers and executives. I've worked with gifted speakers and tongue-tied managers. I've worked with visionaries and die-hard pragmatists, with detail-oriented realists and broad-stroke futurists. Despite their differences, they all reached a similar level of success. They found environments where their abilities were valued and received a commensurate level of success in return. There was good alignment between their strengths and their roles. Either their shortcomings were overlooked, or they were not a significant issue for the responsibilities they held.

Their limitations, however, did become an issue when they wanted to take their performance to a higher level. They discovered they couldn't get by with only short-term thinking. They realized that in order to broaden their responsibility, they couldn't stay involved in all the minutiae that occurred around them. They found that their technical knowledge wasn't as valuable as the people skills they lacked. To take on more responsibility or reach a higher level of performance, they discovered that they could no longer simply use their strengths. They had to develop in new ways. They needed new skills. They had to overcome the limitations that could not be overlooked.

They also discovered that the strengths on which they relied were, in fact, a limitation. The source of value they had leveraged in the past had become a liability. One executive I worked with was a consummate comedian with a quip for every situation. When he was a first-line manager, his team loved his comic relief. Yet when he was promoted to run his division, his peer group was more senior, and the jokes made him come across as professionally immature.

Another executive with whom I worked had a deep expertise in his industry and the services his company offered. His strength was his domain expertise. When he was promoted onto his company's senior leadership team, his focus on the details prevented him from seeing the big picture. He struggled to grasp the company's vision and to articulate it at a level that everyone could relate to.

In case after case, people's strengths at some point become their weaknesses; strengths in one situation become liabilities in another. It is true for any personal characteristic. Creativity is a clear strength for brainstorming new ideas and an asset for advertisers, fashion designers, and artists, but it can be a liability for assembly line workers or for anyone needing to make a quick decision. Patience is a strength for students slogging through difficult coursework but a weakness when immediate action is required. Extroversion is a strength for retail salespeople but a weakness in negotiations where periods of silence are used to gain concessions. Strengths and weaknesses are situational: a strength can be a weakness and a weakness a strength.

Some suggest you should focus only on your strengths. Others say you should only focus on your weaknesses. I say neither is right. To say that you should focus on your strengths or your weaknesses without context makes little sense. Without context, you can't accurately separate the two. In fact, if your reliance on a strength is preventing your self-improvement in another area, your strength is more a weakness. In my experience, you need to be careful about overly relying on any strength or making too large an issue out of any weakness.

Nature Versus Nurture

Talking with people about their strengths and weaknesses often brings up the question of the source of each. Are our strengths and weaknesses developed over time, that is, by experience and nurturing, or are they genetic and natural? The thinking goes that if our abilities and limitations are primarily a result of genetic predispositions, no amount of development could overcome our intrinsic limitations. It would be impossible, and therefore foolish, to invest time, money, and energy into something that doesn't have a legitimate chance. The opposing idea is that if our strengths are primarily a result of our learning, experiences, and nurturing, we can develop new behaviors and overcome our limitations.

This is the classic nature-versus-nurture debate. Do our innate qualities (nature) or our personal experiences (nurture) determine our skills and behavioral traits? If the answer is "nature," then trying to develop in our areas of weakness is all but impossible. It would require a huge investment of time and energy with little return. While some change might be possible, it would be severely constrained by our natural abilities and natural limitations.

This debate has many implications. Is it unrealistic to expect that anyone can be a doctor, long-distance runner, or piano player? Can anyone lose weight, stay on an exercise program, or become a great parent? Can anyone choose to be creative, learn to be a better speaker, or transform into a great leader? Dr. Martin E. P. Seligman, a professor of psychology at the University of Pennsylvania and past president of the American Psychological Association, is considered an expert on what people can and can't change. In his research, described in his book *What You Can Change . . . and What You Can't*, he finds that people absolutely can make lasting change through various techniques such as cognitive therapy (changing the way people think), interpersonal therapy (focusing on social relationships), meditation, and behavior therapy (exposure to physical situations). These techniques have been particularly effective in overcoming anxieties, panic disorders, phobias, obsessions, pessimism, depression, and anger. If these conditions can be changed, then surely people can learn new skills, develop new styles, and change other behaviors.

That doesn't mean change isn't easier for some than others. Overcoming addictive behaviors can be easier for people with higher levels of conscientiousness. Learning social skills is easier for extroverts. Developing organizing skills is easier for those who value efficiency. Being more positive comes more easily to people who believe that their circumstances are under their control. There is no denying that people with personality traits that support their development goals find their development easier. But easier isn't always better, and harder isn't the same as impossible.

In development areas that seem completely foreign to you and at odds with your existing personality traits, be careful about your assumptions. If you say, "I'm not a planner," you are shortchanging yourself. You may not be a good planner *right now*, but that may have little to do with your natural ability. It may be a matter of never having learned, needed, or applied fundamental planning skills. In fact, planning could be a natural ability you've never exposed.

Had you asked me a few years ago if I thought I would be a good executive coach, I would have said probably not. While I managed people for most of my career, I considered my people management skills to be more in support of setting their performance targets, helping them overcome obstacles to those targets, reviewing their performance, and keeping them motivated. I had no idea that I had what now seems to be a natural coaching ability. What makes it more amazing is that I have a strong natural personality preference to use the capabilities of my left brain (logic and reason) over those of my right brain (empathy and compassion). Yet when coaching, I use both equally.

Despite the reality that people do learn, grow, and overcome, the fact that it can be difficult, if not impossible, for some keeps the nature-versus-nurture debate alive. Hard-line nature supporters argue that because our physical makeup is largely determined by inherited genes, then so are our talents, personality, attitudes, and behaviors. Nurture supporters, on the other hand, argue that environmental factors have a more significant influence over our individuality.

Warren Bennis, an expert on leadership who believes leaders are made not born, says in his book *On Becoming a Leader*, that in the debate between "hereditary determinism" and "environmental determinism," little attention is given to "self-determinism." He argues that we are products of all the factors that influence us—including family, genes, education, weather, and chance. He acknowledges that the nature-nurture debate is interesting but inconclusive: "It's about as useful a guide to life as an astrological chart." What distinguishes leaders, he says, is that they create a "new, unique self" out of this "great stew of chemistry and circumstance."

While our genes may predispose us to certain abilities and talents, our environment creates much of what we become. Our attitude, behaviors, values, interests, style, feelings, and other nonphysical characteristics result from circumstances within our control.

Science Sheds New Light

Neuroscientific research explains that our brain cells (neurons) and their synaptic connections (synapses) determine our personality and thinking skills. Our brains are made up of an elaborate array of billions of synapses—junctions through which signals pass to our nervous systems, organs, muscles, and glands. These connections form the architecture for how we perceive, think, feel, and behave. At the most basic level, the arrangement of connections among our brain cells creates our skills and habits.

During our formative years, our brains contain about ten quadrillion (ten million billion) synapses. As we grow, the number of synapses declines and stabilizes at one to five quadrillion. We keep only the synapses that are used and made part of our connection network. These remaining synapses result from how we engage our five senses, as well as from what we do, think, and feel. The unused synapses fade away and die.

Recent discoveries reveal that by actively engaging our brains, regardless of our age, we grow new neurons. These new neurons, in turn, become part of new synaptic networks that continue to affect how we perceive, think, plan, learn, remember, feel, and behave as we grow older. In other words, dynamic abilities, not only genetically fixed abilities, direct how we change as we grow older. Each of us is a product of our inherited makeup, *which includes the ability to continue to change and develop.* The bottom line is that learning and ongoing personal development are possible. Our natural physical and psychological abilities enable them.

Each of us is a product of our inherited makeup, which includes the ability to continue to change and develop.

Because your mind has a natural ability to learn and grow, your development is truly your choice. It depends on factors you control. The more experience and knowledge you acquire, the more synaptic connections you develop, and the more capable you become. You are a product of your own thinking and experience. Your mental makeup is malleable and reprogrammable—by you. Motivational speaker Zig Ziglar put it this way, "You are who you are and what you are because of what has gone into your mind. You can change who you are and what you are by changing what goes into your mind." Fretting over some missing natural talent is a waste of energy. Don't be hostage to your own perceived genetic disposition. Instead, focus your energy on cultivating the traits you need to be successful.

Before attending my company's leadership boot camps, participants complete a battery of assessments. In the assessments, we focus on leadership attributes such as thinking strategically, attracting top talent, communicating more effectively, and inspiring employees. The assessment scores for these leadership attributes among mid- and upper-level executives average around seven on a ten-point scale, which equates to "average performance" in our scoring system. This means most participants have an opportunity for improvement. We create their individual coaching development plans based on how they score relative to where they need to be to achieve their objectives.

We implement and follow these plans for six months and then reevaluate their performance. In eight out of ten cases, the executives make significant improvement in the areas on which their development focused. I regularly get feedback from their bosses along the lines of "John's progress is amazing. He has made incredible improvement. He doesn't seem like John anymore." Let there be no doubt that with the right approach, people absolutely can learn, develop, and overcome.

In the two out of ten cases where the executives don't make significant progress, it is rarely the result of trying and failing. It is the result of not trying. They miss their coaching appointments, fail to complete their assignments, and don't follow their plan.

When people apply themselves and use the right approach, they learn, improve, and overcome. When a whole organization uses the right approach and improves, the whole organization's performance improves. This is the way organizations realize the untapped potential of their people and take their performance to a new level. Ian H. Robertson, a leading researcher in reshaping the way brains perform, summed it up in his book *Mind Sculpture: Unlocking Your Brain's Untapped Potential* by saying, "Almost every human skill—including those measured by IQ tests—can be improved by training and practice."

Don't Wait Another Day

Don't create regrets. Don't wait until the doctor says you need heart surgery to change your eating habits. Don't wait until the oncologist says you have six months to live to quit smoking. Don't wait until your boss passes you over for a promotion to work on your professional development. Don't wait until you are served divorce papers to invest in your marriage. Don't wait until your teenager leaves home to address your parenting skills. Make the choice now to pursue your self-development.

To be realistic, it's easy to postpone reading a new book on improving leadership skills, signing up for a debt-reduction seminar, or initiating an exercise program. We live in a society packed full of activity, much of which seems to be outside our control. Even knowing that dire consequences lie ahead, people keep putting off improvement because they can't find the time to do something about it. They think "I'll just put it off for a day," with full intentions of getting to it tomorrow. After all, one day rarely makes a big difference.

But the clock keeps ticking. Your days quickly turn into weeks, weeks into months, and months into years. Before you know it, you've given up or forgotten about taking any action at all. Looking back, you see a long list of missed opportunities. Even sadder, you can't remember what you did in place of improving. The daily routine that was so important at the time isn't even memorable. In hindsight, it wasn't more important. It was more convenient, more comfortable or more urgent, but not more important.

Successful people make improvement a priority. They invest time and resources in their personal and professional growth. They understand that inaction is rarely the best solution, and that it has definite, undeniable consequences. Successful people have few regrets.

They live a life of continuous learning, development, and purpose. They take charge. They are intentional in what they do. As time goes by, their incremental decisions add up in their favor, and they are richly rewarded for their efforts.

Make the choice to improve. Don't wait another day. Don't let any short-term gratifications overpower what you know are more important longer-term interests.

You Are Worth More than Your Car

Take seriously the choice to invest in yourself. Too many people neglect themselves and their personal development. Some invest more in their automobiles than they do in themselves. They buy high-grade gasoline for their cars yet load up on greasy foods for their bodies. They get a tune-up at the first sign of a sluggish engine but ignore their own indications of stress or poor performance. If they don't pamper their cars, they devote that attention to their clothes, hobbies, sports, novels, or whatever else they find valuable. Clearly your mental health, physical health, attitude, behavior, and competence are more important than your possessions.

Your car and other possessions don't lead to a fulfilled life or the achievement of your goals. Possessions and certain activities may give pleasure, but at what cost? Your career, your family, and your life? Whether you want to earn more money, be a better parent, enhance your relationships, win competitive events, or expand your service to others, invest in yourself. Make self-development your number one priority, and the achievement of your other desires will quickly follow.

2

Prepare for the Challenge

Prosperity is not without many fears and disasters,
and adversity is not without comforts and hopes.

–Francis Bacon

Rick was vice president of sales for a global software company responsible for a large territory in the eastern United States. Seven sales directors reported to him, each responsible for one of seven branch offices. His entire team consisted of about a hundred people.

Rick reported to Jeff, the executive vice president for global sales. Jeff was a seasoned sales executive with a long history in the software industry, whose view of success boiled down to one metric—meeting the current quarter's sales quota. Jeff's short-term, simple approach was common for executives who grew up under a "command and control" management approach.

Jeff left the company to take another job, which left his position open, a position Rick coveted. In Rick's twenty-year professional career, he had enjoyed many successes, won awards, received promotions, and made good money, but had never been part of the "senior leadership team." He considered himself well qualified and a top contender to replace Jeff.

Unfortunately for Rick, as fast as the opening was announced, it was filled. It went to another executive. The company's president hadn't even considered Rick for the position. He didn't see Rick as having the higher-level leadership qualities the position required.

Rick's first reaction was to dismiss the whole affair as an oversight. He was good at his job. He hit his numbers. He rationalized that maybe his current responsibilities were too important to allow him to move up. Or maybe the senior leaders weren't even aware of his capabilities. But the loss of promotion nagged at him. He questioned his role in the company, his contribution, his skills, and his style. He grew sullen as he couldn't get the missed opportunity out of his mind. Despite his achievements, he knew his career had stalled.

In an attempt to take charge of his fate, Rick enrolled in his company-sponsored leadership training program. All participants in the program were given a 360-degree assessment of their skills, behaviors, attitudes, and values. The feedback for the assessment came from peers, direct reports, and senior level managers, and unlike similar performance appraisals Rick had taken in the past, this one was designed solely for his benefit. The purpose of this assessment was to give straightforward, objective feedback on a participant's leadership competency and style.

Rick completed the assessment, and the results were not good. The report identified him as reactive, rigid, and narrowly focused. In his efforts to make his numbers each quarter, he concentrated almost solely on operational execution. He was manically tactical. He was considered inflexible and unwilling to change. He resisted new ideas and opposed any approach too different from standard operating procedure. He was a contributor, not an innovator, a doer, not an influencer. He didn't think strategically, didn't develop his people, and hadn't improved the business in any meaningful way for years, all core competencies for an executive at the executive vice president level. Rick could manage but not lead.

The 360 report was a lot of information for Rick to internalize. At first, he couldn't believe what he read. "Surely there was a mistake," he thought. "I can't be this bad!" Then his denial turned to anger. "How could everyone be so critical of me? I've been a strong performer around here for years," he stewed. "They aren't perfect either." Then he rationalized the findings. "I've been working against huge quarterly targets. There hasn't been any time for leadership training, executive coaching, or other high-level individual development. I have forecasts to turn in, business reviews to attend, customer issues to resolve, performance appraisals to complete, meetings to attend, voice messages to return, and e-mail to tend to. When would I have had to the time to be more adaptable and strategic?"

Unknown to Rick, he had a life-changing choice to make at that point. He could choose to develop or he could rationalize his self-limiting behavior away. He could dismiss the criticism and do as he'd always done, or open himself to the feedback and do something about it.

Unknown to Rick, he had a life-changing choice to make at that point. He could choose to develop, or he could rationalize his self-limiting behavior away.

Before he realized it, the leadership program ended, and he was back at work. His short departure from his day-to-day problems, conference calls, meetings, e-mails, and phone messages was over. He was fully reengaged in busy work. Almost without thought, Rick's leadership-training experience faded out of his consciousness. In effect, he dismissed the feedback that could have been just the catalyst he needed to make some long-overdue changes. Instead, he decided he was good enough.

Enemies of Self-Development

Rick's story isn't a business fable. Names and supporting details were changed, but Rick's story is true, as are the stories that follow in the upcoming chapters. My company's leadership program was the one Rick attended. In it, he received a life-changing dose of self-awareness, which he chose to ignore. He turned his back on the opportunity to develop and chose not to invest in himself. He preferred the comfort of his existing mode of operation—busyness as usual—and resigned himself to being a machine of execution. He elected to stay in his rut. Unknown to him until it was too late, he became a depreciating asset to his company and to himself.

The epilogue of Rick's story is a sad one. Ignoring the opportunity to change caused him to be fired six months later. His new boss reasoned that if Rick wasn't making sustainable improvements to the business, his team, and himself, he was falling behind. Once Rick was out of a job, he found that his skills and knowledge were well behind those who had been keeping up with contemporary management practices and theory. Although only in his forties, Rick was all but obsolete. He had lost his relevance.

Rick succumbed to several of the typical enemies of self-development. While they were not obvious to him, they lurked in his subconscious, guiding him to make the poor decisions he made. His prior success, perceived lack of time, and faulty self-awareness led him astray. He had deceived himself.

Self-deception is a major obstacle to self-improvement, and it comes in many forms. Here are some of the most common culprits causing self-deception and creating barriers to self-development:

1. **Busyness:** As you work diligently to keep up with e-mail, phone messages, conference calls, meetings, and other responsibilities, you overlook self-development.

2. **Resource limitations:** You lack money, approval, flexible work hours, or resolution of other limitations before you can begin.

3. **Time:** Your self-development agenda requires time that you currently don't have.

4. **Procrastination:** You put off anything that's not a huge problem yet. You could make the time, but you don't, because you don't yet feel the urgency.

5. **Fear:** Change is intimidating, and the unknown scares you. The thought of trying and failing is inconceivable.

6. **Prior bad experience:** You've tried before and failed. Why bother? You know you can't do it.

7. **Lack of awareness:** A lack of experience or insight into yourself makes you unaware of the need to develop.

8. **Inadequate support:** You don't have others to help you along your journey, and you lose the motivation to keep going.

9. **Lack of knowledge:** You don't know how to develop and change. You may not have any idea how to get started, or you've been given bad advice or been misled.

10. **Insufficient value:** You are unaware of the potential value of your self-improvement, or you think it's not worth the investment required.

11. **Limited feedback:** You believe that if you really needed to change, others would have told you so. Your family, friends, co-workers and valued advisors have failed to speak up, thereby reinforcing your self-deceptions that all is fine.

12. **Social norms and the herd mentality:** You believe that everyone else does the same thing, so you're not that different. You reject any need to develop because those around you don't develop either. You consider yourself normal, and normal is good enough.

13. **Strengths:** You put all your efforts into using and improving your strengths and work around your weaknesses. You believe your strengths more than offset any weaknesses you have.

14. **Arrogance:** You think too highly of yourself. You take positive thinking to the extreme, making you foolish. You see your shortcomings as being no big deal—or, worse, you see them as assets that need no improvement.

15. **Low self-esteem:** You see everything as difficult, if not impossible. You are naturally pessimistic and lack confidence in yourself.

16. **Relinquished ownership:** You have given ownership of your personal and professional development over to someone else. You don't see the choice of development as yours. Your locus of control is outside yourself.

17. **Short-term thinking:** You rarely commit time or resources to activities that don't produce a very near-term return.

18. **History:** You've always done something a certain way, and you've made it this far. Why change now?

19. **Memories:** Your memories, good or bad, keep you stuck in the past. You feel any endeavor related to events of the past would nullify the good you experienced or reopen the bad.

20. **Success:** Your earlier successes confirm that your current skills and habits work. Your success blinds you to your shortcomings.

The list of enemies to self-development is quite long. Without the proper preparation and ammunition, you are severely disadvantaged. No wonder so many self-improvement initiatives fail!

The good news is that all of these enemies are within your control. They are all in your mind as perceptions, not realities. They are self-deceptive thoughts, and every one of them can be overcome.

The last enemy of development listed, success, is especially troublesome because it can be so misleading and difficult to overcome. When money is coming into your bank account, you are enjoying the trappings of success, you have few unmet needs, and little is keeping you up at night, why bother to embark on a self-development initiative? You're doing fine just as you are, right?

The truth, of course, is that successful people can improve and be even more successful. People can also be successful through association with others or through lucky circumstances. Regardless, success is not a guaranteed, permanent condition. Without ongoing improvement, your success will wither away. Living off current success without investing in your future is not a sustainable strategy.

I've worked with executives who were promoted, given bonuses, and held up as shining examples of great leadership, yet were in truth terrible leaders. In many cases, their success was a result of a fast-growing economy or a well-positioned product; it had very little to do with their contribution. The sad part of misdiagnosing personal success is that while these executives made good money during those years, they actually lost ground. Because they wrongly correlated their good fortunes with their leadership skills, they didn't invest in their development or address their shortcomings and bad habits.

If you are successful, that's fantastic, but be wary. You could actually be in the greatest need of self-development. Marshall Goldsmith, author of *What Got You Here Won't Get You There,* says, "Our delusions of achievement, status, and contributions become a serious liability when we need to change. We sit there with the same godlike feelings, and when someone tries to make us change our ways, we regard them with unadulterated bafflement."

People often wrongly attribute their success to their own contributions or to the wrong facets of their contributions. I've worked with a number of executives who rode a long wave of success that had little to do with their involvement, and when their favorable circumstances ended, so did their success. Don't rely on your past successes or let them prevent you from improving your skills. Know that you can be even more successful. You can take better advantage of your existing capabilities, develop new capabilities, and ensure continued successes for many years to come.

Consistently successful people rise above the enemies of self-development, achieving through diligence and discipline, not coincidence. They invest in improving themselves. They apply themselves intentionally. They don't wait until a boss, doctor, family or friend gives them an ultimatum. They are proactive, spotting opportunities and taking advantage of them on their own. They develop because it's their nature. They don't settle for good enough.

Pay Attention to the Fine Print

In any self-improvement program, you will face one or more of the enemies of self-development. However, every one of them can be overcome, as you will discover throughout this book. A common misperception is that willpower is all it takes to combat the enemies of improvement. Some suggest that the key to success is simply having enough drive and persistence to plow through the obstacles. While a will to succeed is certainly necessary, it isn't enough.

Business performance researcher Jim Collins, author of *Good to Great,* conducted extensive research on what great companies do differently from good companies. According to Collins, great companies are guided by leaders who possess what he describes as *level five leadership,* a mix of personal humility and professional will. Willpower makes it into his top two but doesn't stand alone.

Robert E. Kelly says that to be sure, personal success is about initiative, but that's not all. Kelly is a human-performance scientist and author of *How to Be a Star at Work.* He conducted research on what separates top performers from average performers and found that top performers demonstrate nine characteristics—initiative, networking, self-management, big-picture perspective, followership, leadership, team-work, organizational savvy, and "show-and-tell," his term for persuasion. Initiative makes it into the top nine, but it doesn't stand alone.

Will, initiative, drive, and determination are characteristics of great leaders and of anyone who consistently achieves success.

These characteristics separate people who activate and achieve their ambitions from those who don't. But as the legendary radio personality Paul Harvey said in his daily broadcast, there is always more to the rest of the story.

In my early twenties, I signed a health-club contract that contained an asterisk that led to tiny footnotes, which I ignored. I thought I was signing up for a one-time membership, when I was actually agreeing to a recurring annual commitment. I also recall authorizing a brake job on my car. The repair agreement contained some fine print, which I ignored. That mistake turned an anticipated $79 brake repair into a $900 total brake replacement. The fine print of self-development is no different. It is critical that you don't miss it.

If you expect to achieve success, willpower on its own is insufficient.

If you expect to achieve success, willpower on its own is insufficient. Willpower provides the fuel, but without the engine, transmission, wheels and steering mechanism, it isn't enough. In fact, willpower without its supporting cast looks more like the proverbial bull in a china closet, leaving a trail of destruction. It's all brawn with no brains. Many initiatives are started with drive and stay alive with determination, but those that result in sustainable improvements require the use of a larger cast of supporting characteristics.

Look in the Mirror

"The diet plan wasn't any good." "The exercise program didn't fit my style." "The seminar's suggestions didn't apply to me." "The business consultant didn't understand our culture." Sound familiar? These are pervasive excuses to avoid self-development that can be heard at any water cooler or dinner table.

Most excuses have one thing in common, the *it's-not-me* factor. Whatever the problem, it's not me. Whatever the hurdle, I didn't put it there. If it didn't work, it wasn't my idea in the first place, much less my fault. Given the volume of excuses and bad outcomes, it's perhaps surprising that people continue to attend seminars, buy exercise programs, hire consultants, work with coaches, start diets, and seek help from counselors. If a television series received as many bad reviews, it would be pulled from the network in a week.

While the content of a seminar or book is very important, it is not the predominant cause of one's failure or success. We've all seen people achieve significant improvements from mediocre content. I've sat through basic seminars led by inexperienced hosts and still managed to learn a new principle or two and be better for it. So have countless others. The root of the problem is in the mirror. When we gain virtually nothing from the content, especially when the content is perfectly suited to us, the failure is our own.

How many times has someone you know read an outstanding self-improvement book, received sound training, or been given the wise counsel they needed, only to ignore it? It may be happening to you now, and you don't realize it. As we are masters of self-deception, it happens all the time.

If you're guilty of self-improvement ignorance or the *its-not-me* syndrome, look in the mirror. Consider what you are blaming, and consider the possibility that it may simply be a convenient excuse. Accept the challenge to find something beneficial in what you are reading or hearing. Don't let excuses rob you of achieving your full potential.

It's Not That Hard—Look Forward to It

Developing yourself is one of the most rewarding experiences you can have. It can be truly enjoyable. It doesn't have to be overwhelming or a chore. With the right approach, self-development can be a magnificent journey. You obtain interesting insights into yourself, acquire new knowledge, and meet new people. You feel a sense of accomplishment and increase your self-esteem. These and many other rewards are in addition to obtaining the specific benefits of your goal.

Early in my IBM career, I learned to use and demonstrate IBM's computer-aided engineering software. I remember to this day the great feeling of satisfaction I had when I completed my training and turned the corner in my proficiency. As a result of that training, I didn't have to find and schedule others to perform customer demonstrations; I could do them myself on a moment's notice. It took time and energy to learn, but it was fun and rewarding.

Many of my learning and development endeavors were challenging, but they were still fun, interesting, and rewarding experiences. Collectively, I wouldn't trade them for anything. I've grown in ways that are priceless. And honestly, the investment I had to make wasn't that significant. Most of what you need to know is in a book or someone's head. Self-development seems hard only when you make it that way. It isn't that difficult or complicated when you go about it in a systematic way.

I frequently write business and self-improvement articles for Internet and print media. These articles give me an opportunity to sort out my thoughts, road test new ideas, and gain valuable feedback. People often say my advice is simple. Maybe I'm just simpleminded, but I believe it's because learning and self-development isn't that hard. Staying the same is harder.

Consider Rick, the now unemployed former vice president of sales. He knew what to do—he needed to develop his leadership skills. He knew how to do it; he had step-by-step instructions during his leadership boot camp, plus ongoing executive coaching. Investing time and energy into his self-development would have been easy from that point on. It would certainly have been easier than continuing to be a machine of tactical execution. Had he pursued self-improvement, he might now be sitting in the very position he so coveted. I imagine he would also consider that fun and rewarding.

The changes most people need to make are small. The result they're looking for may be significant, but the change necessary to achieve it is minor. The difference is similar to winning or losing in sports. Winning or losing in sports often comes down to a throw just a few inches lower, a run a tenth of a second faster, a swing a degree to the outside, or a shot at the goal just inside the bar instead of just outside of it. These minor adjustments produce significant results.

The changes most people need to make are small.

You may need to practice a new skill only a minute a day to become an expert. You may only need to avoid one temptation a week to overcome an addiction. You may only need to say one more sentence or listen a few seconds longer to change a relationship completely. If you are like most people, you only need to make the slightest of changes in order to produce the most significant improvement. Don't make it so hard. Rather than dread it, look forward to it. Self-improvement can be not only one of the easiest things you have ever done but also the most rewarding.

Resist Your Resistance

Improvement is a staple of life for enduring success. Improvement and enhanced productivity are the basis of our economy. New products replace old products; new cars replace old ones. Schools add to their learning curricula. Restaurants update their menus, governments upgrade laws, organizations hire new employees, and industries modernize. As recently as 1900, almost half of the United States labor force was employed in farming. By 2000, the number dropped to 2 percent, while the farming output more than quadrupled over the same period. Improvement is everywhere, like it or not.

With so much change around us, such a resistance to change on a personal level seems odd. You might think everyone would be comfortable with change and openly embrace it, but they don't. Think about your natural reaction to getting a new boss, moving into a new office, hiring a new assistant, being paid against a new bonus scheme, or transferring to a new insurance plan. Are you instantly positive about these changes? If you are called into a meeting at work and the first words out of your boss's mouth are something like, "We are going to make some changes around here," do you instantly feel good about what is coming? If you are like most, you would rather keep what you know than take a chance on the unknown. Most people are skeptical of change. They resist, putting off change until there isn't a choice.

We get comfortable with the status quo, even though the status quo is often not as good as other alternatives. We favor the known over the unknown. We learn to cope, adjust, and form habits that give us a sense of security and comfort. We like stability and try to maintain it as long as possible. Even when stability means standing still, the equivalent to moving backwards, we naturally prefer it.

Consistently high achievers, on the other hand, realize the danger of stagnation and view change as an opportunity. They seek it out. They are willing to try new activities, processes, and products. They seek opportunities to learn, to be involved in new events. High achievers view the status quo as the enemy.

One of my clients became chief executive officer of a billion dollar company at the age of forty-two. When he talks about his early career, he emphasizes his focus on taking advantage of change, learning, and developing. While he made a good income, his focus wasn't on making money or being comfortable. His focus was on learning and developing his skills. He welcomed change as opportunity, and it paid off. If you want to be a consistently high achiever, resist your natural resistance to change. View change as the opportunity it is.

Enlarge Your Comfort Zone

I've had more than one debate with an executive about the need for a real and tangible return on a leadership development investment. I certainly agree with the need for a real return, but I dispute that it has to be a tangible one. Clearly, great leadership leads to tangible results, but the competencies that drive those results may not be tangible. You can't dispute the value of making good decisions but measuring it accurately can be challenging. Try to measure the value of a climate of creativity or a spirit of teamwork. Yes, you can measure them, but they are often so subjective that they are relegated to the realm of the intangible. However, that doesn't mean they aren't real and valuable.

Intangibles are what give most companies a competitive advantage over their rivals. With the pressing of a computer's "Enter" button, prices can be lowered. New products can be designed and developed in a matter of months. Tangibles like these are not sustainable sources of competitive advantage. An intangible, like an impassioned group of employees who help each other focus on meeting the needs of their customers, is a greater source of competitive advantage and much more difficult to imitate. Intangibles are important to organizational success. The same is true for self-development.

The big intangible of self-development, and source of advantage, is getting out of your comfort zone. Unlike reading a book, attending a seminar, or enlisting the support of a friend, getting out of your comfort zone is mental, not physical. Your comfort zone is an intangible mental boundary that when crossed causes anxiety and resistance to change. It is at the root of many barriers to success as well as many excuses.

The big intangible of self-development, and source of advantage, is getting out of your comfort zone.

Your comfort zone is an invisible area in which you feel secure and comfortable. You might think of its boundary as a wall around you, akin to the walls of a secure room inside a dangerous place. Inside the room, things are well known and safe. Outside, things are unknown and perceived to be dangerous. Your comfort zone is the limit beyond which you believe there is pain, discomfort, or risk. Just thinking about stepping outside those limits can make you anxious and tense, and it can cause tangible physical reactions too. Reactions to anxiety include a pounding heart, a rise in blood pressure, sweating, and an aching stomach, all very real and uncomfortable reactions that are more than enough to cause you to stop the self-development you might be pursuing.

Even though your desire to change may be considerable, any expectation of stepping outside your comfort zone can paralyze you. Your self-development becomes secondary to your need for security, and you put off your desires in favor of safety, real or perceived.

Early in my professional career, I had a fear of public speaking. Put me in front of an unknown audience, and I'd get a rush of anxiety. My comfort zone was limited to small, known groups and one-on-one interactions. When I needed to give a presentation to a group of twenty or more people, my palms would sweat, my voice cracked, and on occasions my mind froze. All of this made my invisible wall even thicker, the discomfort even greater, and my fear of public speaking stronger.

Public speaking was clearly out of my comfort zone. As my job responsibilities grew, I knew I had to learn to speak in public or accept a lesser role. I decided to step up to the challenge and accept the discomfort. I sought out speaking opportunities. I began to speak weekly, sometimes daily, to small groups. Guess what happened? Speaking got less uncomfortable. Over time, speaking in public even became an enjoyable experience. My invisible comfort area expanded and continued to grow until public speaking became a part of my new comfort zone. Public speaking was no longer outside, in the danger zone.

Today, I look forward to speaking in public. I'll admit that larger audiences still make me a bit nervous, but it's a good nervousness, a combination of excitement and anxiety. It drives me to prepare and makes me a better speaker. If I had not worked as hard as I did to become comfortable with public speaking, I would not be as good a speaker as I am today.

As in my case, the fear of getting out of one's comfort zone is usually unfounded. Presentation audiences present no real threat to our safety. The danger is simply perceived. Yet even though the fear is unfounded, the boundaries we set for ourselves give us a feeling of security.

Feelings of insecurity come from our past experiences, learned responses, values, natural instincts, and habits that have deep roots. Our need to be secure and comfortable is often stronger than our ability to push through the invisible boundary that exists in so many areas of our lives. Giving up an addiction, changing our management style, exercising, learning a foreign language, overcoming negativism, and conquering selfishness are just a few examples of pursuits that require getting out of our comfort zone. The discomfort from any of them can take a considerable level of energy and courage to maintain. When dieting, for example, you have to push back against your natural response to hunger. In practicing a new skill like listening, you have to fight the urge to think ahead or speak up.

Your comfort zone is a self-created mental boundary that can derail any self-improvement endeavor. We will cover several antidotes throughout this book. The first is learning to value discomfort.

Value Discomfort

As a parent, I encourage my children to appreciate the value of their home, way of life, health, and possessions. When I compare the conveniences, comforts, and choices they have today with those I had when I was growing up, I can't help being grateful, and I want them to be grateful, too. Gratitude is easy for me because I come from a different generation and remember a time with less wealth and abundance. My children don't have that contrasting view.

I am even more appreciative when I think about our ancestors. Imagine what it was like a couple of hundred years ago, building a home without power tools. Imagine what it was like when someone became farsighted or nearsighted and corrective lenses were nonexistent. For our ancestors, securing food, putting a roof over their heads, communicating with relatives, seeing a doctor, traveling, staying warm, bathing, and just about every other convenience we take for granted was a major chore.

In contrast, our modern society sets very high expectations. It teaches our children they should have just about anything they want. Cars loaded with convenience features are available in a wide range of colors with multiple financing options. Furniture comes in many shapes, styles, and prices. Food, clothing, and everything else is available in an endless variety of options. We can cure a long list of ailments with pills. We can change jobs, friends, and mates on a whim. Our choices are vast, if not infinite.

While having these options is great, there is a downside to our abundance. We are being conditioned not to settle for less and losing our tolerance for discomfort. We don't expect to eat what we don't like or to work, travel, live, or play in any degree of discomfort. We don't even expect to have to think of uncomfortable things. Many people knowingly prefer to be ignorant about social, political, economic, cultural, and spiritual issues because thinking about them is too uncomfortable.

The problem with avoiding discomfort is that in the process, we also avoid growth. Laurel Mellin, author of *The Pathway* and associate clinical professor of family and community medicine at the University of California at the San Francisco School of Medicine, suggests that for us to grow and earn life's rewards, we must experience our "essential pain." She describes essential pain as the risks and reality of the human condition that we must face to achieve our goals. Work through and overcome these elements, and you receive the fulfillment of life. By accepting that life isn't perfect, that we can't always be comfortable, and that we must incur some pain, we accept a key part of growing and are able to move confidently forward into the uncomfortable.

The problem with avoiding discomfort is that in the process, we also avoid growth.

If you're not convinced that discomfort is good for you, I can't blame you. It makes little sense to seek discomfort when you spend much of your time and money on acquiring comfort. The plain truth though is that discomfort makes you stronger. Working through the uncomfortable helps you grow. Psychiatrist M. Scott Peck described the comfort/discomfort dichotomy this way: "The truth is that our finest moments are most likely to occur when we are feeling deeply uncomfortable, unhappy, or unfulfilled. For it is only in such moments, propelled by our discomfort, that we are likely to step out of our ruts and start searching for different ways or truer answers."

When you're comfortable, you don't look for new opportunities. You don't appreciate what you have. You don't recognize your shortcomings and ask for help. You don't test yourself or take on new experiences. You don't learn or improve.

Discomfort and adversity are an integral part of change and development. They are necessary for growth. Motivational speaker Denis Waitley says, "A dream is your creative vision for your life in the future. You must break out of your current comfort zone and become comfortable with the unfamiliar and the unknown." Only by doing so can we truly reach our peak potential. Successful people learn to move out of their comfort zones when it is time to grow.

Pablo Picasso, one of the most prolific and influential artists of the twentieth century, told followers, "I am always doing that which I cannot do, in order that I may learn how to do it." Personal growth for many people boils down to one thing—having the courage to step out of their comfort zones.

Leadership guru Warren Bennis suggests that an essential element in becoming a great leader is experiencing the crucible. This transformational experience often involves overcoming adversity, so that the leader emerges stronger, more optimistic, and more open to experience.

In looking back on my life, I realize that my crucible experience wasn't a single event but many formative experiences over many years. It was overcoming adversity, spending time outside my comfort zone, learning painful lessons, and choosing to apply those experiences and lessons in a positive way. You, too, have probably experienced adversity and benefited from it. You may be experiencing adversity now. As crazy as this may sound, delight in it. While adversity is hardly ever enjoyable, the lessons learned and the resulting improvements are often worth the cost.

While adversity is hardly ever enjoyable, the lessons learned and the resulting improvements are often worth the cost.

Tony Dungy, American National Football League coach and Super Bowl champion, attributed part of his team's success to what he called *artificial adversity*. Dungy created artificially harsh game scenarios to prepare his team for the situations when genuine adversity arrived. Learning to handle adversity made Dungy's team even more capable when adversity wasn't present. Through adversity training, his team became best prepared and ultimately reached their peak potential.

Achieving your goals and becoming the best you can be requires that you spend time outside your comfort zone learning to face and overcome adversity. Be glad for your adversity. When you emerge from the crucible, you will be a stronger and more capable person.

Find Your Courage

Fear can be a significant inhibitor to self-development. Fear of the unknown or of looking foolish keeps people in abusive relationships, jobs that don't fit them, and other ruts preventing them from improving and growing. Consultant and author Marilyn Ferguson defined people's fear as that nebulous space between their old way of life and their desired way of life that they can't quite grasp yet. It's the place where there's nothing to hold on to, a place that feels like being lost, lonely, and afraid. It is the absence of the familiar. The uncertainty, amplified by imagination rather than by any real danger, frightens us. Roman Emperor Marcus Aurelius told his followers, "If you are distressed by anything external, the pain is not due to the thing itself, but to your estimate of it; and this you have the power to revoke at any moment."

Everyone has fear. Fear keeps us alive by calling our attention to danger. If your fear results from real physical danger, your fear is helping you. It tells you to change your physical circumstances. If, however, your fear is imagined, it is hurting you and telling you to change your thinking. If unfounded fear has power over you, think of it as the acronym: False Evidence Appearing Real.

In my own fear of public speaking, false evidence supported my fears. Had I thought about it logically, I would have seen public speaking as an opportunity, not a threat. Being invited to speak was evidence that I had something to offer, that I would be welcomed. This more reasoned approach to my fears was a much-needed contrast to the self-defeating fears of being on public display, being ridiculed, or simply failing and losing the respect of others.

Eleanor Roosevelt, first lady to the 32nd President of the United States, once said, "You gain strength, courage, and confidence by every experience in which you really stop to look fear in the face. You are able to say to yourself, 'I lived through this horror. I can take the next thing that comes along.'" Susan Jeffers, author of *Feel the Fear . . . And Do It Anyway,* who herself overcame a life run by unfounded fear, says fears don't go away on their own. You must go out and do the thing you fear. Doing it will make you feel better about yourself and help you put fear in its proper place.

If fear keeps you from moving forward with your self-development plans, confront it and take steps to mitigate its hold on you. Here is one approach that works for many people using social phobia as an example:

1. Put your fear into specific words and write it down. If you fear meeting new people and building rapport through small talk, state what you feel, the circumstances that you fear most, and the outcomes of prior uncomfortable situations where you had to talk to a total stranger.

2. Do research. Get the facts. Increase your knowledge in the area of your fear. Prepare and study to convert any unknowns into

knowns. Research social phobia on the Internet. Buy books on social phobia and social anxiety. Talk to people at the Social Phobia Association.

3. List the possible outcomes, both good and bad, of meeting new people. Identify how an impromptu encounter with a stranger might turn out just fine as well as how it might become a disaster for you.

4. Identify the worst possible outcomes in the list and develop contingency plans for each. In doing so, you gain confidence that you can handle even the worst possible outcomes if they happen. If the worst outcome is that someone would stand there looking at you with nothing to say, memorize three to five conversation-starting statements that you could use to get the conversation going again.

5. Identify the best possible outcomes in the list and their benefits. Consider that if you meet someone new who has interests like yours, you could build a great new friendship, or that someone you meet could be in a similar line of work and give you future employment opportunities.

6. Given what you know about the situation, predict the most likely result. This is usually not the worst possible outcome and is often closer to the best. Understand the reality that most strangers you meet will just be people with whom you'll enjoy small talk for a few minutes, and you will never see them again. There are no future ramifications. There is no downside.

7. Create a mental picture of the best possible outcome and dwell on it. Stay positive and focus on the benefits. Picture the positive results of a pleasant meeting. Picture yourself doing

what you must to succeed and make that your default mental picture. See yourself smiling to your new acquaintances and enjoying what they have to say. Consider your other talents and successes to maintain your confidence.

8. Do it. Do it again. Do it some more. Look for opportunities to meet people. Engage in small talk at the grocery store, the hardware store, your place of worship, your hairdresser, and at every opportunity you have. Your experience will increase your confidence that you can handle it, and your fear will subside.

The process of thinking through and writing down logical outcomes will help put your fears in perspective. This simple process replaces uncertainty with a degree of sureness. The writing and list-making replaces your emotional anxiety with logic. In developing a plan to handle your most difficult situations, you gain confidence that you can manage even the worst outcomes. If you can handle them, you can handle anything.

If you want to change your world, change the way you think about it.

Don't let fear steal your success. Your profession, your family, and your health depend on it. Rosa Parks, United States civil rights leader, once said, "I have learned over the years that when one's mind is made up, this diminishes fear; knowing what must be done does away with fear." Easing fear is as simple as making up your mind. Make up your mind to be courageous. If you want to change your world, change the way you think about it. Value a little discomfort. Experience the essential pain needed to reap life's rewards. Overcoming your fear is much easier than living a life imprisoned by it. To quote Zig Ziglar, "Others can stop you temporarily—you are the only one who can do it permanently."

3
Establish Your Objective

The world makes way for the man who knows
where he is going.

–Ralph Waldo Emerson

Once you've made the decision to pursue your ambition, there
is one more step before beginning to apply the eight principles of
Activating Your Ambition. You need to be clear on what you plan
to pursue. Spell out your desire. Napoleon Hill, twentieth-century
American author and pioneer in self-improvement philosophy,
had it right when he plainly stated, "The starting point of all
achievement is desire." Desire is not the end or the means, but it is
the beginning.

What you want to be or do is not always clear. You can have a
general idea of what you want yet struggle when pressed to put it into

specific terms. Or you can have a clear desire but be unsure where to start. This chapter is here to help you remove any uncertainty and add clarity into your objectives, goals, and ambitions. As motivational expert and self-help author Anthony Robbins pointed out, "Setting goals is the first step in turning the invisible into the visible." This chapter will start you turning the unseen into the seen. It will put transparency into your ambitions.

What Do You Want?

Do you have goals? Do you know the areas you need to develop in order to achieve them? Or do you have many interests, perhaps with competing pros and cons, that make gaining clarity difficult? Have you considered what you might pursue if all constraints on you were lifted? If the mythical Arabian genie popped out of the lamp at this very moment and offered you three wishes, what would they be? What, specifically, do you want to accomplish? Who do you want to become? What would you like to learn?

Perhaps something has prevented you from progressing in your career. It could be a "soft" skill, such as strategic thinking or being more direct in your communication. It could be a domain skill like learning project management, computer networking, negotiation, or remodeling. It could be more personal, like overcoming chronic tiredness or improving your mental acuity. It could be stopping an addiction, controlling impulsive spending, quitting gambling, or strengthening your spiritual faith. Or it could be something completely different than your career or anything you do now, like learning a foreign language, playing a musical instrument, or starting your own business. It could be becoming a more caring person or building your self-esteem.

The options are truly infinite, but you can't do them all. You must narrow them down to decide which way to go. As Yogi Berra, Hall of Fame American baseball player and manager, said, "You've got to be very careful if you don't know where you are going, because you might not get there." Having no goals is not a good option, and having too many goals is not a good option, so the obvious answer is to have just the few right ones. The question becomes, how do you pick them?

Setting Goals

In my mid-twenties, I attended a seminar hosted by Lewis Timberlake, a motivational speaker and author from Austin, Texas. It was one of those extraordinary experiences where the speaker said exactly what I needed to hear at that particular time. As a result, it had a major impact on me that has lasted to this day. His message was about the power of setting goals. He explained how setting goals had brought focus and balance to his life. He outlined the high-priority areas of his life and how establishing written goals and plans for each enabled him to achieve them.

The day after the seminar, I took Timberlake's advice and created written goals for my life. Until that time, I had no framework to help organize my aspirations and no guide to help me think through the myriad of options open to me. This process was as powerful as it was simple. At the time, my goals covered five areas of my life. For each, I created short-, medium-, and long-range goals with detailed actions. In my social life, for example, I set a short-term goal (one to twelve months) of putting together a ski trip with several friends. In my professional life, I set a medium-term goal (one to five years) of become a marketing manager. In my spiritual life, I set a long-term goal (five-plus years) to lead Bible study at my church. This exercise helped me in six distinctive areas.

First, it forced me to think about what I wanted. I was already focused on my career, but goal setting pushed me to think about other areas of my life. It challenged me to reflect on what else deserved my attention and forced me to think about my broader intentions. In the end, I did create goals, but the bigger benefit was the direction I obtained. For the first time, I really felt that I had a bearing on which way to head over time. Rather than just setting goals, the exercise helped me set a direction as well.

Second, writing them down forced me to be specific. I couldn't get by with the general and unclear intentions floating around in my head; instead, I had to list specific tasks and accomplishments I could measure and track. Writing out my goals helped me create a new level of self-awareness. I didn't know until then that my previous goals had been so general. It turned out that in four of five areas of my life, all I had was a vague concept of what I wanted. Because writing forced me to translate my ideas into specific words, it gave me much greater clarity in what to do.

Third, written goals and their supporting plans created accountability. Without measurable tasks or milestones, I hadn't been accountable. I had been successful in some pursuits without measures and tracking, but I had been missing an even greater opportunity to improve and be more successful. Having specific milestones enabled me to track my progress, gave me feedback on where I needed to make adjustments, and confirmed that I was on course.

Fourth, the process gave me insight into issues that had been holding me back. By listing specific, measurable outcomes, I exposed my subconscious rationalizations. Setting down my goals made me confront the self-deceptions that were blocking my success. For example, I set what I thought was a modest goal to read a certain number of nonfiction books every quarter. I read daily and didn't expect it to be a big challenge. In the ensuing months, I learned that much of my reading wasn't in books at all. Most of my reading was in current affairs gleaned from newspapers and trade magazines. While I thought I was doing okay on reading, I wasn't. I realized it only after setting the goal and tracking it.

Setting down my goals made me confront the self-deceptions that were blocking my success.

Fifth, establishing written goals gave me confidence. Having a plan reassured me that I was headed in the right direction and on track to be successful. I felt organized and in control of my own destiny. Any doubt about achieving my long-term goals was replaced by hope. Having specific actions and milestones was like finding a map that took away the guesswork and paved the way to my final destination.

Finally, having written goals gave me a sense of accomplishment that sustained me. Checking off the box after achieving a milestone provided a sense of satisfaction. The small achievements encouraged me and validated that I could reach the goals I had set for myself. The incremental achievements made the process fun. From a business perspective, I effectively created my own "business review" in which my boss (me) ran through my accomplishments and praised me for a job well done.

Establishing written goals:

- Compels you to think about your life's ambitions and the direction you want to head.

- Transforms generalities into specifics, clarifying your intentions.
- Creates accountability by giving you something to track.
- Produces a transparent view into your shortcomings and obstacles.
- Gives you confidence that you have an achievable plan and are on a path to success.
- Creates a sense of accomplishment that sustains you.

A study by Dominican University of California psychology professor Gail Matthews found that people who wrote goals and regularly shared them with others were more accountable and achieved on average a third more than people who didn't. Twentieth-century American behavioral psychologist and Harvard professor Dr. David McClelland extensively studied the attributes of successful people. He found that high achievers set goals, sequenced tasks in relation to their goals, and prioritized their tasks in order to attain their goals. Setting goals, and in particular written goals, is characteristic of successful people.

Focus on Life's Important Areas

In my first couple of years of goal setting, I reviewed my goals every few months and updated them at the beginning of every year. I kept the old goals in a written archive in order to look back and track my progress. When personal computer software became available, I put all of it online, which made the goals easier to update and track.

Over the years, I've increased the areas of my focus to the following nine:

- Family
- Faith
- Profession
- Finances
- Fun
- Mental Acuity
- Physical Condition
- Emotional Condition
- Community Service

Family goals relate to enjoying and caring for my parents, spouse, siblings, children, and extended family. Faith goals include maintaining my spiritual objectives: faith, Bible study, tithing, teaching, and obedience. Professional goals embrace my career objectives and career progression. Financial goals relate to increasing my income, budget, cash flow, assets, retirement funding, and net worth. Fun goals involve my social activities with friends, neighbors, and co-workers, as well as other entertainment, recreation, and hobbies. Mental acuity goals deal with maintaining my knowledge, mental energy, and mental alertness. Physical condition goals relate to good health, physical energy, nutrition, and fitness. Emotional condition goals have to do with improving self-control, having a positive self-image, managing stress, and developing social capabilities. Lastly, community service goals include being involved in the community, giving something back to others, and being a good citizen of planet Earth.

These focus areas work for me, but the areas important to you may be different. You may feel that fewer or even more areas deserve your focus. Consider what those areas are before honing in on specific goals. It will help guide you as you funnel down to the objectives, goals, and plans you wish to pursue.

To create focus, gain clarity, and be accountable, capture your goals and objectives in writing. Write down your short-, medium-, and long-term ambitions in each important area of your life. For each ambition, create a plan of the key actions needed to achieve your goal.

When finished, look at your list of goals and actions to see what self-development might be helpful to pursue.

The power of written goals and plans can't be overstated. I couldn't agree more with international speaker and author Brian Tracy when he said, "People with clear, written goals accomplish far more in a shorter period of time than people without them could ever imagine."

Follow Goal-Setting Best Practices

In the goal setting process, there is a tendency to take shortcuts and make the steps too big. The process of thinking into the future and considering what might be possible gets people excited. It is a motivating experience that can end up in overzealous planning. David Allen, recognized expert in time management and author of *Getting Things Done*, says that people need to take it slow, moving forward in little steps that don't take too much energy or time to accomplish. Be careful not to make your near-term goals too big. They should be attainable through the achievement of simple, small action steps. Small goals attained add up to big goals accomplished.

In creating detailed action plans for your goals, know the difference between actions and milestones. Action steps lead to milestones. For example, if you are single and your goal is to find someone with whom you can enjoy a long-term relationship, an action step would be to join the adult singles program in your local church. A milestone, on the other hand, would be to go out on a date by the end of the quarter. Good goal setting and action planning contain both actions and milestones. The milestones are a method to track progress, not the means to get there.

When first setting your goals, don't set too many. One or two may be all you can realistically focus on. Rome wasn't built in a day, and your life's aspirations won't be either. It's better to start small and enjoy a few successes than to start too big and face early defeat that may lead to the cynicism that makes further attempts even more difficult. Avoid overwhelming yourself and setting yourself up for failure and disappointment with the entire process. You can come back to your goal setting exercise in a few months and add more if you feel you are ready.

If, for example, you have an overarching objective to simplify your life, you may have a myriad of short-, medium-, and long-term goals involving several life areas. You may want to fix up and sell your house in order to buy a smaller home. You may want to sell your boats, cars, motorcycles, and all but one bicycle. You may want to pursue fewer but deeper relationships with your friends. You may want to consolidate your investments. The magnitude of these changes and the work needed to accomplish them can easily overwhelm you. A better approach is to concentrate on just one or two areas, make progress in them, and add more as you have capacity to accomplish them.

When selecting which goals to pursue first, pick the ones that provide support to the other ones. If several goals depend on one in particular, pick it first.

Once you get your near-term, high-priority goals under control, consider setting a sizable long-range one. It could be what author Jim Collins described in his book *Built to Last*, a BHAG—a big hairy audacious goal. A BHAG is a stretch goal so far out of your comfort zone that you've never given serious consideration to pursuing it. As impossible as it might sound, BHAGs offer the biggest rewards. Don't discount the possibilities. Once you identify a BHAG, break it down into a series of smaller goals that, when completed, get you to your BHAG.

Whatever goals you decide to pursue, write them down. Identify the small steps you need to take to complete them. Periodically review them, assess your progress, add new ones, change existing ones where needed, and check them off the list when you're done. Make this a regular routine, and before you know it, you will be looking back at the great progress you've made from the accumulation of your many small accomplishments.

When you are trying to change, there is a subtle but important difference in how you think of your goal. For example, if you want to overcome angry outbursts, your initial goal might be to "reduce angry outbursts to one per month." However, stating it in this form focuses on the anger instead of the calm. Instead, reword it to something like "respond to frustrating situations with calm and patience nine out of ten times." Stating objectives positively creates a completely different mental picture than negative statements. Even though your objective may be to reduce anger, you want your mind focused on being calm. How you describe and picture your goal is important because your mind has a mind of its own.

How you describe and picture your goal is important because your mind has a mind of its own.

The mind within your mind is called your subconscious. You can't defeat it, so you might as well work with it to your advantage. No matter how you state your objective, your mind creates mental pictures from the key words you use. Words paint pictures which become archived in your subconscious, and your mind drives you toward those pictures. Select words you want your mind to use, words that create the right mental pictures.

If you are dieting, state your goal in terms like "get to a trim 185 pounds" instead of "lose twenty pounds." If you are developing a coaching versus a telling style of management, state your objective in words like "coach my employees in the core principles that lead to their success" rather than "quit telling my employees what to do when they ask me for help."

In addition to stating your goal positively, use the present tense. Stating goals in the present tense makes them more real. Instead of saying, "I will become a trim 185 pounds," state your goal in the present such as, "I am a trim 185 pounds." Instead of stating, "I will better coach my employees to be more productive," state it as, "I coach my employees to be more productive." Stating goals in the present tense helps create a mental picture of your desired future state now. Present tense makes the attainment of your goal appear closer, as if the journey is started rather than being a distant objective. Present tense makes your mental picture clearer.

Here is a summary of best practices in good goal writing:

- Be realistic in the goals you establish. Don't establish so many goals and actions that you become overwhelmed.
- First work on the goals that provide support to your other goals.
- Break down your objectives into smaller goals and specific incremental milestones that are easier to accomplish and track as you make progress.
- Identify simple, small action steps to support the attainment of your milestones.
- Express your goals in terms of the positive characteristics you intend to attain.
- State your goals in the present tense, as if they have already happened.
- Review your goals periodically to assess your progress and update them.

Visit www.activatingyourambition.com for a free goal-setting worksheet that will guide you through the goal setting process.

Know Your Purpose

If you have difficulty coming up with your goals, take a step back and reflect on your overall purpose in life. Without a purpose pulling you in a particular direction, goal setting can be difficult.

Your purpose is your reason for being, your guiding reason for living, and your answer to "what do you want to do when you grow up?" It is what energizes you over the long-term. Unlike a goal, a purpose may not be a specific accomplishment, but rather the involvement in an ongoing cause that continuously guides and focuses you. It can be related to your family, career, environment or whatever passion you choose to follow.

In companies and organizations, a purpose is synonymous with a mission. It's the reason for existence, the central focus of the organization that drives its objectives, goals, and strategies. Purpose is the cause that rallies people to perform at their best and gives their work meaning. A hospital's purpose might be to make health care more comfortable for patients; a software company's, to make computing more user friendly; an electric company's, to preserve the environment for future generations; and an office furniture company's, to build products that help office workers be more productive. These missions are clear and ongoing.

Purposes are as varied as the people they guide. Those who have overcome serious adversity or a tragedy often take up or create a cause to help others overcome the same. Some simply want to help others by working for non-profit organizations. Others set out to improve their community through political involvement or volunteering. The purpose of a parent of young children could be to raise their children to become good, caring, and responsible adults, or to help their children develop in some special way. A common career purpose is to reach a level of authority or proficiency—senior vice president, chief scientist, or tenured professor—or to start a small business. Other purposes could be to become an exceptional Sunday school teacher, a scratch golfer, a connoisseur of fine wines, a world traveler, or a great gardener. A guiding purpose could be as straightforward as being a loving spouse, a caring grandparent, or a football fan, or to enjoy the loving companionship of a pet.

What do you want to be when you grow up? Based on your unique blend of passions, experiences, influences, education, knowledge, abilities, weaknesses, and values, what purpose suits you best? What is the most satisfying thing you could accomplish in your life? Think about your past experiences that have been especially gratifying and how they might be a part of your future purpose. Consider who you are, how you can express yourself, and on what you can undertake to act on your core values.

If you are young and don't yet have a clear purpose, that's okay. You'll know better after a few more years and life experiences. You just need more time in the greatest learning environment of all, the crucible of life. Take advantage of opportunities to experiment. Let your curiosity guide you. Experience different places and cultures. Get to know different people and how they fulfill their passions. At some point you will find that special interest that completely aligns with your unique blend of values, skills, knowledge, and experiences.

If you are older and don't have a clear purpose, there could be many reasons—some good and some not. Your environment may take up so much of your time that you haven't thought about anything else. You may simply be living on auto-pilot. You've made a choice, unintentionally perhaps, to react to life instead of taking charge of it. If so, take this opportunity to rethink your strategy. Think about what you want to accomplish. Ask yourself what you want to leave as your legacy. Consider your unique combination of talent, knowledge, and experience. Reflect on what you might be the best at in the world with the right focus and resources. Think about living without regrets and the actions required to make that happen. If nothing else, stir up the interest to write a book on what you'd like to share with your family's future generations.

Think about living without regrets and the actions required to make that happen.

As you reflect on your purpose, write it down. It will give you something specific to contemplate, discuss with others, and revise. Establishing a written purpose will help you to form clear goals. Knowing your purpose will help you recognize what is most important to you and help sustain your drive to reach your objectives.

When I was in my thirties, I found myself questioning my goals, my career path, and what I wanted to do when I grew up. I wasn't having a midlife crisis. I had no regrets, I didn't feel I was running out of time, and I didn't doubt myself. I just had a nagging sense that I was doing less than I could. I wasn't sure what "doing more" consisted of, but I felt capable of more. I took out a notepad and starting compiling lists in order to uncover my true interests. I listed my areas of experience, enjoyment, curiosity, concern, knowledge, passion, and talent. I listed areas where I had received encouragement, areas where I had not done so well, and areas that I clearly wanted to avoid. I then circled the items that I most enjoyed and crossed out those I didn't.

The talents and abilities I listed and wanted to develop had little in common. I liked the outdoors and hosting guests. I had earned an engineering degree, spent a year in a Harvard Business School's advanced management program, and been certified in emergency medicine. I had received a number of professional awards for consultative selling and strategic planning. I was good at facilitating meetings and riding motorcycles. I enjoyed building houses and being part of hard-working, competent teams. I had been told that I was good at turning complex issues into easily understandable concepts and that I was a good listener.

At first, the list offered no help because everything seemed so unrelated, so I set it aside and let it simmer in my mind for a while. After about three weeks of jotting down ideas, marking things off the list, and adding others, I had an epiphany. There was, in fact, a common thread among them. In that instant, I conceived two objectives that allowed me to use all my talents, experiences, knowledge, values, and interests while avoiding those areas that I most wanted to avoid.

The objectives were to start a boutique consulting company and to build an executive retreat in the Rocky Mountains of Colorado. The consulting company would use my talents while allowing me the flexibility to live and raise my family where I wanted. The retreat would become a venue to host my clients, family, and friends. This dual objective would allow me to use my home-building and engineering skills to build the retreat, to accommodate my interests in hosting, and to impart my professional experience to others. I could guide my clients and guests in the many outdoor recreation opportunities offered in the national forests surrounding the retreat. Best of all, it supported my family's interests. The fit was perfect.

Realizing this goal took twelve years. As you might imagine, pulling it off required an incredible amount of planning, financial resources, family support, and execution. It also required additional self-development in many areas. As a do-it-yourselfer, I had to learn how to manage a construction project of considerable size. I had to learn how to select and motivate construction workers. I had to improve my ability to partner with others as I went from a corporate world full of resources to a boutique consulting practice that initially had no clients or employees. I had to develop patience, the ability to manage stress, creative ways to overcome obstacles, and many other competencies. In the end, I owned my own business and a venue in which to apply my interests, talents, knowledge, and experience.

Even though my BHAG was clear to me when I started my two ventures, my overarching purpose wasn't. Only after I started my consulting business and engaged in many different areas did I discover the exceptional fit that coaching and leadership development became for me. Sometimes you just have to act and figure it out as you go along. Now I'm certain of my purpose: to help individuals and organizations reach their peak potential. It fits my values, it fits my skills, and I truly enjoy it. And by the way, I still have other interests and pursue other opportunities. Having an overriding purpose doesn't mean you can't involve yourself in other areas.

You will know when you find your purpose because your passions and talents converge to multiply your performance. Your mind will gush out ideas, objectives, and goals. You will envision achievements you didn't know were possible. If you are like me, it will give you meaning beyond yourself, the feeling that you've discovered how to make a real difference in the world. As Roger Williams, seventeenth-century English theologian and author, said, "The greatest crime in the world is not developing your potential. When you do what you do best, you are helping not only yourself, but the world."

You will know when you find your purpose because your passions and talents converge to multiply your performance.

Recall that my purpose originated from my exercise in understanding my own unique set of experiences, interests, social influences, education, knowledge, natural abilities, weaknesses, and values. A similar exercise may help you. If so, visit www.activatingyourambition.com for a downloadable skills and interests worksheet to help you identify your unique skills, interests, and characteristics.

Don't Worry about "How"

You should now have written goals and plans for the important areas of your life. Hopefully the simple process of writing down your goals has given you a new sense of direction, purpose, and confidence. If you haven't identified your goals, create them now and record them. Don't miss out on the benefits and direction they provide. Even if your goals seem impossible at this point, write them down anyway. Impossible today doesn't mean impossible forever. If you give them a chance, the principles you're about to learn in *Activating Your Ambition* can transform the way you see the world. As in the African proverb, "You can eat an elephant—it just takes one bite at a time."

This proverb reminds me of when I first started vacationing in the high country of Colorado. I would see local residents jogging along the mountain paths and think how impossible that would ever be for me to do. We were at ten thousand feet above sea level. Coming from a near sea-level elevation, I could hardly carry my luggage up one flight of stairs to our cabin, much less jog for miles. Even though I was only in my twenties, the thought of jogging at high altitude seemed extraordinary, and I thought it must require a level of fitness well beyond me. Fast-forward twenty years. Now, I work out, jog several miles, ride a mountain bike, or ski at high altitude every day I'm in town.

It's no different than when I first enrolled in college and struggled to come up with the money for my first semester's tuition and books. I remember thinking how hard it must be to save up for a house. As a teenager just out of high school, I lived paycheck to paycheck to pay for rent, food, and transportation. I thought affording a house would be impossible. By the time I reached my mid-forties, I owned four houses and a ranch. What seemed completely impossible became a complete reality.

Most things are not impossible; they only seem impossible. Impossible is a mental construct, a perception. Reality is different.

At this point in your self-improvement endeavor, don't fret over the "how" to achieve your goals. Just write them down. Endeavors that require significant effort, real chutzpah, and extra willpower to sustain in order to succeed are the target applications of *Activating Your Ambition.*

Follow a Systematic Approach to Goal Setting

To put your purpose, important life areas, goals, and action plans into order, here is a commonsense approach to follow:

Step One—Contemplate your purpose. Think about what you want to do when you grow up. Consider your experiences, values, talents, skills, accomplishments, failures, education, knowledge, interests, and any memories that have made an impact on you. Discover that special something you can do that gives meaning to your existence.

Step Two—Based on your overriding purpose, values, and life ambitions, identify the primary areas of your life, such as family, faith, profession, finances, fun, mental acuity, physical condition, and community service, on which you want to focus.

Step Three—Create a list of high-level goals (objectives) you wish to achieve in each area you identified in step two. For now, free your mind of the constraints that might normally prevent you from dreaming; you'll decide how realistic each objective is later. Objectives could include spending more time with your spouse, building a new house, traveling the world, learning how to think strategically, improving your fitness, becoming a better listener, and so on. Time permitting, or at another time, identify objectives in each area for all three time horizons—near-term (less than twelve months), medium-term (one to five years) and long-term (more than five years).

Step Four—Prioritize your goals. From the ones you identified in step three, circle those that offer the highest return on your development investment. Consider moving to the top of your list those goals that most affect other areas or that enable objectives in other areas.

Step Five—Establish specific goals for your high-priority objectives. For each one you circled, define a successful outcome, a measureable milestone. State it positively and in the present tense. If, for example, your objective is: "to teach Sunday school," the outcome might be something like: "I have taught Sunday school six times as of the end of this year." Or if you want to work more productively, your outcome might be: "I complete every item on my daily to-do list four out of five days a week."

Step Six—Look at your list of high-priority objectives and goal outcomes and ask yourself, "What special skills or behaviors do I need to develop to attain these goals, and what do I need to overcome to be able to grow and develop?" Reflect on these questions and identify the core enablers to reaching your goal. Ask others whom you trust and respect for their insight. These questions deserve your most focused attention and will be the key to activating your ambition.

The reason to focus on your self-development is that it is the means to reaching your goal. You wouldn't expect to save the down-payment on a house or a new car if what you needed to do first was improve your skills so you can earn more money. You wouldn't expect to find a marriage partner if you first needed to learn relationship skills. You wouldn't expect to become a scratch golfer if you didn't focus first on improving your aim, stance, and swing.

Make your ambition personal. Make it something you need to do in order to achieve your desires. If your ambition is to become a manager within two years, think about what traits you need to develop in order to achieve that goal and set your self-development ambition on areas like better strategic thinking, improved speaking, or collaborating skills. If you want to pursue a new career, think about how you can become more valuable to a prospective employer. Consider what skills or attitudes you need to develop or improve. If you have any obstacle that you suspect will prevent you from getting to your goal, make overcoming it your ambition.

Your personal development ambitions can be goals in themselves. Don't fuss too much about whether you have set goals, milestones, or objectives. Their differences are minor, and they can frequently be interchanged without impact to the results. Goal setting can be done in many different ways to accomplish the same result. The bottom line is that you have a strong sense of direction, you are accountable to an achievable documented plan, and you know where you need to focus in order to achieve your ambitions.

Common Professional-Development Goals

The list of possible professional-development goals includes just as broad a range of skills, behaviors, attitudes, styles, and competencies as does the list of personal goals. When you consider the number of characteristics a professional can exhibit and the unique combinations of those characteristics, the possibilities are infinite. Common models that human resource professionals use to assess personality include the Five Factor Model and the Myers-Briggs Type Indicator. Even these concise models of five or four basic characteristics, respectively, require that you break them down into subfactors to get meaningful goals on which to focus your development. The Five Factor Model, as simple as it appears, is based on initial research that uncovered 17,953 personality-describing words. When you consider the possible combinations of that many characteristics, there is truly no limit to the uniqueness of our characters and to the areas in which we might develop.

While there is an endless possible list of development options, in my executive coaching, a finite number of development areas recur more often than others. These may be useful for you to review as you think about your goals and developmental needs:

- Thinking more strategically
- Being more focused
- Having more time or energy
- Creating ownership in others
- Inspiring others
- Strengthening decision making

- Dealing better with conflict
- Fostering a climate of cooperation
- Improving social skills
- Raising professionalism and image
- Becoming a better speaker
- Becoming a better listener
- Boosting mental acuity
- Having courage
- Building confidence
- Moving strategies to execution
- Attracting top talent
- Delegating tasks to others
- Being more open and approachable
- Coaching and developing others

- Reducing unconstructive conflict
- Improving teamwork
- Holding employees accountable
- Making weaknesses irrelevant
- Building a positive attitude
- Leveraging resources
- Working more intentionally
- Increasing productivity
- Finding work-life balance
- Confronting performance problems
- Setting priorities and saying no
- Being more organized
- Executing with excellence
- Encouraging innovation

Create Your Road Map

Before moving on to the next chapter, make a choice of the highest priority goal you will pursue. Pick a critical skill you want to enhance, a leadership competency you want to develop, a behavior you want to change, a level of physical fitness you want to attain, an improvement you want to make in your relationships, or a bad habit you want to overcome.

Write your self-development objective down in a notebook or in the companion workbook, *Activating Your Ambition Workbook* (see www. activatingyourambition.com for ordering information). Your notebook or workbook will become your road map to successful self-development. As you go through the remaining chapters, you will be adding information, actions, and milestones that cover each of the eight principles. At the conclusion of this book, you will have created a detailed road map of how to successfully turn your ambition into reality.

Even if you are reading this book with the intention of helping others in your company, family, or community of friends, create your own road map first. You will be a much better teacher, trainer, coach, or helper having applied the approach yourself. Knowing how to do something is no substitute for experience and real-life examples.

If you're using your own notebook, follow these instructions to set up your road map to success. Put a title on the first page of your notebook that represents your endeavor. It might read, "I am a trim 135 pounds," or "I am a confident public speaker and enjoy speaking in front of audiences of one hundred people," or "I am an inspiring coach to my athletes," or "I am considerate to my spouse and do things daily that make her smile." Make your objective specific, measurable, and positive. Write it in the present tense.

On top of the next page in your notebook write the page title "Table of Contents." Below that, write the following bullets that will represent each of the sections of your road map:

- Introduction and Background
- My Purpose, Objectives, and Goals
- My Awareness
- My Motivation
- My Belief
- My Incremental Steps
- My Time and Energy
- My Initiation
- My Others
- My Normalcy
- My Activating Your Ambition Scorecard
- My Journey Journal

On top of the following page, write the title "Introduction and Background." This section will capture your initial thoughts about your upcoming effort. You can include a brief background, why you have chosen this journey, a review of any prior attempts, how you came to your self-development objective, and any other pertinent historical information you want to include. In this section, list the enemies of self-improvement that you expect to contend with. Add any fears you face and your plan to deal with those fears, as explained in the section on fear in Chapter Two.

Skip a few pages, and at the top of a following page write the title, "My Purpose, Objectives, and Goals." Include here the information you created when establishing your goals as outlined in this chapter.

Your road map notebook should now have a title page with your self-development ambition, a table of contents page, a brief introduction and background section, and a completed purpose, objectives, and goals section. The next eight chapters will guide you through the completion of the remaining sections of your road map, which will put the "how to accomplish" detail behind the "what you want to accomplish" objective.

The page you titled "My Activating Your Ambition Scorecard" is provided to assess yourself at the end of each of the upcoming eight chapters. It will give you a comparison of the areas you believe you are strong in to those in which you are not as strong, so you know where to put added focus. Use a simple one to five scale or high/medium/low rating to score how well you believe you do in each area.

The page you titled "My Journey Journal" is provided to record your progress once you fully initiate your self-improvement pursuit.

Good luck!

Part 2

Developing the Ability

4
Build Awareness

An investment in knowledge pays the best interest.

–Benjamin Franklin

Debbie was the chief financial officer for a building products manufacturing company. She came to me with more than a little trepidation. Her boss, the president of the company, had suggested she go through a six-month coaching engagement with me. Debbie wasn't fully committed to the idea, and she was unsure of the coaching process in terms of its time requirements and level of transparency. However, she was open to giving it a try.

When I first talked with Debbie, she explained her needs. By her own admission, she was extremely disorganized. She had piles of paper around her office, on her desk, her credenza, her floor, and even on top of her printer, rendering it useless unless she temporarily moved the piles before printing. Her filing system was not much different. She had files in multiple cabinets with no consistent filing system. Some files were in calendar order, some arranged by topic, and others by project name.

Because of Debbie's disorganization, she was the bottleneck to progress on many company initiatives. As the company's chief financial officer, she was part of the critical path to producing the company's financial reports, reviewing legal contracts, approving capital expenditures, and many other important activities. Co-workers were constantly put on hold, waiting for Debbie to finish her work so they could continue theirs.

As I started working with Debbie, we began with the "why" of her disorganization before plunging into the "what." We dug into the root causes of her cluttered mode of operation. What we found was that Debbie was a people pleaser. She couldn't say no. She accepted every request that came her way, and rather than pushing back or delegating, she simply accepted what was asked of her. As a result, she was completely overwhelmed.

Her disorganization was a symptom of a different root cause. Had Debbie and I focused only on her organizational skills, we would have completely missed the real issue. Without an accurate awareness of her current condition, we would have implemented an inappropriate solution.

Early in my coaching career, I naively asked people how well they knew themselves. I learned to quit asking, because the answer always came back, "I know myself well." Of course, that's the answer people should provide, given they've lived with themselves for their whole lives. The problem is that it turns out to be untrue; our self-knowledge is misleading. We have two issues to overcome when trying to see ourselves objectively and establish an accurate self-awareness. One is getting beyond the psychological filter of biases through which we see the world. The other is teasing apart our intentions from our actions.

Our self-knowledge is biased by our intentions, our rationalizations, and our subconscious, in addition to our actions. These make it very difficult to see ourselves objectively. Our unique blend of experiences, values, talents, personality, and knowledge filters how we take in and process information. Our filters prevent us from seeing what can be obvious to others. As a result, we have a very narrow view of ourselves. If we see anything about ourselves accurately, we see the symptoms. Root causes are all but invisible.

Many people don't even see the symptoms. Debbie's case was straightforward because she was well aware of them. Discovery of her true need was quick and easy. For others who are unaware of their symptoms, the first task is to bring them into view. Many people don't know that they constantly interrupt others in the middle of a sentence, much less why. People don't see how defensive they are when someone offers them advice, much less the reason for it. People don't realize how insecure, out of shape, overweight, angry, or addicted they are until they are made aware of it.

The first task when people don't see their symptoms is to get their attention. You can't expect people to fix something they don't know is broken. People need to realize their need to develop before engaging in any meaningful conversation about deepening their awareness or identifying root causes.

You can't expect people to fix something they don't know is broken.

No matter how smart you are, how unfortunate you are, or how loudly someone is screaming at you, you won't change if you don't perceive a need. If no one has gotten your attention and you feel no sense of urgency to change, you won't. If you haven't yet encountered a situation requiring different behavior, you won't see the need for it. If you've not experienced the negative consequences of your current behavior, you won't see the need. If you have not discovered that you are not as quick, careful, energetic, open-minded, logical, considerate, or capable as you need to be, you won't change.

When you become aware you're having guests over for dinner, you plan the meal and get the house ready. When you learn you'll fail a class if you don't turn in an assignment, you go to work on turning in the assignment. When your boss tells you your bonus is based on your performance, you focus on your performance. It is only when you are aware of your true condition and its consequences that you take it seriously.

Once you become aware of your condition, the focus turns to pinpointing its underlying cause. True awareness requires digging beneath the symptoms and finding their cause. It requires getting beyond your rationalizations and self-deceptions, pushing aside the excuses, and focusing on the truth.

Awareness means looking at your situation objectively and discovering what you really need to do to reach your goals. It is the recognition of your true self, desires, values, and intentions. Awareness is the foundation of your journey, because everything else you do is based on it. Of the eight principles you will learn, awareness is the most likely to bring out epiphanies and new realizations that will provide the basis for tremendous growth.

Awareness is more than knowledge; it is understanding and accepting the reality of your situation, recognizing and admitting a need to change. Awareness starts by acquiring knowledge about yourself, but true self-awareness begins when your knowledge turns into understanding.

Consider your reactions when others comment objectively on your behavior. Let's say you snore in your sleep. If someone says you snore, and this is the first time you hear about it, you react with a degree of shock. You might say, "Are you sure? Are you kidding?" The next reaction, often unvoiced, is annoyance or resentment: "I can't believe she told me that! I don't believe her." After further reflection, you accept that it might be something you do, and it gets your attention. You realize you do snore, and if it's bad enough, you decide to see what you might do about it.

Note that in this scenario you had the knowledge from the first time you heard that you snored. However, only later did you accept it, understand it, and have the true awareness needed to do something about it.

Three kinds of awareness are critical to building a solid foundation for change—self-awareness, awareness of your objective, and awareness of how to get there.

Self-awareness is the honest and accurate assessment of your current self, a genuine understanding of your current reality and your "as-is" condition. It goes beyond any rationalizations or self-deceptions that impede a candid view of yourself, and it includes recognizing you have an opportunity for personal development.

The second awareness you need is that of your true objective—the one that resolves the root cause. This is a natural outcome of establishing an accurate self-awareness. Debbie's initial goal was to be more organized, but her root-cause-resolving objective was to learn to say no and delegate to others. You retain your original objective, but augment it with a secondary objective. The result is a deeper and more realistic view of what your true success looks like.

The third form of awareness is that of how to reach your goal—understanding how to close the gap between where you are and where you wish to be and knowing the important details of the journey. It includes the logistics, resources, methods, supplies, costs, and other details involved in reaching your goal. Where there are multiple options available, it includes educating yourself and making decisions on the best routes to take.

Putting the three dimensions of awareness into action isn't hard. If you are pursuing better health and longevity, self-assessment might be as simple as considering what you eat. Your end goal could be a daily intake of calories, vitamins, and minerals. Your awareness of how to attain that intake basically involves looking into nutritional recommendations, understanding nutritional sources, and selecting the foods and nutritional levels that best suit your needs.

If your objective is to become a great leader, self-awareness might involve understanding how you perform compared to the abilities of other great leaders. This includes knowing both your strengths and your developmental needs. That knowledge would give you insight into the improvements you need to make as well as the courses, seminars, books, on-the-job assignments, and other options available to achieve your desired improvements.

Identify Your Gap

As a consultant, I model organizational processes to improve efficiencies and overcome obstacles. The models apply to processes like selling, customer service, software development, and decision making. The approach starts with modeling the "as-is" environment, the current set of activities in the process before any improvements.

The next step is to create a model of the "to-be" environment, the desired future. The two models define the gap between the "as-is" and the "to-be." The gap is the basis for identifying and analyzing alternative solutions available to bridge the gap. Without an accurate awareness of the gap, selecting the best solution is guesswork.

If you are building a house, first you understand your needs, and then you decide on the features to fill those needs. You go through a process of evaluating, pricing, and decision making to design a home with the features that meet your needs. Building a house without such planning would be foolish. You would end up with a lesser home than you could have had.

Understanding your self-development gap is no different. It is especially important if your objective is less tangible, such as improving your relationship or decision-making skills. Anything you can do to make the intangible more tangible gives you a better chance of improving it. With an unclear gap, you risk heading down the wrong path of alternatives and criteria on which to evaluate them. With a clear gap, your decisions are easier and your confidence in them is greater, reinforcing your commitment to implement them.

Anything you can do to make the intangible more tangible gives you a better chance of improving it.

If you're planning to improve your physical condition, the gap could be something like losing forty pounds. The next step would be to evaluate your best options for losing the forty pounds. You would research the various diets and exercise programs available and select the one that best fits your needs. Had you not known how much weight to lose, your decision on which program to follow would have been a guess, that would have resulted in limited confidence that you had chosen correctly.

The following sections provide various methods of establishing your gap and show how best to bridge it. If you are taking notes in your notebook, title the next page "My Awareness" and list any ideas or actions you wish to take as your read through this chapter. If you are using the *Activating Your Ambition Workbook*, turn to the "My Awareness" page and do the same.

Get Beyond Your Self-Deception

The first of the three dimensions of awareness is self-awareness. Self-awareness is establishing an accurate assessment of your own "as-is" condition. Even if you think you already know yourself, you probably don't as well as you think you do. If you are like most people, you are better at knowing others than knowing yourself. We tend to assess and judge others more accurately because we base our assessment of others on real actions. Our self-assessments on the other hand often confuse our actions with our intentions. Studies on self-awareness consistently reveal that there is little correlation between people's self-assessment and their scores on objective tests.

We are masters of self-deception. We can be totally honest with others but be habitually dishonest with ourselves. Benjamin Franklin once suggested, "Search others for their virtues, thyself for thy vices." We more often get his advice backwards, looking at others with an eye toward their vices but toward our own virtues. We think we look better, behave better, and communicate better than we really do. In the book *Leadership and Self-Deception* by the Arbinger Institute, a consulting firm and scholarly consortium, the authors tell an enlightening story of a leader who had no idea of his selfish motives. He thought he was an experienced and gifted leader while, by all objective measures, he was selfish and internally focused. Because of his self-deception, he had a completely inaccurate awareness of himself. Only through a process of opening himself to objective feedback was he able to discover his true selfish nature and start to overcome it.

Gaining self-awareness means getting to know yourself—not judging yourself, but honestly getting to know the real you. It means understanding your own uniqueness, what makes you good and what holds you back. It is a candid assessment that gets beyond what you think you know and into areas you really don't know. Whether starting a self-development initiative to build a new skill or to overcome an old habit, your success depends on starting with the facts of your current condition. The only legitimate starting point is an accurate assessment and interpretation of the truth about your actions, beliefs, and behaviors. Armed with the truth, your road map to success will be faster, easier, and more conducive to achieving the benefits you desire.

Gaining self-awareness is also a great experience. You will find it not only beneficial but also extremely interesting and satisfying. For many, it produces a series of epiphanies through which, for the first time in their lives, they truly understand why they do what they do.

In my work as an executive coach, I consistently come in after previous attempts at changing people's behaviors have failed. People routinely misdiagnose their conditions. Eight out of ten people come to me describing an issue that, upon deeper discovery, is not the one for which they need help. In a January 2009, *Harvard Business Review Research Report*, a survey of 140 executive coaches by Diane Coutu and Carol Kauffman, found that all but eight of them agreed that the focus of their coaching sessions typically shifted during the course of their coaching engagements. The predominant reason given was a deepening of the executive's goals and self-awareness.

One executive with whom I worked had a problem with low employee morale. His initial request was to help improve his ability to inspire and motivate his team. He believed stronger speaking skills would inspire those around him and therefore boost morale. When we reviewed his feedback from an employee survey we conducted and analyzed the root issues, low employee morale wasn't a result of his speaking ability at all. The root issue was his inability to listen. He didn't listen, didn't ask questions, and didn't seek employee input or involvement in any form. When he met with employees, he spent his mental energy thinking about his next statement, not what others were telling him. This executive could have worked on his speaking skills for years and never improved his employees' morale.

Eight out of ten people come to me describing an issue that, upon deeper discovery, is not the one for which they need help.

What you and I may think are critical obstacles to achieving our ambitions may only be symptoms, not causes. Left on our own without deeper awareness, we would more often than not proceed down the wrong path in solving our problems. Don't assume you know your true self or your self-improvement goals until you have a solid foundation of self-awareness.

You can use several techniques to strengthen your self-awareness. One is to try to separate yourself into two people—the real you and someone observing you. The observer takes notes. She assesses your behaviors and attitudes and records how well you do against measures you set for yourself. The observer in you can also enlist the assistance of audio and video recordings of you in action.

While it's a valid option for getting to know yourself, turning on the mirror of self-observation is difficult and the least effective approach to accurately increasing self-awareness. More effective approaches include soliciting feedback from others and participating in structured assessments.

Conduct Assessments

Structured individual assessments help reveal natural personality preferences, innate strengths, management competencies, work orientations, work styles, values, interest areas, and many other characteristics. They can be found online, within self-help books, and as part of many coaching programs. You need to do some homework, though, because most are context sensitive in that they are designed for a particular situation. Pick the type of assessment that best fits your needs. If you are interested in developing social skills, select an assessment instrument designed to create transparency into your social capabilities like empathy and emotional intelligence. If you want to understand your true capabilities in strategic analysis, select an assessment that reveals your analytical reasoning capabilities. There are assessments for every characteristic you would want to understand better. If you're not sure in which areas you want to dive deeper, broad assessments are also available.

One popular assessment is the 360-degree survey named after the circle of influence in which a person operates. It gathers input not only from you, but also from managers, peers, direct reports, and others within your circle of influence to provide objective feedback about you in a variety of areas. The 360-degree SCOPE of Leadership™ survey my company uses captures feedback on thirty different competencies.

A typical 360 survey consists of twenty to forty questions about a variety of characteristics, including skills, attitudes, values, and behaviors. This type of survey is frequently employed in large organizations. The survey does a nice job of revealing how others perceive you and how those perceptions compare with how you see yourself. The survey is a reliable source of insight as long as its results are not tied to performance appraisals. If the survey has performance appraisal implications, or if an organization gears the survey toward organizational goals rather than individual development, its effectiveness as a self-awareness tool is dramatically reduced.

Self-assessments can also be taken by members of your family and co-workers to help uncover family or team dynamics issues. When members of a family or team take the same self-assessment, they have a common baseline for sharing information. The sharing process requires a degree of transparency—allowing others to see your results, and vice versa—but as long as group members trust each other to use the results constructively, it is a very effective tool. Comparing another's characteristics to your own can be very revealing and help both of you better understand why you behave and interact as you do.

Historically, one of the most popular assessments for understanding personality preferences has been the Myers-Briggs Type Indicator, which has been around for many years and has been taken by millions of people. It measures some of the most fundamental characteristics of personality, your preference for taking in information from the environment around you, how you make decisions on that information, and how these two basic thought processes are oriented either inwardly or outwardly. The results help reveal predictable errors in judgment, activities that drain your energy, unconscious behaviors, and other valuable insights about yourself.

Before evaluating any self-initiated assessment, you must know how to interpret the results. Simple assessments can be easy to understand, but interpreting the more complex assessments usually requires the help of an expert. If you don't have the benefit of a professional coach, an interpretation is often available at extra cost as part of the assessment. I encourage you to spend the extra money and gain the full understanding that is available to you.

Assess Yourself Broadly

A solid foundation of self-awareness is made up of understanding your strengths and your shortcomings. These include your abilities, attitudes, and values. While you may be pursuing development in only one area, such as in controlling emotional outbursts or lowering chronic stress, knowing yourself broadly is nonetheless essential. Often one area affects another; rarely does one characteristic stand completely alone. Characteristics support each other, detract from each other, and sometimes cancel each other. Knowing both your strengths and your weaknesses can reveal how one causes the other. Both have double edges, and knowing what they are explains many behaviors.

Knowing both your strengths and your weaknesses
can reveal how one causes the other.

If your objective is to improve your social skills, a broader assessment could reveal that your strength in working with facts and

97

numbers is what prevents you from focusing on being more social. An aptitude for details or a technical field often prevents people from being socially inclined. They see the world more as objects, numbers, facts, and tasks than as people with emotions and feelings. The same applies in reverse; an extrovert who enjoys gatherings and talking to people may want to be able to focus more on tasks and details. A broad self-assessment could reveal that their people orientation makes detailed work as boring for them as watching paint dry. Assessments deliver valuable insights that will directly affect the approach you take or the goal you pursue.

There are several benefits to understanding yourself broadly. Knowing your aptitudes before you begin a development initiative saves you significant time and frustration along the way. Knowing, for example, that the very competency that makes you good in one area makes you not so good in another can save you countless hours of working on the wrong area.

A broad understanding of yourself answers many questions and boosts your confidence. It offers insight into why you do, say, and think the way you do and value what you value. People discover for the first time why they do things they've been doing for many years. They get answers to basic questions—why certain activities really bother them and certain others are so enjoyable. They learn why people react to them in different ways, for instance, why they set some people off and make others so comfortable.

Assessments boost your confidence not only by answering questions but also by identifying your strengths. When your improvement program makes you feel like a rookie, realizing you are a veteran at something else gives you refuge and makes it more bearable. Assessments can also point out that your weaker areas are not character flaws but simply aspects of your natural personality. This is extremely valuable to know and understand in accepting yourself and knowing what may be hard to change.

Overall, broad assessments enable you to examine objectively the areas in which you want to change. They help you understand other traits that affect the areas you want to change and reveal how your strengths can also be weaknesses. They help you understand how one personality trait can be overused and cause problems in other areas. This information adds up to a much more accurate foundation for your self-development.

Solicit Feedback

One of the easiest and best ways to get to know yourself better is to solicit the perceptions of others who can offer a more objective view of your actions and behaviors than you can. Our unconscious deceptions make us a poor eyewitness of our own behavior. In extreme cases, it distorts the results of structured assessments, even though most have built-in mechanisms to prevent it. To combat the tendency to replace introspection with self-deception, solicit the feedback of others. They are better at seeing how well you do in converting your intentions into actions.

Seeking feedback from others is not only powerful, it's also simple. Gaining feedback is as straightforward as asking a trusted co-worker to give it to you. You simply ask for an assessment of your proficiency in something like listening to or inspiring others, "John, may I ask a favor? I'm examining my listening skills and would value your opinion. How do you perceive my listening skills?" In a matter of a few minutes, you can learn what you've not known for a lifetime. You can learn that you're better than you thought or that you lack the skills you thought you excelled in. While you'd prefer the former, the latter would be more beneficial to know. Either way, you increase your self-awareness.

In addition to receiving feedback when you request it, encourage others to give you feedback on an ad-hoc basis. Tell them what you are working on and that if they see a specific behavior, you want immediate feedback. If you chronically interrupt people, tell your co-worker or friend to point out your offenses as you commit them. Tell them you need their help bringing it to your attention. Give them an incentive, if it would help, like giving them five dollars per occurrence or a free lunch. It would increase your incentive too.

Giving feedback is uncomfortable for some people. They would rather be quiet and unhelpful than speak up and risk coming across as being critical. Some entire organizations and cultures frown upon feedback, even when given constructively. They view it as not being accepting of others or not being a team player. People who work in such a feedback-poor culture rarely understand why they get passed over for promotions or receive low pay raises. They are fortunate to get their perfunctory performance appraisal once a year, and even then the feedback is so outdated or sterilized that it is of little help.

If you are part of a feedback-poor environment or need to accommodate those preferring to withhold their observations, you can get around this by asking them to tell you what others think about you. Put them in the position of a third party by asking their opinion about a recent situation in which you interacted with others. Or ask them what others might say about you if they were sitting in a bar after work having a couple of drinks. Make them feel they are giving feedback as a third person, not a first person.

A word of caution in receiving feedback: Don't be defensive. Don't punish the feedback provider for trying to help you. If you do, don't expect more feedback. Learn to say, "Thank you for that feedback," and leave it at that. Don't try to explain why you said or did what you did. Even if you have a good explanation, this isn't the right time for it.

Another source of objective feedback is video recordings. If you are serious about improving your coaching skills, presentation skills, golf swing, executive presence, or other visibly observable abilities, record yourself. Video is a great source of insight and makes your actions indisputable. Just know that while video evidence may be what you need to understand your current self, it can be humbling. You have to be able to learn from what you observe without taking yourself too seriously.

To create a video recording, ask someone else for help. Let him operate the video camera and worry about lighting, microphone input, and other issues so you don't have to. The environment should be as natural as possible. Position your assistant in the room so he doesn't distract you.

If your improvement program is related to work, find opportunities to video events that would be beneficial for others besides yourself to see. This accomplishes two objectives for the effort of one. If you have remote employees who don't normally see you in person, a video could provide a delightful alternative to a normally boring e-mail or conference call, and you'll have a copy for yourself to review and learn from.

If video is a problem, some projects do just as well with audio recording or photographs. If you're working on your vocabulary or tonality, an audio recording could suffice. If you are dieting, a simple photograph of yourself in a swimsuit might be all you need.

Alter Your Point of Reference

Another method of building your awareness is to change your point of reference. While your view of situations, attitudes, beliefs, and actions seem real to you, they are merely your perceptions from your vantage point.

To illustrate, a valuable technique in negotiation is exploring each party's needs. The aim is for each party to understand the other's needs before taking positions, so each has a full and accurate perspective of the issues and opportunities. You do this by putting yourself in the other's position and stating that position before stating your own. Putting yourself in someone else's shoes changes your point of reference. You view the situation not from your point of view but from his. This is as useful in understanding our own issues as it is in situations involving others. Changing perspectives offers an important opportunity to see a situation from a different vantage point and gain a new level of awareness.

Our minds are quick to jump to conclusions. Based on past experiences that we perceive to be like our current situation, we rush to judgment, but our intuition and unconscious biases are not always accurate. They reflect past feelings and outcomes that do not accurately represent our current reality. By putting yourself in a different position with a different perspective, you gain a much better understanding of an issue.

Based on past experiences that we perceive to be like our current situation, we rush to judgment, but our intuition and unconscious biases are not always accurate.

If your development need involves communication, conflict, or any other people-related area, it is especially important to put yourself in the shoes of others. Try to see the situation from the other person's perspective and feel his feelings. Do your best to understand and even explain his point of view before explaining your own. Explain the situation as he would and confirm that you understand his point of view. When people have strong emotions, opinions, and positions about an issue, there is usually a reason. Seek to understand the reason and ensure you are not basing your awareness on your own inaccurate perceptions. Successful self-development is based on reality.

Change Your Surroundings

Another method for changing your perspective is to alter your surroundings. Your perceptions result not only from what you think but also from what you do, whom you associate with, where you work, where you live, what you play, how you socialize, and all other elements of your physical surroundings. Your environment defines your view of reality.

I have great respect for people who work for one organization for their entire career. If you are one of these, congratulations. Lifelong employment with one company is a testament not only to stability but also to resilience. No doubt you've experienced many situations where you were tempted to leave. You've likely persevered through bad bosses, failed projects, and difficult situations, yet you've chosen to endure or fight back rather than quit.

There is a downside, though, to working for only one employer. It limits your view of how other organizations operate. People who have worked in only one organization tend to see everything from one perspective. They have missed opportunities to expand their experience and knowledge. They see their work from a single viewpoint. Since they have been exposed to only their own organization's policies, procedures, processes, and values, they are largely unaware of those of other organizations.

This is not to suggest that you should change jobs every few years, as that causes other issues which more than offset any benefit offered by different experiences. If you work in a larger organization, however, consider expanding your perspective by taking on special assignments in other regions or divisions. Or if you must stay in your current role, participate in special projects. Organizations typically have many special projects and understaffed initiatives that would benefit from additional resources. Special projects and assignments also give you valuable exposure to other departments and managers.

Changing your surroundings to gain a different perspective does not require serious sacrifice. It can be as simple as getting out of a routine or habit. If your self-development initiative is to deal more effectively with conflict, find an assignment that puts you in surroundings where managing conflict is unavoidable. Customer service is full of opportunities for resolving conflict. Working a few days in a customer service department would give you valuable experiences without the upheaval of changing jobs.

If you are stuck in one of life's ruts, particularly one preventing your development, you may need to make an even greater change in your surroundings—one affecting where you live, where you work, or with whom you socialize. When I started high school, I hung out with kids who believed life was all fun and play, a common perspective held by many teenagers (my own included). My view was that high school was the place to spend time with friends during the day, so you could figure out what to do when the school day was over. If you had to work, you worked with friends to make it fun.

The problem was that my friends and I took it to the extreme. Our fun-loving behavior became shameless. We had fun at others' expense. My selfishness went on for a couple of years until I noticed that kids outside my group who exercised more restraint and discipline were also having a good time, but without the collateral damage. They were achieving more too. They made better grades, performed better in sports, received school recognition, worked in better-paying part-time jobs, and drove nicer cars. These more mature kids saw the world not as a playground, but as an environment to learn, gain experience, be successful, and have fun.

At first, I resisted the temptation to change what I did and who I hung out with. These were my best friends. But as time passed, I knew I had to change my surroundings. Although it wouldn't be easy, I knew it was the only way I could mature as I needed. I made the decision, and from that point forward, I disengaged from my circle of friends.

Distancing was difficult at first, but within a few weeks, with my new sense of freedom and time, I put myself in situations where I met new friends. After a few months, I had a new circle of friends who were more mature, had higher ambitions, and to my delight, were better friends. By the time I graduated high school, my intentional change of surroundings had given me a diverse set of acquaintances and experiences. I uniquely had friends among most of the main groups including the geeks, jocks, druggies, car buffs, scholars, and socials.

I've applied this same strategy many times since. I've changed jobs, moved from one neighborhood to another, found new hobbies, joined new churches, and changed friends. While sometimes painful and inconvenient, changing my surroundings has been invaluable in my development.

Staying in the same surroundings too long creates a rut and desensitizes you to the broader reality around you. Even good routines that you would be foolish to give up desensitize you to your surroundings. If you drive the same route to work each day, stop at the same coffee shop, go in the same door of the office building, use the same elevator, and sit in the same office, much of what you do becomes so habitual that you become blind to it. You can make it to your office with little memory of how you got there. But if you take a different route to work, try a different coffee shop, choose another door to your building, or start your day in someone else's office, you stay much more aware. Different experiences increase your sensitivity to and awareness of your surroundings.

New experiences leave strong and lasting impressions. They can be as strong as a memory of a national disaster or lifetime accomplishment. I remember being riveted to the television on July 20, 1969, when Neil Armstrong stepped out of the *Apollo 11* lunar module and walked on the moon. I recall the college lab class I attended on March 30, 1981, where I heard the news that U.S. President Ronald Reagan had been shot. I remember the discount superstore I was in when I walked past the television aisle and saw the news of the space shuttle *Challenger* disaster on January 28, 1986. I can picture looking down on the desk in my office on September 11, 2001, when I got a phone call about the terrorist attack on the World Trade Center in New York City.

When you experience something new, it grabs your attention in ways that routines don't. Driving past a beautiful flower garden every day on your way to work might be something you appreciate and enjoy, but as it becomes part of your routine, its beauty diminishes and is all but forgotten. However, when you drive by a scene for the first time, especially if it is one of unexpected beauty in the middle of an otherwise drab drive, you are much more aware of the experience.

The more experiences you have, the more attention you give yourself and your environment. The more attention you give, the more aware you become, and the more you grow and develop. To heighten your awareness and learn more about yourself, do the unexpected. Get out of your routine. Look for new and different opportunities. Seek out new experiences. Accept invitations from colleagues, friends, and family to visit new places or participate in new activities. Look for occasions to experience new surroundings. Seek out training programs that are experiential or have an element of adventure. New experiences get your attention and turn on your learning switch. They increase your awareness of your strengths, weaknesses, habits, values, and other traits that aid in your development. Out-of-the-ordinary experiences can be life changing.

To heighten your awareness and learn more about yourself, do the unexpected. Get out of your routine.

It's also important to know the difference between a good rut and a bad one. As we will discuss in the final principle of *Activating Your Ambition,* routines can be your friends as well as your enemies. Self-defeating routines and stagnating surroundings that prevent your growth deserve a shake-up. Yet stick with routines, such as good eating habits and daily exercise, which promote good health. Some surroundings, such as the support of an encouraging family, facilitate your self-development. Others may not. Changing your surroundings is intended for those situations that prevent your improvement. Know the difference.

Improve Your Physical and Mental Condition

One of the most important ways to change your surroundings is by changing your physical condition. Your body is a permanent part of your surroundings and has a huge impact on your perceptions. Your physical condition is inextricably linked to your mental condition, and it affects all aspects of your awareness. Your thoughts, perceptions, attitudes, and behaviors are all by-products of your physical condition.

If you believe you're functioning below your potential but can't get excited about taking action, it may be your body telling you it's time for a tone-up. You are feeling the effect of poor physical conditioning. A poor physical condition makes you feel chronically tired, weak, and dull. You can't muster the energy, mental capacity, or confidence required to take the action you perceive is needed.

If you work in a job where much of your day is spent sitting, live a generally sedentary lifestyle, or simply eat more calories than you burn off, your body rebels. You feel lethargic. Your physical condition saps your physical and mental energy.

Not long ago, the mind and body were considered two separate entities; diet and exercise strengthened the body, while mental exercises improved your mind. Now we know that your mind and body are tightly connected. What you do for your body benefits your mind, and what you do for your mind benefits your body. Your thoughts and ambitions are directly linked to your level of physical conditioning.

Physical exercise benefits you in many ways. It increases blood flow and oxygen to your brain, improving its health. It releases two essential neurotransmitters, dopamine and serotonin, which help sustain attention and increase brain-derived neurotrophic factors—a family of proteins that actually regrow neurons. Regular exercise plays a role in increasing the number of synaptic connections in your brain and increases the density of your cortex, the outer layer of your brain responsible for numerous functions, like movement, perception, memory, and speaking. Regular exercise also strengthens other parts of your brain that are responsible for reasoning, emotion, coordination, and learning.

Routine workouts improve muscle tone, increase bone density, lower body fat, reduce cholesterol, and increase immunity to disease. Exercise enhances lung capacity and strengthens your heart, boosts energy capacity, and lowers stress. Exercise increases your metabolism, slows the aging process, and improves the quality of your sleep. It lessens the chance you'll get hurt in recreational sports or when playing with your children. It heightens your self-esteem, improves your confidence, and promotes a can-do attitude. It makes you feel strong, mentally and physically. Physical exercise provides innumerable benefits to your mental health, your physique, and your physical health.

Mental exercise also plays a role in your overall health. Studies have shown that people who do daily crossword puzzles, play memory games, engage in conversations, and constantly learn continue to grow new synaptic connections. This happens regardless of age, which means you can begin doing mental exercises in your senior years and regain memory and cognitive ability that you thought were forever lost.

In addition to mental and physical exercise, a good diet with proper amounts of vitamins and minerals helps your mind and body. Healthy foods and supplements strengthen your immune system, reduce plaque buildup in your blood vessels to increase blood flow, help regulate your hormones, and prevent some types of degenerative diseases.

The indisputable bottom line is that proper diet and exercise can help enhance your energy level, cognitive skills, confidence, and self-development. Without the benefits of exercise and good diet, you lack peak mental acuity and peak energy. When you're out of shape, the mental and physical activities required to achieve your goals can seem completely out of reach.

The indisputable bottom line is that proper diet and exercise can help enhance your energy level, cognitive skills, confidence, and self-development.

Many exercise and nutrition programs are available. The program I've used with great success alternates cardio workouts with strength workouts every other day. Each workout lasts about an hour and includes a variety of routines that together strengthen my heart, lungs, and muscles. Every day's routine includes stretching to improve flexibility as my muscles grow stronger. The program includes diet and nutrition recommendations that, combined with the exercise, produce rapid improvements in fitness in just ninety days.

If you maintain a good level of fitness and nutrition, yet still feel chronically fatigued or suffer from other ailments, see a doctor. Chronic pain, allergies, and other illnesses can suppress your energy level, dampen your enthusiasm, and hinder your mental acuity. When you are ill, distracted by pain, or simply don't feel right, you don't want to do anything, much less pursue a change in behavior.

For much of my own life, I suffered from terrible allergies. They caused chronic sinus infections, making my head pound from the sinus pressure, which in turn debilitated my thinking capacity. Allergies made me chronically tired, and when I took antihistamines to combat them, I couldn't stay awake. When I finally found a way to control them, my new attitude and energy level gave me much higher expectations for myself and my future.

I have friends who put off having knee replacement surgery for years, only to discover after the surgery that not only did their knees feel twenty years younger, but their whole attitude on life changed.

If you suffer from any chronic illness, mental or physical, see a qualified specialist or doctor for treatment. Treatments are available for many conditions that in the past were thought incurable, and treating your illness can give you a whole new attitude. Your improved health can make what you might have thought impossible completely within your ability. It can give you a new perspective on your life and yourself. If you don't feel well, do something about it.

If you aren't active, don't exercise regularly, or don't maintain proper nutrition, make exercise and improved nutrition a part of your self-development plan. Energy and good health can be the difference between seeing your goals as achievable or impossible. They can create the change in surroundings you need to gain a more accurate view of your reality. They can give you a new level of confidence and make all aspects of your self-development much easier.

Relax and Reflect

Another valuable benefit of physical conditioning is that it relaxes your mind. When you are riding a bike, jogging, or swimming, you get into a soothing rhythm. Your muscles and mind go on autopilot. Your body does the work with little mental intervention, and your mind gets a break. Yoga offers a similar experience. Outside of eastern religions, where yoga is more a spiritual practice, yoga exercises are valued as much for the sense of calm they provide as for the physical conditioning. While you barely move beyond a two-foot by six-foot area, your focus on physical balance, breathing, posture, and stretching keeps you in the present, thus freeing you from worry and responsibility. Aided by the increase in oxygen to your brain, physical activity gives your mind a great boost of clarity and allows you to get beyond the daily distractions and responsibilities of life.

Slowing down your activity level has a similar effect. When you take a shower, sit in a sauna, watch the sunset, or take some time off work, letting the world go by without you, your mind calms. Your worries take a break. Your responsibilities, to-do lists, and phone calls get a hiatus. As in a routine exercise that gets into a rhythm, slowing down and enjoying the sunset relaxes your mind.

Besides relaxation's stress-reducing and physical-recharging benefits, it gives you increased mental capacity to think of new ideas and increase your self-awareness. To develop a deep self-awareness, you need to free your mind of distractions and reflect on what, why, where, when, and how you do what you do. You need uninterrupted time to consider what you believe, value, and think. You need down-time to contemplate your feedback, feelings, motives, experiences, circumstances, and decisions. Have a board meeting with yourself from time to time to assess your progress, appraise your performance, and evaluate your opportunities.

People who have no blank space on their calendars have little chance of truly getting to know themselves. Those who think they always have to be engaged in a book, newspaper, phone conversation, e-mail, or other activity miss important opportunities to think and reflect. Like a cashier at a coffee shop during the morning rush hour, your constantly busy mind has no time to reflect and think about your personal development.

> People who have no blank space on their calendars have little chance of truly getting to know themselves.

Learn to relax. Find opportunities to reflect. Use reflection as a tool to contemplate your actions and thoughts and to understand yourself better. Get in touch with your thoughts and feelings. They have a lot to tell you if you will make the time and mental space to listen.

Take the Chance

You may be unsure whether you want a deeper awareness of your current self. Even though you need to improve, you may be afraid to let go of any self-acceptance or coping skills that give you confidence. You may not look forward to opening yourself to the potential humbling that can come with feedback and critique, or you may hesitate to reveal your true nature for fear of what you may discover. Recognize that any short-term dent in your self-confidence or unwinding of the past will be more than offset by the improvements you make.

Early in my career, I enrolled in a presentation skills workshop about which I had great anxiety because it included videotaping three of my presentations. I wanted to improve my presentation skills but didn't look forward to seeing my own shortcomings on video. I knew I would look foolish and incompetent, but I attended anyway.

When the workshop was over, it turned out my presentation video footage did reveal areas for improvement, but my deficiencies were unworthy of the level of anxiety I'd created. The improvements I needed were minor. As a result, the workshop encouraged me and boosted my confidence instead of embarrassing me. It also made me aware of some talents I didn't know I had. I saw for the first time several good speaking characteristics, such as my disarming style, of which I had no prior knowledge. As a result of the experience, my self-confidence went up, not down.

Few good things in life come for free. Your self-development is no exception. Part of the cost is facing your imperfections. Yet there is no good reason to fret. You can still retain dignity and accept yourself. In fact, you're probably better than you think. Anyone else with your genetic makeup, nurturing, unique experiences and constraints would have the same capability. Don't be over anxious. Face your short-comings, whatever they may be. The awareness you gain will be worth it. You will benefit from it for a lifetime.

Here is a summary of the methods of increasing your self-awareness:

- Be your own observer and assess your behaviors and attitudes.
- Participate in structured assessments, such as a 360-degree survey, the MBTI, or an assessment based on the Five Factor Model, along with the appropriate debriefs on the results.
- Seek feedback from others.
- Capture yourself in action on video or in audio.
- Change your perspective by putting yourself in someone else's position.
- Change your surroundings.
- Seek out new experiences.
- Increase your energy level and mental acuity by improving your physical condition.
- Find time to relax and reflect.

Discover the Root Causes

With a baseline of self-awareness, you are almost ready to turn your attention to how you will pursue your desired behavior change. But you're not quite there. Understanding yourself won't always make obvious what you need to develop. You could be seeing a symptom and not a root cause. For example, a 360 assessment may reveal that you're a poor listener. While that may be true, something else could be causing it, and that cause could be a better place to focus your attention. Poor listening could be the result of poor hearing, being too busy, or narcissism. These causes would obviously lead you to very different courses of action. Properly diagnosing the cause of your symptoms is the core of creating awareness.

To ensure you don't misdiagnose yourself, look for deeper causes hiding behind your initial findings. Think about the possible reasons you do what you do, say what you say, value what you value, and feel what you feel. Look for the "why" behind the "what." Ask yourself, "Why do I behave in this way?" If you are a poor listener, ask yourself, "Why don't I listen well?" If you avoid conflict, ask yourself why. Or if you have the support of a coach, manager, or someone else you trust, ask them to help you figure out the source of your behaviors and opportunities. You will usually discover a deeper reason that is more deserving of your self-development attention.

Generating a list of ten to twenty possible causes for a given problem is not uncommon. Once you start the process, one idea leads to another. It helps to substitute words and ask the question in different forms. Asking "Why am I not calm?" can prompt a much different set of ideas than "Why am I so angry?"

When you have a list of potential sources of the behavior you want to change, pick those that are the most likely. This is a good time to enlist the help of others. Rank the causes from high to low. Once you have narrowed the list, pick the one on which you want to focus. To be sure there is not another, deeper issue, ask yourself again, "What is causing this behavior?"

If you are digging into why you are a poor listener and you've narrowed the root cause down to being too distracted, ask why you are distracted. The answer might be that you're overwhelmed with work and too busy to give anyone proper attention. Asking why again might reveal that you fail to delegate work to others. Asking why again might reveal that you want to control all aspects of your work. Asking why again might reveal that you lack trust in your employees or peers. Asking one last time might reveal that your lack of trust is due to your employees' dishonesty. With that insight, your best course of action might be to address the dishonesty first instead of your poor listening skills.

The best practice in root-cause discovery is to continue asking "why" until you feel you have arrived at the root cause. Be aware that this process of discovery can lead you back to other issues you've already uncovered. Root causes and drivers of behavior don't usually fit into an organized hierarchy. They can be circular or linear or branch off into parallel paths. If you find yourself coming back to previously identified ideas, you've probably found the primary drivers of your behavior, and you're ready to pick the one that drives the others. Once you've resolved one issue, you can come back to your list and pursue others until you're satisfied with the results.

What you learn in probing for root causes is that many causes drive your behaviors. Had you not continued to ask "why," you would have failed to discover the basic barriers to achieving your original goal.

Here is the summary of the process of root-cause discovery:

- Identify the symptoms that prevent the actions, attitudes, behaviors, values, or strengths you want to develop.

- Seek out the causes of those symptoms by repeatedly asking why until you get a map of root causes that accurately identifies all the likely possibilities.
- Isolate the top few causes that best attack the issue or opportunity you are planning to work on.
- Focus your attention on these causes. Accept that they may point out a need to change your original objective.

Know Your Longing to Belong

Abraham Maslow, a twentieth-century psychologist, developed a model of the hierarchy of human needs. The model asserts that certain needs take precedence over others. As in the layers of a pyramid, lower-level needs create the foundation for the upper-level needs. At the bottom layer of the pyramid are our basic physiological needs—breathing, eating, and drinking. Once these needs are met, we need safety—to feel protected, secure, and stable. On top of that are our needs of belonging—relationships, acceptance, and love. The next level of the pyramid is esteem—respect from others and from ourselves in the form of achievement, competence, and recognition.

At the top of the pyramid is self-actualization. Self-actualization is our instinctual human need to be the best we can be—to reach our peak potential. In contrast to the other four levels of needs, which are about satisfying a deficit, this highest level is about growth. Our motive at this level moves from satisfying an unfilled need to growing in a new way. Not until we have accommodated our lower-level needs do we discover an innate desire to achieve a higher potential. Growing and developing are natural human needs. As long as we feel our development is incomplete, we will feel unsatisfied.

Another interesting aspect of our humanity this model highlights is our desire to belong. After our physical needs are satisfied and we feel safe, we long to belong. We need human contact, relationships, and acceptance. These needs prevent many people from changing.

If your sense of belonging comes from a group of people who exhibit the very character, style, or image you want to change in yourself, you will have to break from the group, at least temporarily, while you go through your transformation. This is especially hard because you must let go of the sense of belonging you feel through association with the group. A good solution is to acquaint yourself with others who possess the new competencies that you are pursuing. Seek relationships with people who help you become the person you want to be. If, for example, your goal is to become a better coach to your employees, join a coaching organization with like-minded members. If your ambition is to improve your relationship with your teenage son, spend some time with other parents who have good relationships with their teenage sons.

The desire to belong is a basic human need that can work for you or against you. Make it work for you by finding your sense of belonging with those most like what you aspire to become. Learn from them how they bridged the gap that you hope to bridge.

The desire to belong is a basic human need that can work for you or against you.

Another relevant aspect of this model is the dependency that one need has on another, which raises a caution. If your goal is a self-actualizing one, but you find yourself without the resources to satisfy your basic physiological needs, you are skipping levels. Without satisfying your lower-level needs first, your goal is unrealistic. Refocus your attention on your unfilled basic needs first. Once you've fulfilled those, you can work on the higher-level needs.

Be aware of the hierarchy of needs. Assess where your goal sits relative to your other needs, and if you have unfilled lower-level needs, address them first. If you don't have food to eat, air to breathe, or a roof overhead, it doesn't make much sense to spend time on improving your strategic-thinking skills.

Do Your Research

When you have established a solid self-awareness and validated your self-development objective, the remaining aspect of awareness is determining how you will bridge the gap. If you plan to improve your physical condition, research available exercise programs. If you plan to learn a foreign language, research your local community college course offerings. If you want to improve your marriage, inquire about marriage enrichment programs or marriage counselors.

Before I began building our retreat in Colorado, I did a lot of awareness building. I knew my final goal, but had little idea how I would make it a reality. I didn't know exactly what, where, when, or how I would build it. All I knew was that I needed to figure it out, and I began a knowledge-building journey that lasted ten years.

For ten years before I started construction, I did research to learn how to build a house in the harsh conditions of the high country in Colorado. Although I had built three houses before, I had never built anything of this size or complexity. To make the construction project succeed, I needed to take my knowledge and awareness up a notch. I read magazines on mountain living, on mountain home construction, and on architectural design. I cut out and filed away how-to articles, advertisements, and pictures of anything I wanted for later reference. I attended home shows, talked to material and appliance suppliers, and talked with others who had built homes in the mountains.

Had I not developed this in-depth awareness before proceeding in my endeavor, I could easily have failed. I would likely have had structural problems due to the unusually large snow loads on the roof, water leakage problems due to ice dams on the eaves, and water drainage issues related to melting snow. I would have wasted money in redesign and rework. I'd have missed out on other valuable features such as high-efficiency fireplaces, instant hot-water faucets, fifty-year guaranteed paint, battery-free smoke detectors, passive solar heating, and self-closing kitchen drawers. The effort I put into research was returned to me many times over.

This final facet of building awareness can be as simple as stopping to think about a few key details or as complicated as the collection of insights over a period of ten years. The guideline is to do what you need to do to be confident that you are taking the right approach. Conduct research. Read books written by the experts in the field of your endeavor. Go to the library or use the Internet to learn about the different approaches available. Make sure you understand all the important details about your current condition and the nuances of your aspiration. Remove uncertainty by building your knowledge. Put yourself through a self-directed education process. The more you learn, the more prepared and confident you'll be.

Two other approaches to deciding how to bridge your gap are learning from the past and performing a trial run.

Learn from the Past

Whether understanding your current self, establishing your desired future, or researching the best way to bridge the gap, exploring history provides valuable insight and awareness. The attempts, failures, and successes of those who came before you reveal valuable lessons, as do your own prior attempts and failures.

Explore your personal history for lessons learned. If you are in sales and your goal is to sell to higher-level decision makers, think about your earlier attempts. Ask yourself, "Why didn't they accept my invitation for a meeting?" "Was my invitation not aligned to their interests?" "Did their administrative assistant have anything to do with it?" If you are building new competency in executive coaching, assess your earlier attempts at helping and mentoring others. Ask yourself, "In my past coaching attempts, how did my protégés react to my advice?" "Why didn't they apply my advice?" or "How might I have better helped them?" Ask those whom you've coached or mentored for their perspectives.

Explore the experiences of others. Ask those who have accomplished your aspiration to share their lessons learned. Ask seasoned coaches what they did to develop their coaching skills. Ask people who successfully gave up smoking how they kicked the habit. Ask others who have successfully reconciled their conflicts how they overcame the hurt and anger. You don't have the time or money to experience every lesson yourself. Benefit from the lessons learned by others. A rich history of insight is available for the asking. Ask for it.

You don't have the time or money to experience every lesson yourself.

As a note of caution, use the past as a learning tool, not as a refuge from the present. You can become so enamored by its glory (or mired in its gloom) that you can't get out of it. For many people, letting go of the past is paramount to eliminating the core of their identity. Yet when you're hanging on to the past, it's difficult to grab on to the future.

See the past for what it is—a learning experience. Of course, it also provides many fond memories, but don't let it prevent you from creating new fond memories. Don't dwell on past successes or mistakes to the exclusion of living the here and now. Don't let the past beat you up or turn your focus to pessimistic thoughts. Don't let the new day's sunshine be overshadowed by the clouds of the past. History is extremely valuable in building knowledge and establishing your awareness, but it can also rekindle thoughts and emotions that are counterproductive to your endeavor. Use the past to the extent it helps you move forward.

Perform a Trial Run

How can you confirm that the approach you've researched and selected for your endeavor is the right one? How might you validate your needs? How could you test the expected benefits? How might you test the key assumptions your goal depends upon? Consider a trial run. A trial run can help you validate the value of your pursuit, quantify its potential benefits, disprove your assumptions, or confirm your plan, saving you tremendous amounts of time and energy that might otherwise be wasted. Working in the computer software industry through much of my career, I've seen more than one organization install a software package that didn't give the expected benefits. In most cases, had the organization done a trial run in a small department before installing the software company-wide, they would have discovered the problems much earlier, allowing necessary adjustments to be made before full-scale installation.

One of my biggest professional failures might have been avoided had I conducted a trial run. In the middle of my IBM career, I led a task force of several senior managers charged with reengineering a critical front-end process to our sales approach. The goal was to improve the process of identifying and qualifying sales opportunities so we could best use our sales resources. We spent a couple of months modeling, debating, and documenting our "as-is" selling practices. We then crafted new "to-be" practices that significantly improved what we did. To wrap up the project, we assessed several software applications to automate our new processes and documented their key features.

In the final task-force presentation and executive review, our work was well received. Our processes were best-of-breed and approved with little debate. The problem was with the software applications we reviewed and the expectations we set. The executives became so enamored with the software's forecast-reporting features that they all but forgot the actual process the software was designed to improve. At the end of the meeting, the executive team authorized us to begin the software implementation immediately, which we did.

The sales management process we'd designed to help the sales staff better manage their sales opportunities became, instead, an automated sales-forecasting system. This was nowhere close to what we had originally been charged to do or intended. After several years and millions of dollars in software modifications, the sales management and forecasting systems were merged into a single comprehensive system using the best practice processes we designed.

In the end, the processes and system worked very well. Unfortunately, it took years longer and much more money than it needed to. Had a legitimate pilot implementation been performed and thoroughly assessed, the gap between what we did and what we needed would have become obvious, and the changes needed could have been made before full implementation.

This same principle applies to our self-development projects. If your goal is to change roles in your organization, request a temporary assignment before making the final decision. If you plan to join a fitness club, ask for a thirty-day trial membership to make sure the club meets your needs. If you aspire to overcome a fear of boating, attend an orientation meeting or a test ride before committing to a two-week, fear-killing rafting trip. If you want to sell your house to travel around the country in a motor home, rent a motor home for a month first.

A trial run can be your best method to gaining knowledge and verifying critical details before finalizing the plans of your self-development program.

Be Wary of Easy

When you have identified the alternatives available to you to bridging your gap, be wary of the allure of "easy." We all prefer something easy over something hard, but easy is often accompanied by disappointment. You usually get back what you put into something. If it doesn't take much of your time or energy, you will probably not get much out of it. There are exceptions for sure, but be careful, especially when following the biased advice that comes in marketing messages and advertising.

Weight loss offerings that don't require any real change in eating habits or exercise are a hoax. Degree programs that don't require any homework or class attendance are not a genuine education. The advice of so-called experts who suggest that you need only to stop worrying or deal with what is effectively a symptom instead of a root cause will only prolong your development.

Dan Ariely, author of *Predictably Irrational,* found in his experiments at MIT that "when choosing between two products, we often overact to the free one." He adds that "most transactions have an upside and a downside, but when something is free, we forget the downside." Don't be fooled into thinking that you can achieve something for nothing. If there is little effort, cost or time required, be wary. There probably isn't much of a return.

Be Prepared

If awareness-building sounds like planning and preparation, it is. It's the first step, the foundation of your self-development initiative. It's the longest chapter of this book for a reason. If you don't get awareness right, the rest of your journey will be either a very short exercise in futility or a long-term waste of your valuable resources. As the proverb says, "Failing to plan is planning to fail."

If you don't get awareness right, the rest of your journey will be either a very short exercise in futility or a long-term waste of your valuable resources.

Early in my IBM career as a salesman, my team and I skimped on the preparation step before conducting a complex, computer-aided engineering demonstration for a sales prospect. Right from the beginning, we found ourselves fumbling to answer the engineering manager's basic questions. The presentation was supposed to be a half-day demonstration, but in a few minutes, it was over. Our prospect walked out. We weren't prepared, and it showed. The same happens every day to self-development initiatives. Before people barely get started, their initiatives are over.

Before embarking on any important self-development initiative, do your homework. Identify your gap, get beyond your self-deception, conduct assessments like the 360-degree survey, solicit feedback, and learn from the experience of others. Alter your point of reference. Put yourself in someone else's shoes to see the situation from their vantage point. If necessary, change your surroundings, friends, and associates, at least temporarily. Improve your physical condition and learn to relax. Learn from the past and arrange to meet others who have accomplished what you wish to accomplish. It could take you several weeks or even months, but the return will last a lifetime.

Don't underestimate the importance of building your foundation of awareness and preparing for your journey. It will have more impact on the outcome than anything else you can do. Studies have shown that every minute spent in proper planning saves up to ten minutes in implementation.

Activating Your Ambition

On the page of your road map titled "Activating Your Ambition Scorecard," score how well you currently do in applying the concepts of awareness. On the page of your road map titled, "My Awareness," list the things you need to do to build your awareness in preparation for your self-development endeavor. Include an accurate assessment of your "as-is" condition, your desired "to-be" condition, the key actions for bridging the gap between them, and what you need to do to be fully prepared and knowledgeable about the effort that you are about to pursue.

5
Secure Your Motivation

People often say that motivation doesn't last. Well,
neither does bathing—that's why we recommend it daily.

–Zig Ziglar

Greg was the chief operating officer of a Midwestern manufacturing company. He was a man of sound character with strong family values, but also a man on the verge of complete burnout. Greg's typical workday started at 7:00 a.m. and rarely ended before 7:00 p.m. He often brought his laptop home in the evenings and on weekends to put in even more work hours. He had two children and a wife who seldom received his undivided attention. Greg knew he couldn't sustain his current way of living; he knew he had to find a better work-life balance, or he would snap. He decided to do something about it and hired me to be his coach.

We started by assessing his current needs and building an accurate awareness of his strengths and developmental areas. When we probed into the causes of his marathon work schedule, we discovered he was reluctant to delegate work. He either did it himself or assigned only small portions of projects to his team. He rationalized that others were already busy and he was more capable anyway. He reasoned the work would be of a higher quality if he did it himself.

Based on this assessment, we developed the objectives of his coaching engagement: 1) I know when and how to delegate work properly to my employees and 2) My employees' skills have improved, increasing the quality of their work to my standards.

After several coaching sessions, Greg learned the art of delegation—when it was appropriate to delegate, when it wasn't, and how to stay on top of the details even though he wasn't doing them. But despite his newfound knowledge, he made little progress, assigning only a small number of projects to his staff. He remained in the critical path of three-fourths of the projects under his responsibility.

In probing for the reasons why Greg was so reluctant to empower his staff to do more of the work, we discovered that we needed to move our focus from the how of delegation to the why. What we uncovered was a lack of motivation. He was not convinced that delegating his work would offset the extra time it was taking him to teach his team what to do and check on their progress—that the time he was investing now would lead to his desired work-life balance later. Since his workload had not decreased much, he hadn't received any confirmation that he was heading in the right direction. He hadn't yet grasped how much his job would improve.

We spent some time creating a mental picture of his improved future. It was a picture of his employees having more skill and needing less of his time than they did now, while getting the work done even better than he could. We then focused on developing a mental picture of benefits that lay ahead for him, including having dinner with his family, enjoying an occasional date with his wife, and so on. Only then did the proverbial lightbulb in his head turn on. Greg became excited and motivated enough to continue despite his concerns. That motivation enabled him to move forward in our plan until his progress supplied the motivation.

Motivation is a fundamental factor behind achievement. People who are motivated succeed. People who aren't, don't. Motivation is critical to starting, sustaining, and completing any initiative, particularly a difficult one. Fundamentally, motivation answers the question, "Why would I pursue this objective?" It's the reason for your effort—understanding and internalizing how strongly you want something. The more you want something, the more likely you will pursue and stick to it.

Motivation comes from understanding and anticipating the benefits of your effort. It is the mental link between your effort and its reward, the true understanding that your endeavor is important and that its benefits will be worth your investment. Motivation is the core of your commitment and decision to move forward.

Motivation comes from understanding and anticipating the benefits of your effort.

People are generally motivated in one of two ways. Some have an enduring predisposition to achieve, referred to as *trait* motivation. Their motivation is largely part of their character. For others, motivation is a temporary attitude called *state* motivation. Their motivation depends on their situation. The lack of natural ambition is not a problem as long as your goal motivates you sufficiently.

If I was your boss and I told you to improve your leadership to your team, my statement would probably motivate you to improve. The degree of motivation would depend on other factors, such as how much you respected my opinion, how serious you thought the problem was, and how conscientious you were. However, if I told you that if you didn't improve your leadership, you would lose your job in ninety days, your motivation would increase. Why? Because now you know what's at stake. You know the consequences of not improving.

For any self-development effort, the consequences are the same whether or not you know what they are. If you don't become a better leader, knowing or not knowing the consequence doesn't change the fact that you will lose your job. Knowing can, however, greatly affect your motivation. When you know you are gambling with high stakes, you take the game more seriously. Truly understanding the importance of your endeavor's consequences and benefits greatly strengthens your motivation and increases your likelihood of success.

Motivation is doubly important when your self-development requires not only the learning of new behaviors, but the unlearning of old behaviors. Authors Daniel Goleman, Richard Boyatzis, and Annie McKee, in their book *Primal Leadership: Realizing the Power of Emotional Intelligence* suggest that while the human brain continues to "sprout fresh connections," the effort and energy required to master a competence are greater because we are overcoming "ingrained patterns." The task becomes "doubled" because replacing old habits that don't work well for new ones that do requires greater motivation: "We have to work harder and longer to change a habit than when we learned it in the first place."

That it's never too late to break an old habit or learn new habits is great to know. The key to making it happen, though, is ensuring you have enough motivation. When you have an urge to grab a cigarette, indulge in a diet-busting dessert, lash out in anger, or revert to whatever behavior it is you want to change, you need motivation to remain strong and resist those temptations. Your desire to resist or change must be stronger than your desire to fall back into old habits. Motivation doesn't change the reality of your situation, but it helps you deal with it.

Rely on Internal Motivation

When motivation comes from external sources, such as other people's actions or the threat of their actions, it comes from outside you. When it comes from your own beliefs, desires, and expectations, it's internally produced. External motivation pushes you; internal motivation pulls you. Either source working alone can move you to action, but when you have both, your motivation is the strongest. If you are unsure if you are externally or internally motivated to do something, ask yourself if you are doing it because you want to or because you have to. If you are doing it because you want to, your motivation is coming from within.

The problem occurs when you become so accustomed to external sources that you turn off your own internal sources. Then, if an opportunity arises without the external push, your stimulus is nowhere to be found. When both your push and your pull are gone, developing and sustaining a self-improvement mind-set is impossible.

The old saying, "You can motivate with a carrot or with a stick," suggests two generally accepted methods of motivation—incentives (dangling a carrot in front of the donkey) and punishment (hitting him from behind with a stick.) For many people, particularly old-school managers, these represent the two alternatives to motivating people—reward good behavior or punish bad behavior. They miss the fact that in either case, the source of the motivation is external. They overlook the power that comes from tapping into people's internal sources of motivation.

Relying only on external motivation has several drawbacks. On the receiving end of the stick approach, you feel degraded. You become resentful and fear the next encounter. Instead of applying your energy productively toward the next project or opportunity, you spend it in fear, anxiety, and avoidance. Pursuing the carrot, you are motivated only to the extent that the incentive continues. When the incentive ends, so does the desired behavior.

Another problem is that incentive-based systems have to be very specific and carefully designed or people will trick the system and achieve the goal without doing the intended work. The goals are met, but without employing the desired behavior. The carrot causes people to perform, but not to grow and develop. Overreliance on incentives represses initiative and individual ambition. It hinders genuine ownership of and responsibility for the goal.

Both the carrot and the stick motivate people to perform in certain ways, but they exclude independence and creativity. People accustomed to external motivation don't think outside of their incentives. They follow orders and do what they're told, essentially turning off their own thinking. Then once the incentive is gone, so is their direction and motivation.

To be self-directed and reliably reach your own goals, you need internal power. When you are motivated from within, your drive to develop is the strongest. You have more passion and strength to overcome fear and anxiety. You take more responsibility, feel more ownership, think for yourself, and demonstrate more creativity. You will never work as hard for someone else's objectives as you will your own.

You will never work as hard for someone else's objectives as you will your own.

Many professions and environments condition people to give up their own motivations. Environments that are overly controlling or undemanding destroy self-motivation. Undemanding environments create a dependency similar to that created by unconditional social services. At the other extreme, bosses, athletic coaches, and parents who yell and demand instead of inspire and encourage do the same damage.

Professions like sales have historically overly relied on external motivation. Sales professionals succeed by focusing on their quotas and incentives. They know that every year, every quarter, every month, and every day they must make new sales in order to earn their salaries and keep their jobs. This is the nature of their environment, and to be successful, they adapt to it. While it's a great profession, the constant bombardment of sales incentives and external influences over time reduces their internal motivation and produces an overreliance on external motivation.

If you are accustomed to external motivation, pursuing your own goals without the external forces of the stick or carrot will be difficult. As you have repeatedly let others set your goals for you, you have become unconsciously programmed to rely on their pushing instead of your own pulling. You've developed a pattern of thinking that makes pursuing your own self-development very difficult.

Nonetheless, regaining and securing your own motivation is possible. Building a strong inner drive to lead you on your endeavor is well within your ability. Even well-ingrained habits can be broken as you generate new neural pathways in your brain. The sections in this chapter offer several methods for regaining and strengthening your own sources of motivation.

Think Long-Term, Focus Short-Term

If your self-development effort produces results quickly, that's wonderful. Stopping an addiction and starting to exercise, for example, offer immediate rewards. You quickly see the benefit. The efforts are still difficult to sustain until you get through the essential pain, but the almost-instant progress helps motivate you to continue.

Other self-development initiatives don't pay immediate dividends. If you are pursuing a college degree or professional certification, your investment won't be returned for several years. If you start your own business, your outlay won't be returned to you for many years. Or if you pursue a lifelong purpose, a mission without an end, your investment may never return to you; it may go to your children, your community, your church, or people you will never meet. When you pursue long-term and lifelong goals, you can't rely on short-term improvements to sustain you. You must adopt a different outlook.

Such goals mean deferred gratification and deferred encouragement. They are like the law of the harvest. You prepare your soil, sow your seeds, and take care of your plants before you expect to harvest your crop. The bigger the yield you expect, the greater the work. So it is with long-term self-development. You invest time, energy, and money up front, knowing that the return won't come until later. Incremental progress won't be enough to sustain you.

Long-term initiatives call for setting your mind on the journey, rather than on achieving a quick win. It's the difference between running a marathon and a hundred-yard sprint. You have to set your expectations differently. In a marathon, you set a pace that you expect will get you to your goal of 26 miles and 385 yards, and then you turn your attention to the race, not the finish line. You focus on your stride, technique, breathing, and the terrain. The five-, ten-, fifteen-, and twenty-mile markers become your progress indicators. In a hundred-yard sprint, your technique is just as important, but your focus from the start is on the finish line.

For long-term initiatives, the easiest approach is not to concentrate on the harvest at all. Anticipating the final outcome of a long-term journey creates anxiety and stress. Setting your mind on the finish line makes your race—particularly the end—more difficult. If your goal is to become a chief executive officer, set your sights on a division manager's job first. The shorter-term ambition takes the pressure off becoming a CEO and puts your focus where it needs to be for the present moment. Pursue your goal, but stay in the present moment. When you focus only on the finish line, you make your journey seem longer and harder. Having a short-term perspective takes the pressure off your long-term goals.

Conversely, a long-term goal makes shorter-term goals seem easier to attain. Having a long-term perspective takes the pressure off your short-term goals. If you set your mind to run a mile, you will probably find yourself getting tired around three-fourths of a mile. If you set your mind to running five miles, you will get through the first mile easily, but the fifth mile will be much harder. If you have a short-term goal, set a longer-term goal to take the pressure off it. If your objective is to go back to school and earn an MBA, put it in the context of an even longer-term goal, such as becoming a company division president. The longer-term ambition takes some pressure off the MBA.

When you focus only on the finish line, you make your journey seem longer and harder.

Suppose you plan to learn a foreign language, with the long-term goal of working overseas. When the thought of working overseas in a foreign country feels overwhelming, turn your attention to your shorter-term goal of learning the language. If studying for a test in your foreign language class seems overwhelming, consider the overall context of where you are headed. A long-term perspective with short-term milestones allows you to enjoy incremental successes without the stress of closing in on the finish line, all while you still are closing in on the finish line.

If you normally expect quick results and immediate gratification, you will struggle with this long-term mind-set. Your short-term orientation may have prevented you from ever embarking on a long-term initiative before. This talk of setting longer-term goals may seem like nonsense and may make you anxious just thinking about it. However, you will be doing something in the future anyway, so you might as well think now about what that will be. It increases your motivation to perform at a higher level in the present. Combining the short-term and long-term perspectives gives you two sources of motivation.

Build Your Excitement

Excitement drives internal motivation. If you're not excited about your journey, your motivation will be lower, and so will your chances of success. You should look forward not only to the results but also to the journey itself.

Think for a minute about what you do, say, feel, see, sense, or think that excites you. What makes you forget your problems? The source of your excitement could be personal or professional. It might be learning a new skill, solving a complex business problem, or becoming more self-sufficient. It could be doing something that makes your children, spouse, or parents happy. It could be taking a vacation, completing a project around the house, reading a book, engaging in a hobby, or simply enjoying the companionship of a loved one. Or it could be painting, writing a poem, or running a marathon. Take a minute to reflect and record the activities, thoughts, and feelings that get you the most excited.

As you think about what excites you, probe deeper for the root cause of your excitement. Dig beneath the activities themselves for the elements that you most enjoy. If you like swimming, why do you like it? Do you feel relaxed or free because you enjoy the feel of the water on your skin? If you like participating in a certain sport, consider whether you like the physical activity, the social engagement, or the strategy of the game best. With a little concentration, you will uncover the recurring elements that make you enjoy many different activities. Knowing these will not only help you build motivation but also enhance your self-awareness.

Now think about your past successes. Write down as many of these successes as you can recall. They might include overcoming a pesky problem or applying a skill in a way that resulted in a considerable achievement. Successes could be related to building skills, overcoming obstacles, attaining a level of proficiency, or completing a project. List anything you worked diligently toward and felt a sense of pride and accomplishment in when completed.

Reflect on your list of successes for a moment. Why did you embark on those endeavors to begin with? What drove you to accomplish them? Dig in and identify the drivers that were working on your behalf behind the scenes. Look for elements of fun, enjoyment, gratification, or anything that made your endeavor exciting.

What excites you and makes you happy plays a pivotal role in your performance and heavily influences what you choose to do with your discretionary time. Being enthusiastic, while not an absolute prerequisite for achievement, goes a long way toward enabling and maintaining your motivation.

Once you've identified the thoughts, feelings, and activities that drive and excite you, find ways to put them into your endeavor. The more elements of excitement you add, the more you will enjoy it, and the more motivation you will have to sustain your effort. If your goal is to write a book but you don't look forward to writing at your desk, consider where else you might write that is more enjoyable. If you love the outdoors, write outside. If camping is your thing, write on a camping trip. If you prefer to be in the company of others but want non-intrusive company, write at a local coffee shop.

Once you've identified the thoughts, feelings, and activities that drive and excite you, find ways to put them into your endeavor.

If you want to improve your golf game by hitting thousands of golf balls, but the prospect of practicing at the driving range seems dull, consider what you enjoy that you could tie into your practice. If you enjoy the companionship of a certain friend, invite that friend to go with you. If you like the smell of flowers, find a practice range with flowers.

If your goal is to become more fit, but walking on a treadmill bores you, consider what elements of your joy could be included in your workouts. If you enjoy reading, read while you walk on the treadmill. If you like to watch sports on TV, put a TV in front of your treadmill. If you love art, put pictures around your treadmill.

Understand what drives you, and put those things to work to build and sustain your motivation. Here are a few "excitement" drivers to get you thinking:

- Gaining respect
- Experiencing deep emotion
- Feeling love
- Increasing security
- Receiving or giving praise
- Improving yourself
- Increasing wealth
- Gaining knowledge or learning a skill
- Escaping stress
- Applying knowledge or skills
- Averting a medical condition
- Conversing or debating
- Avoiding mental or physical pain
- Spending time with friends or family
- Avoiding a fine or penalty
- Being part of a team
- Helping others
- Engaging in physical activity
- Using talents and strengths
- Playing games that engage the mind
- Being entertained
- Stimulating the senses
- Listening to music
- Experiencing nature

You can incorporate any of these drivers and countless others into your endeavor. Know the elements that drive you and embed them in your plans. Energize your effort with the hope of something exciting, something better, something new, or the avoidance of something painful. The more enjoyable and exciting your endeavor is, the more motivated you will be.

Avoid Destructive Motivators

The prospect of attaining fame and fortune has driven many people to great achievements. It has also driven many into serious dysfunction, divorce, bankruptcy, jail, and suicide. News accounts abound of professional athletes, preachers, professors, chief executive officers, and actors who couldn't satisfy their desire to become rich and famous. In the end, their insatiable drive for recognition and wealth led them down a path of selfishness, deceit, and corruption, destroying whatever fame and fortune they had achieved.

The prospect of fame and fortune is an intoxicating motivator, but its side effects can be devastating. Because the root causes of these desires are greed and obsession, they come with undesirable consequences. Unbridled, their toxicity more than offsets the benefits of the achievements they drive. The insatiable desire for money, recognition, or an adrenaline rush overpowers restraint and self-discipline and leads to dishonesty, deceit, and criminal behavior. Greed and obsession have no end; they can never be satisfied. *Greed motivation* drives people to seek more and more, ultimately destroying what good they originally achieved.

I had a boss who had an insatiable appetite for his own promotion and praise. Every idea he conceived was geared for his own benefit. In any decision, he took the option that made him look best. When he spoke about the accomplishments of his organization, his pronouns of choice were "I" and "me" instead of "you" and "we." He was totally consumed by his own selfish desires. As you would expect, he was a poor manager and an even worse leader. Ultimately, his greed and selfishness caught up with him, but it took a few years because we worked in a company whose constant reorganizing hid his shortcomings. Finally, he had worked with the same boss and direct reports long enough that his selfish motives were exposed, and he was out of a job shortly thereafter. His selfish and manipulative reputation then made it difficult for him to find a new job that offered the level of responsibility and compensation he had before.

Not only motivation but also the nature of your motivation is important to your self-development. Don't depend on motivation rooted in greed or obsession. Look in your self-assessment for any greed or insatiability, and if you have it, replace it with other motives.

Many others can move you toward your objective just as well, without the collateral damage. If you have obsessive tendencies, make your next self-development goal to eliminate them. You will discover they are probably at the root of other issues you need to address anyway.

Another motivator to be careful with is fear. To be sure, in certain circumstances fear is a very effective motivator. Fear of danger or pain keeps people from getting hurt; and fear of consequences keeps people from hurting others. Fear of embarrassment and looking foolish drives people to be more prepared. Fear raises people's attention level and deepens their learning. Fear motivation can be used in sports, the home, military, and industry with great success. But fear has its downside. When fear becomes chronic, its effect is more negative than positive. Over time, its cost outweighs the achievements it drives. Old-fashioned "command and control" parents or managers who consider fear the only way to motivate do more harm than good.

Chronic fear shrinks your comfort zone, making you less comfortable, less capable, and more isolated. It sucks up your energy and leaves you exhausted. The greater your fear, the more energy you expend contending with it. The more you concentrate on fearful consequences, the less attention and energy you have for your work or life. Operating under threat, you become so absorbed in the fearful potential that you can think about nothing else. It drives you and everyone around you crazy.

The fear of looking foolish, one of the strongest motivators behind being prepared, is fine as long as it motivates only an occasional event. When it drives people continuously, it is unhealthy. People obsessed with looking foolish don't speak up in meetings, don't ask questions, overprepare to the point of becoming mechanical, remain disengaged from opportunities, and avoid conflict so assiduously that they lose their jobs. People with a chronic fear of looking foolish can't walk, talk, dress, work, play, eat, or sit without worrying about what others will think.

> **People with a chronic fear of looking foolish can't walk, talk, dress, work, play, eat, or sit without worrying about what others will think.**

Chronic fear creates not only chronic problems but chronic stress. Chronic stress is a leading cause of high blood pressure, heart disease, autoimmune diseases, and other physical ailments. Stress reduces mental acuity, clouds your thinking, and is, according to some medical studies, the root cause of most doctor visits. Fear ruins your health.

Unchecked, fear becomes part of you, fading so far into your subconscious that you don't recognize its existence. Its side effects take their toll on you without your knowing. You snap at your spouse, kick the dog, overeat, overdrink, and engage in all sorts of self-defeating behaviors, all because your mind and body are reacting to your unconscious fear.

Being driven by fear also makes people angry and resentful. The longer they operate under threat, the more they resent the person or environment that threatens them. Over time, resentment turns into apathy and disengagement. When people become so resentful that they stop caring, they disengage.

I hold another unpleasant memory of a sales manager who said to me, "Mike, either you win the deal, or I'll find someone else who can." Had I been underperforming, it might have been a deserved, selective use of fear. But I wasn't; I was one of his top performers. It was just his typical technique and, I might add, a testament to his poor leadership skills. He bullied his employees instead of inspiring them.

His threat had the exact opposite effect to what he'd intended—it de-motivated me. Like most people, I am motivated more by the lure of positive results than by the threat of negative ones. A more effective approach with top performers is to encourage them, be their advocate, act as their coach, and lead them by positive example. This boss could have helped me and improved my odds of success, but instead, by threatening me, he lowered them. Looking back, I can't remember whether I won the deal or not. I just remember his heavy-handed approach. His threat was so undeserved and inappropriate that I thought more about it than about closing the deal.

Being driven by fear results in stress, dysfunctional behavior, lasting resentment, and ultimately, ill health. Use motivation by fear selectively. Don't rely on it over the long-term. It is a valid tool for getting someone's attention or moving them to take action, but is not a good substitute for other motivators over the long-term. Fear's best long-term application is in keeping people out of situations that risk personal injury or property loss.

Enthusiasm and excitement, *fun motivation,* secures healthier results than fear or greed. Fun motivation produces energy instead of eroding it and leaves pleasant memories instead of resentment. It makes your journey a joy instead of a chore. Adopt the attitude of Colleen Barrett, president of Southwest Airlines, when she said: "Work is either fun or drudgery. It depends on your attitude. Me, I like fun."

To sustain your motivation, make your work fun. Embed activities that make your effort exciting and enjoyable. Expect it to be pleasurable and satisfying. Avoid overly relying on your obsessions and fears unless you are facing a real danger of injury or loss. If that's the case, use whatever motivation you can find.

Motivate through Generosity

The opposite of greed is generosity. The drive to help and give to others has driven many people to great achievements. Unlike working for money or personal gain, when you do a favor for someone else, you work out of your sense of responsibility, a higher level of intrinsic motivation.

The Nobel Peace Prizes received by Mother Teresa and Nelson Mandela for their unselfish roles in helping humanity are two examples. Mother Teresa's accomplishments, including establishing an organization that has cared for millions of indigent people, were driven by her desire to help others. Nelson Mandela's accomplishments, including his role in ending apartheid, were driven by the same desire. There is no better feeling or inspiration than *generosity motivation.*

The drive to help and give to others has driven many people to great achievements.

Generosity comes from being kindhearted. A kind heart enjoys caring for others, helping, and seeing others receive. Not everyone, though, is gifted with a kindhearted nature. "Left-brained" people (of which I am one) who depend more on logic than on emotion, find caring and compassion less natural. But being naturally logical doesn't mean you aren't caring. Compassion in action is about the only thing that brings me to tears. It creates one of the strongest emotions I have.

Being logical just means you have to pause and think about your actions. When you do, and you realize that you have the opportunity to be generous and grateful, generosity becomes a rich source of satisfaction and motivation—not to mention a tremendous benefit to the receiving party. By the way, studies show that being kind lowers stress, boosts confidence, improves sleep, and increases longevity.

Generosity also comes from gratitude. Find your *gratitude motivation* by recognizing the good deeds of others. If your family, friends, neighbors, or co-workers have helped you or those you care about in some way, let the pull in your heart be your source of motivation. Dwell on it and keep it in the top of your mind so that it moves you to action. If you won't do something for yourself, do it for others in appreciation for who they are, what they've been through, or what they've done.

To develop your "attitude of gratitude," consider what you are thankful for. Think about how you could demonstrate your thankfulness through your self-development initiative. Identify activities that would demonstrate your generosity. Cater to your desire to help others through your own self-development.

If your objective is to manage conflict better in your office, consider how more constructive conflict would help others in your office. If your goal is to quit smoking, consider how your family and others would benefit from inhaling less second-hand smoke. If your goal is to improve your marriage, consider how a better relationship with your spouse would benefit your children. If your goal is a more positive attitude, consider how that attitude will encourage and uplift others.

Maybe you've hurt someone and that memory has had a lasting impact on both of you. The lack of the very development you are now pursuing may have caused the problem. You might have been unsympathetic, quick tempered, rude, greedy, selfish, or unruly. The most sincere apology you could offer would be to change your behavior. Accomplishing your goal would be a great way to demonstrate your genuine remorse. Your self-development could be what you need to restore the relationship.

Pursuing a goal that benefits others may be more about the future than your past. Becoming an elevator installation technician will give you a new source of income, but if you view the career change as giving mobility to the disabled, you have another and possibly stronger reason to pursue it. Becoming a certified financial planner might enable you to quit your boring day job, but it could also help others enjoy a higher quality of life during retirement.

The desire to help others motivated Zig Ziglar, one of the most successful motivational speakers of all time, to become a great public speaker. This motive drove his desire and persistence to work through many discouragements. In his book *Success for Dummies,* Ziglar says that the connection between desire, persistence, development, and excitement lies in helping others: "I believe that whatever your chosen profession, if you make a strong commitment and have a burning desire in your heart—combined with the conviction that you can make a difference—dogged persistence provides you the best insurance for success. Remember that persistence enables you to develop other skills as you go along, provided that you're always 'on the grow' and are genuinely excited about benefiting the people you're dealing with."

In 1952, Ziglar set his self-development goal of becoming a great public speaker. He did not feel he accomplished his goal until 1972. Sticking with a twenty-year self-development program takes strong motivation. For him, that motive was helping others.

Think about whom you owe and what has helped you and your loved ones. Make giving appropriate thanks a part of your journey. Use your endeavor as a way to express your gratitude. Think about how your achievement will benefit others. Use helping others as a source of motivation and make it a win-win for you and them.

Build Your Gain and Pain Motivation

Anticipation, a component of motivation, comes from the expectation of gaining something you want or eliminating something you don't, or both. The prospect of gaining and eliminating are important to maintaining your motivation. They represent tangible benefits and hope for a better future.

When you first join a new company or department, you anticipate acceptance by your new colleagues. Your desire to gain their trust and respect, and to become a meaningful part of the team, drives you to come in early, stay late, work harder, and perform at your best. At the same time, you perform at a higher level because you want to rid yourself of feelings of being an outsider. By working harder, longer, and smarter, you increase your contributions and give yourself the best chance of becoming an integral part of the team. You are gaining something you want and eliminating something you don't.

Like a coin, motivation has two sides. The strength of your motivation will benefit by looking at both. You can essentially double your motivation by considering what you hope to gain and what you expect to eliminate by accomplishing your goal.

For a diet, your gain motivation could be the prospect of wearing new clothes, renewing your confidence, increasing your energy, and participating in recreation with friends and family that you long ago gave up. Looking at the other side, your pain motivation could be the prospect of quitting snoring, reducing your high blood pressure, eliminating your blood-sugar disorders, reducing lethargy, and stopping prescription medicines with bothersome side effects.

Of the two sides, the one that is often ignored is gaining something new. The strongest motivator is usually eliminating or avoiding something you don't want. The pain you endure now, rather than the joy you have yet to experience, is a stronger driver for most people. Stephen R. Covey, author of *The Seven Habits of Highly Effective People*, says, "If you aren't feeling pain, there is rarely enough motivation or humility to change." Pain, or the threat of pain, is more likely to create a sense of urgency to change than just about anything. The hope of eliminating physical, financial, or emotional pain is a strong motive.

The pain you endure now, rather than the joy you have yet to experience, is a stronger driver for most people.

As you identify the sources of motivation to keep you going toward your goal, consider both gaining and eliminating. If your goal is to build a new house, identify the new features you are gaining. Give attention to the benefits of having a new workshop, a larger closet, a built-in coffee maker, and a griddle on your stove-top. At the same time, note the problems you are leaving behind and the pain they have caused you. Think about how nice it will be when you've eliminated your lawn maintenance, avoided the cost of repeated plumbing repairs, and removed the clutter in your old, undersized garage.

Benefits also have two sides. Some changes require giving up something in order to gain something. If you aspire to take on more responsibility at work but feel it will cause you to lose friendships with your current co-workers, the change could feel more like a loss than a gain. The perception that you will give up friends and fun creates a strong disincentive. No matter how many new benefits achieving your goal provides, if you perceive that the benefits you'll give up are greater than those you'll gain, the losses win.

Uncover any perceived loss of benefits that might prevent you from committing to your goal. Put them into perspective. Consider both the benefits you lose and the benefits you gain when building your motivation. The net difference becomes your gain motivation to go forward.

Push yourself beyond the obvious when thinking about your endeavor's benefits. When people reach their goal, they often realize many more benefits than they originally anticipated. You hear, "Wow, if I had known this was going to be this good, I would have done it a long time ago!" Ask others for input. Strive to come up with all the benefits you can expect. The new benefits you come up with could be the breakthroughs needed to find the motivation to move forward.

Develop Your Value Motivation

Building your motivation requires that you identify and grasp the benefits of reaching your goal. Hope, anticipation, and motivation come from a genuine appreciation of the benefits that lie ahead. These include gaining something good, eliminating something painful, helping others, and experiencing joy. When these benefits are not clear or their value does not seem great enough to drive you toward your goal, you can bring them to life by considering their quantitative value.

Many people, particularly those more logically minded, need to go beyond a qualitative understanding and establish a quantitative understanding of their benefits. They need facts, not general ideas or feelings, to be convinced that their investment of effort and resources is worth the expected return. They need to assess the value of their expected benefits. They need *value motivation*.

Value is often expressed in a monetary form but doesn't have to be about money. Self-improvement will help you make more money and save you money, but it can also reduce risk, lengthen your life, and provide many other benefits. The process of identifying and quantifying these benefits helps you realize how important your self-improvement really is.

In terms of monetary value, determining the value of something like an anticipated pay raise is straightforward—simply multiply the amount of your annual raise by the number of years you will benefit from it. To be more accurate, add to that any other financial benefits you would gain from the extra money. If you plan to put your increased income in an interest-bearing or dividend-paying investment, add in the additional interest. On the other side of the motivational coin, if your salary increase allowed you to pay off a debt, include the reduction in interest expense. If you plan to quit smoking, quantify the savings in cigarette expenses and add the savings in health care costs. If you are learning to respect the diversity of people, as intangible as it is, you can quantify its effects on your ability to earn a raise, keep you out of a lawsuit, prevent a government fine, and increase your odds of a promotion.

Nonfinancial value is also quantifiable. Improvements to your quality of life and happiness may be priceless, but you can come up with specifics that will help you see their value more clearly. You can quantify improvements such as feeling better physically, reducing your stress, increasing your free time, and increasing your happiness. Physical fitness improvements can be put in terms of how many new activities you can enjoy with your friends, children, or grandchildren. If your current condition limits you to playing checkers and watching movies but your anticipated improvement enables you to play golf, go hiking, ride a bicycle, and go skiing, then you are expecting a 200 percent increase in the activities you can enjoy.

Adding to that, your increased self-confidence from your better conditioning will enable you to wear swimwear, go to lake parties, go on beach vacations, and play sandlot volleyball with your church singles group, increasing your social encounters by three times a month for the entire summer. Your increased mental acuity will enable you to read an extra book a month, prevent you from having to buy more eyeglasses (because you can now remember where you put them), and increase your memory of what you need at the grocery store, avoiding two trips a month. These are all clear and specific benefits, although not simply monetary ones.

Most benefits have both financial and nonfinancial value. If you are working on improving your marriage, a financial benefit is the avoidance of a costly divorce and paying child support. A nonfinancial benefit is the extra hours and days you get to spend with your children. Both are easily quantified.

Most benefits have both financial and nonfinancial value.

If you are unsure where to start in identifying the value of your benefits, refer to the primary areas of your life—family, faith, fun, profession, finances, social, mental/physical fitness, and community service. Consider how your goal affects each area. Put a monetary value on all the benefits in each area impacted. Then assess the nonfinancial benefits in terms of time saved, risks reduced, new activities that will be enjoyed, stresses decreased, anxieties eliminated, and so forth. The process will not only move your anticipated benefits from the vague and general to the clear and specific, but it will uncover new benefits you had not considered before.

If you clear your mind and focus, you will think of many benefits. As you do, add them up to see their overall magnitude, particularly those that provide financial value. If your goal is to become a top-producing real estate agent, add up the commissions you expect to earn over and above your present salary for the number of years you expect to be in the business. Add to that the profit of any houses you buy and turn around yourself. Add referral fees you earn from satisfied clients. Add the expenses you would avoid by having a company car and a company phone.

If you are on a journey of serious consequences or need a higher degree of precision in your analysis, put the financial value of your benefits in present-day monetary terms using the net present value function on a financial calculator. Net present value is based on the "time value of money" principle that the value of today's money is different from that of the money in the future. The net present value calculation progressively decreases or increases future values, depending on how much inflation or deflation is expected and how far in the future you will receive the expected benefits.

Another method to use to increase the precision of your return-on-investment calculation is to reduce the monetary value by any risks that can affect your estimated benefits. You do this by identifying the risks, assigning them a risk factor that reflects their probability, and multiplying the risk factor against the affected benefits. This applies to both benefits and costs that are at risk of changing.

If, for example, you believe an economic slowdown hurts your chances of earning $100,000 in bonuses over three years, reduce the bonus to reflect the risk. If your confidence is 80 percent that you will get the bonus, the amount at risk would be 20 percent. You would then multiply $100,000 by a risk factor of 0.2, representing the 20 percent risk. The resulting risk reduction in your bonus would be $20,000.

So instead of using the original $100,000 bonus in your estimate of benefits, reduce it by $20,000 to $80,000.

If the $80,000 bonus would be received three years in the future, you would reduce it further if you expect the time value of money to decrease. If you estimated the value of money to decease by 5 percent a year, based on expected inflation and cost of living increases, a financial calculator would reveal that today's $80,000 will be worth $69,107 in three years. Combined with the impact of your risk assessment, this is a significant difference from the $100,000 you initially calculated.

Carrying this example to its conclusion, when you finish establishing the value of your benefits, compare them to the costs you would incur in creating them. If the benefits total $69,107 and the level of incremental effort required to earn them is $40,000, your effort would be worth a net $29,107, based solely on financial considerations.

Now with clarity of the financial impact of pursing your goal, your remaining considerations are the nonfinancial impact of achieving your goal and the impact of your other options. If pursuing your goal would make you unable to pursue another goal, you would take into account the opportunity costs—the costs of not doing something else. If the net result of your investment is $29,107, it would only be worth pursuing financially if there were no other options that created more than a $29,107 return. If pursuing this option prevented you from pursuing another with a $50,000 net benefit, you would have to add the $50,000 cost to this option to accurately reflect the cost of the lost opportunity. It would then no longer make sense to pursue this endeavor on its financial merits alone.

This detailed financial modeling is pure excess for most situations. I'll be the first to admit it borders on the analytical extreme. However, for pursuits for which you're considering taking out a loan, quitting your job, or employing other extreme measures, the hour or two you invest in this analysis is more than justified. It adds a measure of objectivity to your decision making that makes the comparison between important alternatives much easier. When you consider that many decisions are made on emotion and later regretted, a little extra analysis could provide peace of mind both now and later. Take advantage of the opportunity to put objectivity into your decision making by assessing the value of achieving your goal.

Build Up Your History Motivation

Influential events and experiences from the past can be another source of motivation, *history motivation*. Especially good or bad experiences leave lasting imprints. Recalling them moves you to action. It could be an event that scared you or one that caused physical pain or mental anguish, such as the loss of a friend. It could be a wake-up call like being fired from your job, receiving candid words from your doctor, or suffering a setback in a relationship. Or it could be a deep emotion created by an exhilarating, enlightening, or encouraging experience. You might have helped or neglected someone in a way that has left a deep emotional imprint on you. Bringing it into your consciousness and concentrating on it could be the motivation you need.

One such experience happened to me while I was living in Flower Mound, Texas. A friend and I decided one year to make our upcoming Christmas more than the normal exercise in materialism. Rather than going through the ritual of buying and receiving gifts only for ourselves, we decided to do something for those less fortunate.

We addressed our church's Sunday school class one morning that November and announced that we would act as a clearing house, matching people who had something to give with people in need.

We solicited donations of time, goods, and money from people who wished to give and collected names and information about people who needed help.

A friend and I decided one year to make our upcoming Christmas more than the normal exercise in materialism.

At the end of the class, a woman walked up to us and said she was a school teacher in a rural area north of Dallas. She told us about one of her students who belonged to a very poor family. Her student was a teenage girl who lived with her working single mother and five siblings in a camper trailer. The camper was nothing like those you see being pulled down the road behind an SUV. This camper wasn't road-worthy—it wasn't even accommodation-worthy. Before becoming this family's home, it had been deemed unfit for use as a hunter's camper.

I remember the emotion I felt when I first pulled up to this camper to meet the family. The camper was dilapidated; it had a two-foot hole in the floor and holes in the roof that leaked buckets of water when it rained. It had one working electrical outlet that powered a hanging lightbulb, the only source of light. The camper once had several working outlets, but they'd shorted out; smoke from one had stained the wall above the outlet. The camper had been abandoned as junk, yet it became this family's home. A mother was raising six beautiful kids in it. I'll never forget seeing the kids playing in the dirt out front with this junky camper they called home in the background.

Our Sunday school class gave the family new clothes, toys, food, and other items that Christmas. After the holidays, we conducted a fund-raising campaign, and within nine months, our class raised enough money to buy the family a new mobile home. That experience has forever made me appreciate what a few people can do to make a lifetime impact on others. That experience still motivates me to volunteer for community service projects. It motivated me to start a Habitat for Humanity affiliate with a friend, to tithe more at church for benevolent causes, and to be a better father to my own children.

Consider experiences that have left you with strong memories and deep emotions. Recall a vacation, camping trip, accident, or other event that could be used in some constructive way in your current pursuit. If you have a strong childhood memory of something enjoyable, think about how to make it part of your journey. If your fondest memory is camping at the lake and your goal is to get into better shape, add hiking around the lake with your children to your plan. Or add harvesting your own Christmas tree, growing food at Grandma's farm, hiking the Grand Canyon, playing touch football in the backyard, or skiing in the mountains to your exercise plan.

Merge your inspiring memories into the pursuit of your goal to make your pursuit more meaningful, enjoyable, and thus sustainable. Your past experiences and memories can be powerful motivators. Make them part of your plan of action.

Make New Influential Experiences

In addition to using your existing influential experiences, take your motivation up another level by creating new ones. If your pursuit is to improve your parenting skills, go visit a county jail or a juvenile detention center. Gain the mental image of what happens when kids aren't properly parented and become wayward. If your goal is to quit smoking, visit a hospital's cancer ward. If you want to reduce your anxiety and stress, visit the cardiac care unit. If you're working to overcome vices such as greed, materialism, or ingratitude, spend some time with the less fortunate. Take a trip to a Third World country, visit a homeless shelter in an inner city area, or go on a medical or dental missionary trip. Volunteer for a local nonprofit charity that serves the indigent.

Even less moving experiences, such as visiting with an expert in your developmental area, are also influential. If you are considering a new career in sales, talk to successful salespeople. If you are a senior executive hoping to change your management style from "command and control" to "motivating and coaching," visit other senior executives who have mastered the coaching style.

Your aim is to experience a glimpse of the success you anticipate or the pain you will encounter should your endeavor fail. Both are tremendous sources of motivation. They build your enthusiasm and excitement, clarify your vision, and sustain your other sources of motivation. They add the extra drive you need to complete your journey.

Your aim is to experience a glimpse of the success you anticipate or the pain you will encounter should your endeavor fail.

Employ Symbols

Symbol motivation is another powerful motivator. Pictures, signs, charts, figures, and stories help create moving mental pictures. If you are dieting, post a picture of a trim and fit person you've cut out of a magazine by your computer or stick it to your lunch box. Using the other side of the motivational coin, use a snapshot of yourself in your bathing suit exposing the extra thirty pounds you plan to shed. I know it seems unthinkable, but a quick glance will keep you from eating that second helping or that dessert. Or if you are trying to quit drinking alcohol, attach the international skull-and-crossbones sign for poison to your cans and bottles. It will totally change your view of what you are drinking.

Your symbol could be a video clip. If you are working on your public speaking skills, a good motivating symbol could be a video clip of a presentation you did that went extremely well (or poorly). Store it on your personal computer and watch it periodically.

If you are quitting smoking, carry in your wallet a picture of a smoked-out, black lung from a dead cancer patient. It's morbid, but if it works . . . If you want to quit chewing tobacco, print a picture of someone who had half his face cut away to remove his mouth cancer. If you are cutting out carbonated beverages from your diet, carry with you a picture of your soda can with a poison symbol on it.

If you wish to earn a promotion, print out a picture of the new car or piece of jewelry you plan to buy. If you're working to become an industry expert, print out a picture of the industry award you hope to win. If you aspire to become a great leader, write a hypothetical future biography outlining the legacy you left during your career.

Even if you have a solid list of benefits, quantified values, and formative experiences to rely on, create your symbol as a backup. If it's a picture, tape it to your bathroom mirror so you see it every morning. Put it in your purse, tape it to your credit card, clip it to the visor in your car, or pin it on your office wall. A simple image makes a big difference in how you view things. Symbols are great reminders when temptations to fall back on old habits crop up.

Consider All Sources

Another motivation is *regret motivation*. The prospect of regrets moves many people to action. Think about your final days in your job, as a parent, or in your life. What legacy do you want to leave? The time will come when it's too late to do anything more about it. Think how you'll feel when you become unable to pursue your objective ever again. The effort required by your endeavor now is not as hard as dealing with your regret later. Regret is one tough emotion to contend with. There is no more helpless feeling than being out of options when it's too late to do or correct something. Contemplate your regret for not giving your goal a solid try.

The effort required by your endeavor now is not as hard as dealing with your regret later.

Another motivation is *spiritual motivation*. The faith that a supernatural creator is watching over you or giving you strength is a powerful motivator. My own faith gives me strength and confidence. When the going gets tough, I don't worry; I know God will provide what I need. It gives me a peace of mind that would not otherwise be available. I also believe my unique combination of talents and experiences are God-given, and part of my responsibility is to put them to work for His benefit. If you have not made up your mind about your faith, now might be a good time to do so. Talk to others about their faith. Read your holy book. Study the history of the world's different religions. Decide for yourself what to believe, and put your faith to work in your journey.

The sources of motivation presented up to this point come from your thinking. Assessing the benefits of your goal, considering the

Activating Your Ambition

possibility of regrets, recalling strong memories, and being grateful are all thoughts. Another motivation, however, is as much physical as mental. It is experiencing the results of your effort.

Progress motivation happens with success. Realizing the positive impact of your effort becomes a new source of motivation to continue. If your goal is to start your own consulting business, completing two or three successful consulting engagements drives you to continue. The ability to carry on a basic conversation in your newly learned foreign language motivates you to continue. Improved relationships with others motivate you to continue working on your social skills. The experience of progress creates a new source of motivation that helps you sustain your journey.

Here is a summary of the motivation sources available to you:

- Fun and Excitement
- Value
- Fear
- History
- Fame
- New Experiences
- Fortune
- Symbol

- Generosity
- Regret
- Gratitude
- Spiritual
- Gain
- Progress
- Pain

Activating Your Ambition

As a caution, when using any incentive, whether the carrot, the stick, or your internal drive, be careful to understand what behaviors you are driving. Motivation is critical to activating your ambitions, but it's so powerful that it can push you just as hard in the wrong direction as it can in the right one. In the workplace, for example, you may be driving so hard for respect and acceptance that you cover up your mistakes or try to blame others. You can be so driven to reach a sales quota that you alienate customers through unbridled persistence.

160

Be careful not to alienate your employer, your family, your neighbors, and your friends. Motivation is not a license to be stupid. Use good judgment. Don't let your drive push you to extremes.

Before beginning your endeavor, get yourself up for it. Get excited and enthusiastic. Think about the success you will attain and the pain or hassle you will overcome. Anticipate the benefits you expect to achieve. Create a symbol or mental picture to remind you to stay on course. Recall past experiences and plan to create new ones too. Employ your faith. Think about the legacy you want to leave. Picture the benefits to others as well as to yourself. Bury the possibility of regretting inaction.

On the page of your road map titled "Activating Your Ambition Scorecard," score how well you currently do in applying the concepts of motivation. On the page of your road map titled "My Motivation," list the sources of your motivation. Write down why you want to embark on your endeavor.

6
Believe You Can

Believe in yourself! Have faith in your abilities!
Without a humble but reasonable confidence in your
own powers, you cannot be successful or happy.

–Norman Vincent Peale

Sara was overweight and out of shape. She had been an athlete in high school, but since then had turned the attention she had once put into training into raising children, and now she was putting it into her profession. Over the years, her fitness had seriously deteriorated. When I met Sara, she weighed much more than her doctor's recommended weight. She drank carbonated sodas throughout the day, ate fast food, and snacked on sweets between meals.

Sara had long ago accepted a lower level of physical fitness and attractiveness. As time went on, though, she was increasingly unable to ignore her declining energy level. Her management position required her to stay upbeat and sharp, which often took more energy than she had. She found her mental quickness, memory, and overall performance falling as her energy level fluctuated. By late morning and most afternoons, she felt drained. Occasionally, she had to shut the door to her office or go home and take a nap. If she made it through the day without a nap, she would come home exhausted and unable to give any quality time to her family until she slept.

Sara and I spent some time building an accurate awareness of her situation, reinforcing the benefits of improving her level of physical fitness, and developing a coaching plan that would help her achieve her fitness goal. The plan included regular exercise and proper nutrition.

Sara was plenty motivated to improve her fitness, knowing that if she didn't, her ability to do her job—and, ultimately, her career—were in jeopardy. However, that motivation wasn't enough. She was unable to stay on her diet and stick to her exercise program. Going to a meeting with a soda and a snack had become such a routine that she couldn't do one without the other. Believing that she wasn't a morning person, she also struggled to get up in the morning and exercise.

Sara had tried several diets over the years but was never able to sustain them. Now she doubted that she had the ability to overcome the temptations that had derailed her prior attempts. Fundamentally, she didn't believe in herself. The cycle of eating and sleeping that kept her energy level on a roller coaster seemed unstoppable. Sara needed proof that she could resist her temptations. She needed mental reinforcement to complement her motivation. She needed to replace her skepticism with a positive, can-do attitude.

To help her develop a genuine belief in her ability to sustain a diet, we listed the causes of her earlier failures and created plans to deal with them when they occurred again. We studied her successes in other areas and built up her overall confidence, her belief that she really could do anything she put her mind to. We dealt with her skepticism and created a frame of mind that would allow her to confront and overcome temptations and obstacles as they cropped up.

Sara went on to become a "gym rat," as she called it, waking up every day at 4:00 a.m. to go to the gym. As a result, she regained her vigor and mental acuity. She was able to maintain her energy level for a full day, increase her patience, and improve her performance in a number of other areas. After completing her coaching program, she called to tell me she was handling a number of difficult issues at work and that if she were not in such good physical condition, she wouldn't be able to do so.

Accurate self-awareness and motivation are insufficient for most people to overcome an addiction or to sustain the discomfort required to change their habits. In a study led by Dr. Edward Miller, CEO of Johns Hopkins University, researchers found that only one in ten people changed their lifestyle of diet and exercise after open-heart surgery or angioplasty. Fully 90 percent of post-heart-surgery patients reverted to the lifestyle that had created their unhealthy condition to begin with. In other words, nine out of ten people chose to risk enduring another surgical procedure or *dying* rather than change! Even though they had more than enough awareness of their condition and motive to change, they didn't.

To overcome a habit as engrained as eating junk food or smoking, knowing the benefits of change—or the consequences of not changing—is not enough. You need more. You need a genuine belief in yourself and your ability to reach your objective, along with confidence that you can resist temptations. All doubts need to be replaced with a can-do attitude.

The third principle after *awareness* and *motivation* is *belief*. Belief is knowing in your mind and heart that you absolutely can do what you've set out to do, a positive attitude based on certainty of achievement. Belief is your basis for optimism. It is the self-confidence that keeps you focused on what you can do, not on what you can't. Belief is the root system of your persistence. It keeps you going through the inevitable discouragements that changing behavior deals out. It enables you to overcome your built-in mental programming which makes you want to quit.

Much of the material covered in section one of *Activating Your Ambition* demonstrates that people can change. Now it's time to ask yourself: Do you truly believe you can change and achieve your goal? Do you believe you can maintain your change? If the answer is no, you are right. As the pioneer automaker Henry Ford said, "If you think you can, you're right. If you think you can't, you're right." If you believe something will be hard or impossible, it will. If you believe something will be possible, it will. You accomplish what you think you can accomplish.

Many people's beliefs fluctuate. They answer the question about their confidence with, "It depends." When their circumstances change, so does their confidence. It seems normal, since we all experience people and events that impact our mood. We are clearly more capable in some areas than in others. Things go our way on some days, and on others they don't. But while it is natural for our mood and circumstances to fluctuate, our confidence doesn't have to.

When your confidence is founded on an intrinsic belief in yourself and your goals, it remains stable. Conversely, when it's founded on circumstances and people that fluctuate daily, it fluctuates. Fluctuating confidence and belief lead to a fluctuating journey, which leads to derailment. To prevent the best-laid plans from derailing, having a secure and stable core belief in what you are doing is vital.

You will inevitably encounter a setback along your journey— probably more than one. Someone will try to discourage you. A much-needed resource will be in short supply. A key assumption on which you base your plan will change. An unanticipated event will require a change in your schedule. If you don't maintain your belief as these setbacks occur, you will get sidetracked. You will chase after distracting circumstances, let your missed due dates slip further, misplace your focus, lose belief in yourself, and abandon belief in your goal.

When your belief wanes, you eventually quit. Projects are left incomplete, college degrees are left unfinished, and dreams go unfulfilled every minute of the day because the belief in them wasn't strong enough to survive the inevitable setbacks that challenged them. Just because circumstances change and setbacks occur, your belief in yourself and expectations of success don't have to.

Dreams go unfulfilled every minute of the day because the belief in them wasn't strong enough to survive the inevitable setbacks that challenged them.

History is full of people who encountered setbacks yet persevered because of their belief. Our lives today would be very different had they not. Ulysses S. Grant, the eighteenth president of the United States and the leading general in the Union Army's victory in the American Civil War, could easily have turned his back on his military service. After a good start in the military, he encountered several setbacks.

Grant attended the U.S. Military Academy at West Point before he served as a Lieutenant in the Mexican-American War, where he was decorated twice for bravery. After that war, he became a civilian. He tried his hand at farming but failed. He tried running a real estate agency and failed again. He ran for the office of County Engineer and was defeated. In desperation, he went to work for his family in the leather-goods business. Despite his misfortunes, he never let go of his belief in his military leadership ability. When the American Civil War broke out, he enlisted, and the rest is history.

Thomas Edison, inventor of the incandescent lightbulb, the motion-picture camera, and hundreds of other devices, suffered many setbacks. His first famous invention, the phonograph, created in 1879, earned him the title, "the Wizard of Menlo Park." Yet after becoming a successful inventor and doing what he most enjoyed, he met ridicule when he announced his goal to invent an inexpensive replacement for the gas lamp. More than ten thousand experiments failed to produce a working electric lightbulb, but in the end, he prevailed.

Problems will interfere with your goals too. Your beautiful daughter, with whom you are working to improve your relationship, will suddenly turn into a rebellious alien after a simple quarrel with her boyfriend. Your home-remodeling project will be delayed for weeks when a hot-water heater leaks on your new wooden floors. Your confidence in your budding sales skills will be severely tested when nine out of your first ten contacts have no interest in your offering. Your plans to move into management will come under attack when your jealous peers discover and contest it.

The longer your goal takes to complete, the more disappointments you will encounter. If your belief wavers when you meet disappointments, the motivation you spent so much time identifying and developing will turn into hopelessness and despair.

Belief must include two elements—yourself and your pursuit. Success depends on believing both in your own ability and in the merits of your pursuit. Your can-do attitude is confidence that transcends the pursuit itself—not a temporarily hyped-up attitude, but a genuine belief that survives the circumstances that will confront you. This attitude fuels your persistence and carries you through ridicule, frustration, disappointment, or any other seemingly insurmountable obstacle that comes your way.

Wanting to believe is not sufficient; you must actually believe. You might want to believe you have the courage to skydive but find yourself clutching the door when it's time to jump. You might want to believe you can resist a drink if offered, but find yourself at the hotel bar after a long out-of-town seminar. You may want to believe you have the patience to spend every night for a year writing a book but find after a couple of weeks that the patience isn't really there.

Out of the eight principles of *Activating Your Ambition*, your belief is the predominant predictor of your success.

To pursue a goal reliably, you must truly believe in the goal, not merely want to believe in it. Only true belief will sustain you. You may have calculated a long list of benefits, but if you don't truly believe you can achieve them, you won't. When your belief is sure, it will sustain your motivation, drive you, reassure you, excite you, and carry you. Out of the eight principles of *Activating Your Ambition,* your belief is the predominant predictor of your success.

Think Your Way Forward

What you believe drives your attitude, your actions, and the results you attain. People regularly fail because they don't believe in themselves and their ability to achieve. People also succeed against all odds because they believe and don't stop believing.

You might not be able to do something, at least initially, but if you believe you can, studies have shown that your belief will carry you further than would otherwise seem possible. You are more likely to succeed at an "impossible" goal if you believe in it than you are at an easy goal in which you have doubts. Beliefs and expectations become self-fulfilling prophecies.

Almost anything you accomplish is the result of a chain of events that starts in your mind. Your thoughts create your feelings and emotions. Your feelings drive your attitudes and behavior. Your behaviors drive consequences, events, experiences, circumstances, and habits. Your behaviors determine whom you meet, the situations you encounter, the resources that become available to you, and the results you attain. What starts as a simple thought becomes your reality. Results are a direct consequence of your thinking.

If you think you will enjoy a certain project, if you anticipate it with enthusiasm and have a positive, can-do attitude, you will engage it with eagerness and complete it on time and at a high level of quality. With no changes other than thinking you won't enjoy it or can't do it, the same project will be completed late, if at all, and at a much lower level of quality. Regardless of your actual ability or the nature of the project, a simple change in attitude changes the project from a chore to a delight. Your thinking changes your reality.

Your thoughts show up in your communication too. What you talk about, how you talk about it, your choice of words, your voice inflections, and your body language originate from your thoughts and feelings. The messages people hear from you and their reactions to them are the result of what you think. No matter how hard you may try to convey something other than what you're truly thinking, your thinking comes through. If you talk long enough, people hear what you're thinking, not necessarily what you're saying.

Even when you don't want something, thinking about it builds thoughts and feelings that attract you to it. As Carl Jung, a twentieth-century Swiss psychologist, said, "What you resist persists." You gravitate toward your dominant thoughts. What you focus on, whether you want it or not, becomes your reality. Put another way by author Robin Sharma in *The Greatness Guide, Book 2,* "What you befriend, you'll transcend."

Your thoughts also impact your body. Your thoughts and feelings initiate physical processes in your body that release chemicals into your bloodstream. When you perceive danger, fear causes your adrenal gland to secrete adrenaline to prepare your body for action. The adrenaline increases your heart rate, your oxygen supply, and your blood sugar, which increase the power of your muscles—all begun by your belief that you're in danger.

Our thoughts are our most powerful capabilities. They drive our emotions, our words, our physiology, our behaviors, our circumstances, and our life. The people we attract, the opportunities we encounter, the experiences we have, the habits we form, the achievements we enjoy, and the rewards we take pleasure in all start with our thoughts.

Our thoughts are our most powerful capabilities.

If you want to change your current reality, change your thinking. Since you have to think about something, you might as well think in helpful ways. Replace your disbelief with belief. Create the feelings, attitudes, words, and chemicals that work for you, not against you.

Put the power of belief on your side, and it will help you reach your goals.

In the late 1990s, doctors in Texas performed a study on patients who needed arthroscopic knee surgery. The patients all had sore, worn-out knees. Each one was assigned one of three operations— scraping out the knee joint, washing it out, or doing nothing. In the third category, they made small incisions so the patient would believe that the operation had been performed. Two years after the surgery, patients who had the placebo reported the same level of relief as did other patients.

This is not exceptional. Numerous other studies in other areas have shown the same astonishing results. People have believed their way out of cancer, asthma, baldness, and innumerable other illnesses. Some studies have even found placebos actually to be more effective than drugs or surgery. The patients' optimistic thinking created chemical and neurological activity that were more beneficial to them than the proclaimed cure! You talk, walk, drive, learn, heal, behave, feel, and go in the direction of your dominant thoughts. What you believe is what you become. What you believe creates your reality. Perception truly is reality.

Learn to Believe

At the most basic level, our beliefs come from two sources— nature and nurture. Of the more than five hundred defined phobias that humans deal with, some are simply an inborn part of being human. Claustrophobia (fear of confined spaces), acrophobia (fear of heights), hydrophobia (fear of water), ophidiophobia (fear of snakes), and nyctophobia (fear of the dark) are common fears that are genetic. However, they don't have to be permanent. As with the natural fear of animals that we turn into a love for our pets, natural fears can be overcome just as our learned fears can be.

Our learned fears and beliefs are those we teach ourselves through repeated experience, reading, self-talk, and listening to others. They are not genetic. No one is born afraid of public speaking, although seven out of ten people learn to become so. No one is born with clothes, yet most people are uncomfortable walking around naked, even in their own homes. We are not born afraid of electrical shock, terrorist attacks, driving in heavy traffic, or most other things, yet we learn to fear them.

Because we can learn, we can unlearn. You can teach and desensitize yourself to counter both natural and learned phobias. Many children are afraid of the dark, but through gradual desensitization of repeated exposure to the dark, they learn that their fear is unfounded. For some kids, it takes a progression from a nightlight in their room to leaving a light on down the hall to the moonlight through their window to becoming comfortable in total darkness. For others, it comes faster, but all can eventually learn to feel safe in the dark.

The same principle applies to believing in yourself and your goal. You can teach yourself to believe, regardless of your history. You might not fully believe now that you can accomplish your objective, but disbelief can be turned into belief. Apply the concepts in this chapter, and you will learn to believe. Pursuing a goal with a strong foundation of belief is much more reliable than having an "I'll fake it until I make it" attitude. As Samuel Johnson, the eighteenth-century English writer, said, "Self-confidence is first requisite to great undertakings."

Believe in the Outcome

Part of the conditioning to believe involves convincing yourself that the desired outcome is truly desirable. If you are in sales, you won't convince others that your product does what it claims if you don't believe in it yourself. If you are replacing a directive style of management with a coaching style, you won't be a good coach just because someone told you it works; you must believe with your whole mind that coaching people to perform versus telling them what to do will result in higher-performing employees.

If you don't truly believe that the outcome of your goal will deliver benefits greater than their cost and effort, your belief won't sustain you when the going gets tough. Instead, as competing priorities creep into your schedule, you'll fall back into the comfort of your old behavior.

Identify the benefits of your goal, as covered in the last chapter. Identify both the qualitative and quantitative benefits, both the tangible and intangible values. Understand the goal's value to yourself and any positive impact on others. Dwell on these benefits. Create symbols to remind you of them. Remove any remaining doubt that your expected benefits are possible. Believing in them helps your confidence as well as your motivation.

Obstacles create fear and doubt.
They are the enemy of belief.

Plan for Obstacles

If your goals were straightforward and easy, you would already have accomplished them. Obstacles and risks exist in the pursuit of all goals. You may have lowered your expectations by considering your expected risks, but you also need to consider the mental impact. Obstacles create fear and doubt. They are the enemy of belief.

Knowing how to deal with obstacles removes doubt and gives you confidence that you can truly achieve your goal. If you anticipate constraints or temptations that will slow or halt your journey, knowing how to handle them ahead of time gives you peace of mind. It makes you better able to handle them when they arise. An essential tool to increasing your self-confidence and belief in your pursuit is having a realistic plan to deal effectively with expected obstacles.

Start by identifying any anticipated temptations, threats, or obstacles to achieving your goal that you did not already identify when figuring the impact of your risks on your benefits. If you plan to quit smoking, a temptation to light up when going fishing or out for drinks with your buddies would be an obstacle. If your goal is to pursue a deeper spiritual faith, a risk would be getting into a discussion about your faith with an agnostic relative who has tried for years to undermine your faith. If you are a manager working to hold your poor performers more accountable, an obstacle would be the need to approach the poor performance of an employee who is also a personal friend.

Identify anything that will tempt you to quit your journey or slow your progress. Think ahead about external influences that will work against you. Anticipate difficult encounters with people, unpleasant situations, dispiriting memories, and anything that puts your plans at risk.

When you have identified your obstacles, temptations, and risks, create a contingency plan to deal with each of them. First, plan how you can avoid them altogether. Where you can't avoid them, plan how you can overcome them. Carefully planning how you will react to a given obstacle before it occurs prepares you to deal with it.

You remove the element of surprise and engage rational instead of irrational thinking. You are much more likely to conceive a good response to a situation when you are calm than when you are scared, hungry, tired, angry, or otherwise emotionally aroused. In your planning, you gain both the confidence and the ability to conquer.

Contingency plans are straightforward. You use them in many ways already. Having an extra set of car keys is a contingency plan for the event of misplacing your keys. Having a spare tire is a contingency plan for a flat tire. Having flashlights and candles around the house in the event of a power outage are contingency plans. Contingency plans are part of life and just as applicable to handling temptations to fall back into old behaviors.

A contingency plan to resist a drink or unwanted social encounter is to have your car handy so you can leave early. If you are working on controlling your anger, a contingency plan is to know ahead of time that you will turn and walk away when your nemesis says something upsetting. If you are working to reduce your distractibility at work, plan to shut your door or not answer the phone when working on your project, or to ask the requester politely to come back later or set an appointment through your assistant.

If your goal is to reduce weight and going out to dinner with your boss or client is a risk, plan to order a salad topped with salmon or chicken, or to have the wait staff put half your entrée in a to-go box before they serve it, or to bring a piece of dark chocolate to replace your normal dessert. If your goal is to work more intentionally and less reactively, plan a response to counter a risk of receiving a last-minute, urgent assignment from your colleagues. Rather than letting their lack of planning become your emergency, plan to say, "I need to keep working on this. I can discuss your situation in the morning. If you can't wait until then, I suggest you talk to someone else."

Physical exercise is an excellent contingency for many frustrating or tempting situations. Rather than lash out at someone or pick up a cigarette, plan to step on the treadmill, go for a brisk walk, or pump some iron. Exercise is a great tool to have in your emergency response toolkit. It lowers stress and diverts your attention, putting matters back into their proper perspective. Craft a plan to go home or to a gym when the need arises. If that's not convenient, take your running shoes or weights with you to work. Do whatever you can to pedal, run, lift, stretch, step, or swim out of your temptations and frustrations.

Contingency plans are powerful, but early in your journey, it is better to avoid obstacles and temptations altogether. Your resistance to temptation isn't as well developed in the early stages. If you can navigate around your obstacles instead of confronting them head on, do so. If you know you will be tempted to smoke while talking with your colleagues at their smoke break, have lunch with them at a non-smoking restaurant instead.

Think about what has triggered temptations or false starts in the past, and create a plan to deal with them.

With a little thinking and creativity, you can plan for almost any obstacle. Think about what has triggered temptations or false starts in the past, and create a plan to deal with them. Know beforehand how you will respond. The process will build your confidence and solidify your belief that you can succeed.

Confront Negativity

You may be uncertain about this positive self-talk. You may think contingency planning for obstacles is unnecessary. You may be unconvinced that digging into the benefits is worth the time and effort. You may want to believe, but having tried a similar effort before and failed, you doubt another attempt. You may be naturally skeptical, or you may be reading this book under duress. Whatever the reason, if you are going into an initiative with a negative attitude, you are doomed from the start. Succeeding when you lack positive and reassuring thoughts is almost impossible. Save yourself from the frustration. Deal with your negativity first before engaging in your pursuit. Otherwise, you will be making excuses, blaming others, saying "I told you so," and merely reinforcing why you shouldn't be doing whatever you're doing.

Pessimism, like most learned characteristics, can be overcome. Martin E. P. Seligman, psychologist and best-selling author says, "A pessimistic attitude may seem so deeply rooted as to be permanent. I have found, however, that pessimism is escapable. Pessimists can in fact learn to be optimists, and not through mindless devices like whistling a happy tune or mouthing platitudes, but by learning a new set of cognitive skills."

Seligman says three perceptions most affect whether a person has a positive or negative outlook. One is whether the individual believes his misfortunes are caused by others or himself. The second is how strongly he believes his misfortunes are permanent and unlikely to diminish over time. The third is whether he believes his misfortunes are limited to an isolated event or are pervasive across all aspects of his life. When people believe their misfortunes are their own fault, unlikely to diminish over time, or span broad areas of their life, they have little room for optimism.

In Seligman's book *Learned Optimism: How to Change Your Mind and Your Life,* he offers five cognitive-therapy and positive-thinking tactics to help people change their attitude from pessimism to optimism:

1. Recognize the thoughts flitting through your mind when you feel most pessimistic.

2. Question the validity of your automatic negative thoughts and dispute them with contrary evidence.

3. Make different explanations of your circumstances to defend yourself.

4. Distract yourself from dwelling on negative thoughts when in the midst of self-doubt.

5. Recognize and question the assumptions that govern what you think and do.

Employing these five principles helps turn a normally pessimistic attitude into a habitually optimistic one.

If believing in your ability to reach your goal is taking a great deal of effort, read Seligman's book and follow his detailed instructions on how to become more optimistic. Surround yourself with the wisdom of successful people. Read and memorize the positive-thinking quotes of contemporary leaders, historical figures, and the kings of antiquity. Subscribe to positive-thinking online newsletters. Listen to self-help audio books. Hang out with positive people. You won't be able to escape becoming an optimist.

Anchor Your Confidence

Remaining confident during your journey is essential. Yet one of the main components of confidence—competence—could be temporarily sidelined if your journey involves building new skills. You don't feel very competent when you keep making mistakes, as you do when plying a new skill. If you are learning to dance for the first time, you will undoubtedly leave the dance floor feeling as if you have two left feet. To combat feeling incompetent, anchor your confidence in other competencies or elements. Remind yourself of all the other areas in which you are competent. Remind yourself of your existing skills and expertise. Accept that no one has ever become an expert overnight. Accept yourself.

If you are a great speaker but a lousy listener, remind yourself of your great speaking abilities while you learn to listen. If you are great in social gatherings but poor at detail work, remember your social strengths while you develop your ability to focus. Stay centered on your strengths while you develop in new areas. Use your strengths at every opportunity to keep yourself positive. Keep believing in yourself. Confidence in one area rubs off on others. Knowing that you have achieved in other areas boosts your confidence that you can achieve again.

Only you—your abilities, experiences, faith, values, and knowledge—can be the enduring anchor for your confidence.

Just be careful where you ground your confidence. Don't build it on characteristics outside your control. Positions, possessions, and the perceptions of others are fleeting. If you use these as your anchor, you will find yourself drifting at the whims of others. Only you—your abilities, experiences, faith, values, and knowledge—can be the enduring anchor for your confidence. If you lack confidence, or if it seems to go up and down, you may have been looking in the wrong places.

Make a list of your accomplishments, skills, and strengths. Recall all the obstacles you have successfully overcome in the past. Recognize that your unique combination of talents, experiences, values, and knowledge makes you uniquely competent. Keep these accomplishments in your mind when you make mistakes or feel dejected.

Visualize

A great way to reinforce your belief in something is to visualize it. Creating a vivid mental picture of a successful outcome reinforces it in your mind. Seeing yourself doing what you aspire to do reinforces your belief by activating the same mental activity that would have occurred had you actually experienced the outcome. Visualizing molds the neural network of synaptic connections that drives your desired behavior. Thinking in pictures also marshals new mental resources to aid you. Visualization taps into a different part of your brain than thinking of tasks, facts, and numbers.

Mental pictures give your thoughts direction. They are guideposts that steer your thoughts, your feelings, your behaviors, and your reality. Mental pictures fortify an otherwise vague sense of belief. They bring to life what otherwise seems unreal. They give substance to your ideas.

Visualizing creates and strengthens the same patterns of connections in your brain as doing does, so your brain benefits as much from thinking as from doing. Visualize your desired outcome. Feel the benefits of achieving your goal. Picture yourself experiencing the benefits you want. Mentally invoke your senses of touch, hearing, taste, and smell in addition to sight. When you think hard enough about your favorite meal, your mouth waters and you taste it. Visualize your success as often as you can and imprint it in your brain. The mental picture will eventually seem real, conditioning you and reinforcing your belief.

If you're pursuing a coaching style of management, picture yourself as a successful coach. See yourself confidently coaching others, sitting comfortably in a conference room with your protégé across from you. See her listening intently as you ask questions, and hear her respond with well-thought-out answers. Feel the confidence and the satisfaction of a successful encounter. If you are working on your organization skills, picture your workspace clean and uncluttered. Picture yourself effortlessly finding exactly what you need in your orderly file system. If you are developing your listening skills, picture yourself sitting across from someone, leaning forward, making eye contact, giving him extra time to finish his thoughts, probing to understand, paraphrasing his responses, deferring judgment, and taking notes.

Mental pictures have the added benefit of clarifying your goal and helping you stay focused. A well-developed mental picture helps sort out inconsistencies, resolve questions, and add detail to your outcome. With a little concentration, your general intent becomes a canvas of details. What might have been a mild interest becomes a much more detailed and exciting one.

Visualization is so powerful that you have to be careful what picture you create. Avoid mental pictures of your past failures and mistakes. If you are going on a diet, think thin. If you are working on your marriage, think of the good times. If you are building your patience, see yourself being calm and relaxed. If you expect to change, picture yourself as being different from how you are now. If you picture yourself as an individual contributor at work, it will be difficult to do what you need to do to move into management. If you can picture yourself only in poor physical condition, it will be next to impossible to initiate an exercise program.

In motorcycle riding and biking, there is a phenomenon called target fixation. When you focus on an object on the road or trail while you ride, the object becomes your target. You may be looking at it because you want to avoid it, but because you are looking at it, your brain makes you head for it. I've hit rocks, fallen into a lake, driven into a river, and hit trees all because I so badly wanted to avoid them.

Your mental picture is no different. Create a picture that you want to go toward, not one you want to go away from. You'll gravitate toward whatever mental picture you create and head in that direction.

Picture yourself as a successful pastor, athlete, partner, leader, or in a happy relationship. Envision yourself being free of your bad habits or having become what you desire to become, and your belief happens naturally. Don't worry if the image isn't perfectly clear. Don't worry if you're aiming at a job or position or situation you've never experienced before. As you keep looking at your mental picture, it becomes clearer.

Find a time and place where you can close your eyes and relax. Picture yourself having achieved your goal. Picture yourself in your new house. Picture yourself lean and fit, eating salad instead of chicken-fried steak. Picture yourself reacting calmly to someone else's emotional outburst. Picture yourself speaking confidently to your audience. You will know you have succeeded in visualizing your success when you can smell, taste, hear, feel, and see the outcome in your mind's eye.

Think about your mental picture regularly. Write it down in detail. Make it easy to recall. When you think of your goal, think of your mental picture. Replace any pictures of your "old self" with pictures of your anticipated "new self," and feel the excitement of the new you.

Exercise Your Faith

Religion and faith are powerful drivers of belief. Belief in God, or belief that beneficial unseen forces are at work in the world, strengthens your ability to believe in yourself. Faith provides a rock-solid foundation of belief. With God on your side, believing in yourself and your desired outcome is much easier. Solomon, king of Israel in the tenth century B.C. said God "is a shield to those who take refuge in Him" (Proverbs 30:5). Faith can be a significant enabler in starting and sustaining your belief and self-development.

Consider your faith-based values and how they apply to your goal. Put as many of them to work in your goal as possible. Some typical ones to think about include:

- Concern for others
- Creating unity
- Service to others
- Living by moral standards
- Unselfish giving of your resources
- Following an absolute truth

- Living in moderation
- Honoring life
- Promoting peace
- Loving others
- Obedience
- Applying your spiritual gifts

Put your faith into action. The more your goal aligns with your values and faith, the more your faith will help you and the more strongly you will believe in what you are pursuing. If your goal is to become a better leader, position your leadership as an act of service. Create a mental picture of yourself as a servant leader. If your goal is to be a better spouse, consider how being a better spouse is a reflection of your faith and obedience.

In addition to applying your faith-based values, let your faith sustain your confidence. If you believe you can depend on God and your goal is aligned to His will, you should have little doubt you can succeed. Having God on your team is as reassuring as having an old friend by your side. The belief that your endeavor is blessed can comfort and stimulate you. Spiritual belief has a calming effect that creates inner peace. Faith that someone or something is watching over you and guiding you frees you to concentrate on getting things done and liberates you from worrying about things you can't control. It makes what might look like an impossible obstacle seem a minor detour.

Use your faith to remove any anxiety or stress your goal might generate. Pray for guidance. Ask God to help you select the right goal, to support you on your journey, and to secure your success. Seek His blessings and depend on Him. Reflect on how your goal is aligned with His will, and secure your belief in your goal through your faith. You can then focus on the execution of your journey, not on the discomforts, anxiety, or obstacles you might experience. And when you are finished, give Him the glory.

Pass the Foolish Test

What if your goal is unrealistic, perhaps even impossible? Is it foolish to convince yourself that you can do something you can't? Yes, it can be. There is a point at which your pursuit can go from ambitious to foolish. Ambitious is okay—foolish is not. To embark on a journey and commit your time and effort toward a goal that has little chance for success is irrational.

While a goal may be achievable, it can be so far out of your reach that it just isn't worth your time, money, and effort. Or it can be too risky to pursue under current circumstances. Goals should pass the *foolish test*, which starts by applying common sense. If you have no natural ability, no experience, and little knowledge of the goal you want to pursue, it may be foolish. If the effort and cost are excessively high, it may be foolish. If the journey is full of high-risk activities with low odds of success, it may be foolish. If any of these are the case, put more thought into your goal. Do more research. Talk with others who offer you an unbiased perspective. You may need to rethink what you are doing.

Not only your goal but also your approach to achieving your goal should pass the foolish test. While your objective may be logical and doable, your approach to achieving it may not be. The eight principles in *Activating Your Ambition* form an approach that makes the attainment of your goal easier and more reliable. If you are not planning to follow the principles, your plan doesn't pass the foolish test. When you don't take advantage of proven methods that put reliability into your pursuit, you are being foolish.

Not only your goal but also your approach to achieving your goal should pass the foolish test.

Passing the foolish test doesn't require that you tone down your goals or dampen your enthusiasm—it simply requires that you use logic. Suppose your objective is to move into management, and you're technically skilled, but you have to compete with more socially capable colleagues for a management position that requires strong social skills. Suppose you think the only way to compete for the promotion is to schmooze your way up the corporate ladder. This just doesn't pass the foolish test. You're not a schmoozer.

You don't have to abandon your goal of going into management, but you would be wise to rethink your approach. A better option would be to use your technical skills to win the favor of the boss and offer to build your social skills when in the position. If that didn't work, then you might reevaluate the goal itself. Perhaps another department in the company offers career-growth opportunities in a technical field that would be more realistic for you to pursue.

If your pursuit marginally passes the foolish test, conduct a trial run. If you want to play the guitar but you lack experience, knowledge of music, and musical skills, try it for a while. Instead of buying a guitar and making a music studio out of your basement, borrow a guitar and commit to three months of lessons. If after three months you're making good progress and enjoy the experience, then great—buy a guitar, convert your basement, and commit to a longer-term pursuit. If, on the other hand, you are frustrated and have made little progress, give the guitar back and focus on something more worthwhile.

Activating Your Ambition

If you pass the foolish test and you've tried every method to secure your belief but still can't muster a true belief in your goal, reconsider your goal. The upcoming chapters may give you the extra insight you need, but if you've followed the ideas offered in these first chapters and are not confident, you may be pursuing something you shouldn't. Go back to your original life areas and objectives. Contemplate other alternatives you may have uncovered. Widen your options. Becoming a doctor or a lawyer may not be your best option. Accept that and apply your energies to a pursuit to which you are more suited.

As a caution, carefully consider others' beliefs about your journey as well as your own. You may believe your journey passes the foolish test, but your colleagues or family don't. Your belief might be rock solid, but others see you as a fool for considering it. While the same was said of the Wright brothers and Martin Luther King, Jr., you would be wise at least to give their point of view some reflection.

Review your approach. Conduct a trial run. If your plan has significant risk, it may be more foolish than you think. Before quitting your job, selling your house, moving away, or doing anything extreme, reassess your risks and rewards. Seek to understand better the objections you are hearing. You might continue, but the extra attention and understanding could uncover something that will save you substantial effort and expense.

On the page of your road map titled "Activating Your Ambition Scorecard," score how well you currently do in applying the concepts of believing. On the page of your road map titled "My Belief," list the confirming elements of your belief. Write down why you believe so strongly in your goal. Craft your contingency plans to deal with your risks and obstacles. Describe in visual terms the outcome you expect to achieve. Describe how your goal aligns with your faith. Embed elements of your faith into your journey.

7

Plan Incremental Steps

It is better to take many small steps in the right
direction than to make a great leap forward only to
stumble backward.

—Old Chinese Proverb

Doug was an achiever who had succeeded in almost everything
he did and was widely respected for his ability to get things done. As
executive vice president of sales for a regional distribution company, he
was considered one of the top members of the company's leadership
team. His peers would say, "If Doug can't get it done, no one can."

All was not positive for Doug, however. His strength was also his
weakness. His no-nonsense, logical, problem-solving approach, which
served so well in making good decisions and completing projects on
schedule, made him seem insensitive and uncaring. His lack of people
skills prevented him from being trusted. He spent most of his energy

and attention on carrying out tasks and showed little concern for how the tasks affected the people who performed them. His lack of empathy and compassion made his team feel more like objects than people. They rarely felt inspired to give their work their best effort. Doug got things done, but he often left people feeling mistreated.

In his late forties, Doug had known for years he was considered a "hard nose." He had tried a couple of times to soften up, but between the urgency of getting things done and his continued success in achieving his numbers, he'd found little reason to put much focus on tempering his style. Recently however, several high-performing new hires had found his management style overly repressive, and they'd quit. Doug hired me as his coach with the goal of improving his people skills.

We developed a coaching plan that included visualizing his role more as a people job than a task job, paying attention to people, putting himself in their shoes, putting people terms in his vocabulary, and so on. He bought into the plan, immediately put it into practice, and got off to a great start. After about two months, I reviewed his progress with his boss, the president of the company. The president said that Doug had initially made some progress but was falling back into his old habits, driving his people so hard again that the frequency of complaints was as high as before.

When I addressed Doug's apparent relapse with him, it turned out he had become impatient with his progress, tried to do even more than we had agreed, and then been overwhelmed by it all. His high-achiever mentality had pushed him to make his changes too quickly. He was accustomed to embarking on projects and seeing them completed within a few days or weeks. A six-month coaching program was almost intolerable for him.

The root problem was that Doug had set his sights on the end of the journey instead of on its milestones. He got away from accomplishing the incremental steps we developed that would enable him to retain what he was learning and make it comfortable. When we reset Doug's sights on near-term, incremental milestones, he quickly got back on track and made tremendous progress.

About two years after Doug and I started working together, I got a call from his boss. He said Doug was a different person. Doug had softened his management style to an extent that his boss thought would never be possible. And Doug had done it without compromising his "results" orientation. In fact, he made his numbers just as quickly and confidently as he ever had, yet with less collateral damage and less of his own involvement, thereby increasing his employees' self-sufficiency and job satisfaction.

While a few people might measure their success only by achieving their final goal and getting there in one big step, most success comes a small step at a time. You can't realistically expect an engrained habit developed over years to be overcome in a few days. People who pursue incremental steps instead of large or long, drawn-out ones are much more likely to achieve their final goal. They are likely to achieve it sooner and with less anxiety, to maintain it longer, and to end up with greater competency. Slow and steady are more reliable than fast and erratic.

In Robert Maurer's book, *One Small Step Can Change Your Life: The Kaizen Way*, he says that he found people who pursued their achievements in small, gradual steps were much more successful than those who tried to take steps that were too large and outside their comfort zone. He explains, "Small steps circumvent the brain's built-in resistance to new behavior." Small steps avoid moving us too far and too quickly outside our comfort zone. They limit the stresses and fears that make us retreat back to old bad habits.

Incremental steps are easily-started actions that can be completed without triggering your brain's built-in resistance, yet when completed, are big enough to create a sense of accomplishment. They don't alarm you, overwhelm you, or take you so far out of your comfort zone that you feel you have to race back to it.

Incremental steps are easily started actions that can be completed without triggering your brain's built-in resistance.

Incremental steps make many accomplishments easy and comfortable, like the increasing comfort you feel (without realizing it) as you get to know someone, adjust to a new car, or sleep in a different bed. Studies show that people are four times more likely to buy from someone they have come to know than from someone they don't know. The same ratio applies for products that people have tested versus those they haven't. Small, gradual steps make us more comfortable and are more likely to result in our signing a contract, buying something, or successfully reaching our goal.

Create a Plan

Incremental steps translate your intentions into specific actions. They transform your ideas into specific tasks to execute. If you are a planner by nature, you will find the idea of incremental steps easy to apply. If you prefer spontaneity and intuition, you might find this principle challenging. Just remember that moving outside your comfort zone is part of your development.

You complete a trek taking many weeks one day at a time. Similarly, you will most reliably complete your goal through planned, manageable steps. If you have ever planned a large wedding, corporate relocation, product launch, or other complex undertaking, you know the value of breaking plans down into manageable tasks. The bigger and more complex the undertaking, the more important breaking it up becomes. As the proverb goes, "Mile by mile is a trial; inch by inch is a cinch."

The words "plan" and "planning" are commonly used in business. The outcome of just about any meeting you attend is a plan. Statements like, "We need a plan to overcome the XYZ obstacle," or "Let's create a plan to win the ABC account," emanate from conference rooms daily. Yet, ironically, such ideas frequently fail to make it past the planning phase. Plans often resemble intentions, needs, and goals rather than thought-out, actionable steps. Meetings lasting hours are regularly adjourned without translating the key decisions into documented tasks that can be implemented and tracked. That's like working for hours on a report on your computer and then hitting [Delete] instead of [Save].

Being accountable to a plan turns many people off. Plans seem like black holes—places where nothing that enters is ever seen again. Organizations routinely use a "plan" to set aside ideas that deserve future attention but never get to them. People use the word "plan" to refer to something they hope to do in the future, but know they probably won't get to. They interpret phrases like "strategic plan" as thick binders of esoteric information that collect dust until other strategic plans replace them. People rarely associate near-term actions with the word "plan."

As a consumer, you may also be put off by the word "plan." Perhaps you've talked to a customer service technician or a sales person who said something like, "Your request is a known requirement, and we *plan* to add it to the product." Like most, you probably understood that to mean, "Not in your lifetime." While these examples make us chuckle, at the same time, we talk about our goals for years and seldom create a doable plan to pursue them.

Some people do legitimately plan. Successful product launches, relocations, and other projects are accomplished on time, on budget, and to expectations because they are run by project managers who manage them to a well-crafted plan. The problem is that this type of planning is more associated with our professional lives than our personal lives. When planning is part of our personal lives, it is usually more in the context of coordinating resources or deciding what to do than in that of self-development. And when our personal projects, like building a home or remodeling a kitchen, miss their due dates and go over budget, we seldom see the problems as planning problems, although they often are. Well-crafted remodeling plans go a long way in preventing issues such as underestimated resources, resources brought in out of order, insufficient time allocated to certain tasks, tasks being left out, unplanned-for obstacles, and unclear responsibilities—the same issues that plague improperly planned self-development.

When you don't plan, you are winging it—depending on luck. You only hope things will go as you would like. More often than not, though, people end up being inconvenienced, due dates are missed, and tasks that would otherwise have had plenty of time become urgent fire drills. In the end, things don't fit, don't coexist, don't work, take longer, cost more, and don't look right. They don't achieve the level of success that a little up-front planning would have made possible, putting your goal at risk of failure.

Planning identifies dependencies, exposes issues, and uncovers limitations. It identifies resources that need to be secured and reveals permits, approvals, obstacles, constraints, conflicts, resources, and countless other considerations. Planning is the link to quality implementation that reliably turns ideas into accomplishments.

Planning identifies dependencies, exposes issues, and uncovers limitations.

In defense of those who don't regularly plan, it's not like there isn't anything else to do. Few people with the initiative to improve themselves have a lot of spare time on their hands. That's the reason you need a plan. Planning saves more time than it takes. An hour or two of planning can prevent problems, any one of which can cost much more time than you've spent planning. Little else yields as high a return on your time investment as planning. Think of it like the five minutes you spend writing a grocery list before going to the grocery store; that list can save an hour trip back because you forgot something.

When thought through beforehand, plans specify incremental actions to be executed, reducing worries about how well they will work, fit, cost, or last. The deliberation, coordination, and debate are done beforehand, removing confusion during the project. When the plan is done, most of the thinking is done. You simply execute the tasks with confidence.

A good plan not only lists milestones but also lays out specific tasks that methodically move you forward. Say you want to improve your communications skills and have set a goal to speak effectively to audiences of five hundred people. A plan with only milestones might include three or four steps that take you from reading a book on presentation skills to joining a speaking club to presenting to a small audience to signing up for a keynote speech at an industry convention. While this may work for a skill at which you are already semi-competent, it doesn't work well for developing new capabilities. The steps are too big. They are milestones rather than easily started actions.

Many people would never execute this type of high-level plan. Even if they started, they would abandon it before completing it. A reliable plan employs small, specific steps that include the "how," not just the "what." More gradual and easy-to-start steps could be doing Internet research on Toastmasters International, calling Rotary International about speaking opportunities, and talking with a colleague at work who teaches communication skills workshops at your local community college.

When translating your ideas into actions, make your steps as specific as possible. Instead of "work out everyday" or "work out fifteen minutes every other day," say, "Wake up at 6:00 a.m. and work out from 6:30 to 6:45 a.m. on Monday, Wednesday, and Friday." Specific actions remove confusion or the need for follow-on decision making. Because they are more measurable and more likely to be accomplished, they create better accountability.

Develop Your Root System

Small steps give your mind and body the time to absorb change and acclimate before going to the next level. People who climb Mount Everest don't reach its peak in a day, or even a week. They slowly make their way to the top by stopping at up to five base camps. They stay at the first base camp, at about 17,000 feet elevation, for a couple of weeks just to acclimate to the altitude. Then they work their way to the 29,028-foot peak by stopping at incrementally higher camps.

Weightlifters who bench-press 250 pounds don't get there in two or three steps. They start with seventy pounds or less and work their way up to their desired level, adding as few as five pounds each time they increase their weight. This gives their bodies time to adjust. By gradually increasing the weight they lift, they give their muscles time to develop so they can support the next level of weight.

Such development is no different from how a tree grows. The taller a tree becomes, the deeper and broader its roots grow. If you transplant a large tree, you have to take with it as much of its supporting root system as you can if the tree is to live. If you don't, the first heavy wind or snow will topple it over. The root system doesn't only support the tree but also nourishes it. A tree without a strong root system will quickly wither away in a drought.

You, too, must develop a strong root system to withstand the winds and droughts that will come your way. You must be able to support the breadth and depth of change you expect to make. That root system reliably comes from incremental steps; slow, steady development builds the deepest roots of capability. It gives you the time to internalize what you are learning, the repetition required to adapt, the small wins that build your confidence, the experiences that solidify your skills, and the conditioning that makes your change sustainable.

If your steps are too big, you fail to build your root system and miss out on core parts of your development. You lack experience and conditioning. You may have grown on the outside, but your root system is stunted.

If your steps are too big, you fail to build your root system and miss out on core parts of your development.

You may prefer to jump right in and get things done quickly. That's great when you're focused on short-term gains, but for long-term, sustainable results, small steps are the more reliable path to success. Remember the tale of the race between the hare and the tortoise. The rabbit jumped out to an early start, but the tortoise's steady progress and discipline won the race. As in marathons, the winner is rarely the one who jumps out first. Pacing yourself is the key.

Two years ago, my wife and I selected our exercise program, which had six levels of increasing difficulty. When we started the first level, we could barely do the routines, and we would end them exhausted. We both figured we were too out of shape and, in our late forties, perhaps too old ever to get beyond that level. One day we watched part of the video of level five, just to see how different it was. We'd never laughed so hard. People were doing push-ups, pull-ups, wall squats, and other exercises, each for several minutes at a time, nonstop, for an hour. We thought it would be impossible to do those ourselves. We turned off the video and decided we'd just focus on our little novice routine at level one.

Fast-forward two years later, and we're both exercising at level six. We do the full complement of exercises, including everything we thought would be impossible. The reason for our progress is the levels. Had we started at level six, we'd have failed miserably. But since we worked our way to level six slowly, one level at a time, we made it with surprisingly little difficulty. Our success wasn't from our determination or motivation. It was from the ease with which the incremental steps allowed us to improve.

In the long run, methodical, incremental steps toward your goal will result in more progress than inconsistent giant leaps. Don't cheat yourself out of proper development by setting yourself up for discouragement and failure. Create an action plan with small, gradual, realistic steps that build your root system. "Gradual" is your friend, the key to forming good habits. Just as a bad habit gradually sneaks up on you, a good habit can gradually sneak up on you to reverse the trend. Steady work always outperforms hard work. Give yourself the opportunity to experience, learn, internalize, and apply as you grow. Your progress may feel slow on occasion, but trust the process. It works.

Don't Confuse Milestones with Actions

You can start your plan by listing either milestones or actions. The difference between the two is that actions are what get you to the milestones. Your plan needs both, and the order in which you identify them is up to you. Many planners prefer to start by identifying the major milestones they want to accomplish and then inserting the actions needed to attain the milestones. Many individuals prefer to identify the actions they need to take and then aggregate them under periodic milestones. The approach you select depends primarily on the complexity of your goal.

If your goal is relatively straightforward, like improving your physical condition, and you know what you need to do, you may prefer to start listing actions. You'd list an action such as working out fifteen minutes every other day for the first two weeks, then working out thirty minutes every other day for two weeks, and then working out thirty minutes a day five days a week, and so on. The only rule to concern yourself with is that the actions need to be small enough to be easily done, yet big enough to give a sense of accomplishment. When you finish the actions, you add in the milestones you expect your actions to accomplish. They might be to lose five pounds, then ten pounds, and finally fifteen pounds.

If you have a more complex goal, start by listing the milestones. In the example above, you would start your plan by listing the milestones of losing five pounds, then ten pounds, and ultimately fifteen pounds. Then you would come back and insert the actions needed to accomplish those milestones.

Good plans include both milestones and actions. Be careful not to substitute milestones for actions. Milestones are important but not enough. They measure progress but don't tell you how to make it. A plan that provides only the *what* and not the *how* is hard to start, like a to-do list full of items like "fix car," "paint shed," and "update Web site." It makes you want to hide from your list. The to-dos lack clarity about both where to start and how to finish.

Stand-alone milestones make tasks hard to start because they seem overwhelming. Unless they're broken down into smaller actions, they make you feel you need the better part of a day to do anything with them. Instead, divide each milestone into the actions required to complete it. To paint the shed, break it down into "scrape off old paint," "mask off windows," "select and buy paint," "apply coat one," and "apply coat two." These smaller tasks are clearer and easier to start. You'll be less likely to procrastinate because you don't need a whole day to do any of them. You won't feel as overwhelmed by the enormity of the overall project. Before you know it, you will have made steady progress, one step at a time, and the shed will be finished.

Stand-alone milestones make tasks hard to start because they seem overwhelming.

If you are working to create a better work-life balance, start by creating a milestone like spending four hours a day with your family twice a week. Decide how to achieve that milestone and back it up with clear, actionable, written steps: you will leave the office by 6:00 p.m., toss the ball with the kids for thirty minutes, help them with their homework for an hour, cook dinner with your spouse, and end the evening playing a board game or watching a movie with the whole family. When that milestone has been adequately backed-up with specific actions, create another milestone like spending one full, uninterrupted weekend a month with your family. Create the detailed actions to support it and continue the process until you have a plan that gets you incrementally to your desired goal.

If your goal is to save enough money for a down payment on a house, list specific actions that put money in your savings account, not just how much you expect to save. List actions like putting $125 of each bi-monthly paycheck into your savings account, reducing your dining out by $150 per month, and saving $25 per week in unnecessary expenses. Your milestone for these actions would be "increase savings by $500 each month." The actions provide the details, and the milestones give you a way to measure and track progress.

To make your milestones most meaningful, break them into increments that make sense for your plan. Increments can be events, performance thresholds, or progress checkpoints. They can span days, weeks, or months. A daily milestone might be your calorie intake. An element like your weight would more likely be tracked weekly. You could track saving money or spending time with your family either weekly or monthly. The key is to set milestone intervals that allow you to make corrections along the way. Don't set up a monthly milestone when the adjustments you need to make are daily. Likewise, don't set up daily milestones where it takes a month to see a real difference.

For both milestones and actions, assign a due date. Select a date that you realistically expect to meet. Having documented deadlines creates a higher degree of responsibility. When you set a specific deadline, no matter how arbitrary it might have been when created, you are more likely to hold yourself accountable to it.

It's your plan; make it work for you. Keep yourself as accountable as you need to be. You know best what level of detail you need to keep your focus. Include both milestones and the actions needed to reach them. Make the milestones measurable and the actions specific.

Make It Fun

If you dread your journey, you will find every possible excuse to put it off. If you look forward to your journey, you will find every possible excuse to pursue it. Make your action plans something you look forward to. Embed elements of fun into them. Make them engaging.

Studies have shown that when you are having fun, your mind operates at its best. When you enjoy what you do, you become more engaged in what you are doing—time flies, you stay connected, and your mind doesn't wander. When you don't enjoy what you're doing, time creeps by, and it is difficult to maintain your discipline. The benefits of your effort may sustain you if they come quickly, but when they don't, the work becomes drudgery, and it's hard to keep slogging through.

Look back at what excites you from the chapter on securing your motivation. What can you do to make your actions fun, or at least more tolerable? In losing weight, consider different ways or places to exercise. If you like the outdoors, include exercising outdoors in your plan. If you hate the monotony of an exercise bike, plan to ride a real bike around the park. If you hate the thought of learning how to type on a computer in the dark recesses of your basement, add a desk to your den so you can type in a space with windows. If you enjoy spending time in your workshop, move your computer there to practice typing.

If you're working on your public-speaking skills, set up opportunities to speak to small, friendly groups on topics that you know well and enjoy talking about.

If your goal is to become more productive, yet you hate the thought of sitting at your desk all day, design your schedule so you can work in different settings. I can't sit at my desk for more than about an hour, so I keep a daily to-do list that includes tasks that need to be done both at my desk and in other places nearby. If my meeting schedule doesn't get me out of the office, I engage in an "away from my desk" task when I get restless. By alternating desk tasks and away tasks, I accomplish my list in a much more pleasurable way.

Think about your objective and what you might do to make the journey enjoyable. Involve people you like, places you enjoy, and activities related to your hobbies and interests.

Plan for Temptations

You will encounter situations on your journey that will tempt you back into old habits. If you're working to control your anger, you will encounter someone who makes you angry. If you plan to quit smoking, you will be invited to go outside and have a smoke with others. If you're developing your executive presence and professionalism, you'll inevitably be tempted to go out with the guys after work for a drink and the usual office gossip. If you plan to develop a new account in your territory, a crumb of business from an old account will pop up and tempt you away from the new one.

Anticipate your temptations and obstacles ahead of time.

Remember this key principle—*anticipate your temptations and obstacles ahead of time.* If you didn't take your anticipated obstacles into consideration in the last chapter, do so now. Include them in your plans. If you haven't planned a response for a specific situation, record a specific action in your plan of incremental steps to figure it out.

Recording a well-thought-out action plan will help you identify areas that you would otherwise miss. Putting ideas on paper forces you to get your thoughts in order. A written plan doesn't let you get away with vague concepts. You will discover equipment, supplies, activities, and assistance you would otherwise have overlooked. You will better pinpoint when you need equipment and assistance so you can give others valuable notice of your needs. You will know better how long your journey will take and how much it will cost.

Activating Your Ambition

On the page of your road map titled "Activating Your Ambition Scorecard," score how well you currently do in applying the concepts of *incremental steps.* Go back over your notes under the principles related to *awareness, motivation,* and *belief.* Transfer any elements or ideas you listed there to your action plan on your roadmap page titled "My Incremental Steps." At this point, you should have a detailed list of the activities and milestones you need to complete in order to reach your goal. The next four principles build on this list, adding concepts that will make your actions even easier to accomplish.

8

Reserve Time and Energy

Time is the most precious element of human existence.
The successful person knows how to put energy into
time and how to draw success from time.

–Denis Waitley

One issue derails more self-development initiatives than any
other: time. This was Mark's case. Mark let his perception of time
keep him in a prison of self-development stagnation for many years.
Mark wanted help to improve his strategic thinking, but his lack of
time kept him in handcuffs. By most standards, he was competent
and successful. He had a strong work ethic and enjoyed his job with
an East Coast telecommunications company. He was on the senior
leadership team, and his industry knowledge and experience made him
a highly respected and sought-after resource.

However, he restricted himself to tactical matters and operated more as a manager than a leader. Creating new initiatives and thinking strategically were not his forte. Mark dealt in the here and now and would often refer to himself as a firefighter—a person who spent his time putting out the organization's proverbial fires. He rarely thought ahead because tactical issues consumed his attention.

Mark and I agreed on a coaching objective—to improve his strategic thinking. We put together a plan of incremental steps to help him focus on long-term issues and strategic opportunities. As we got started, I discovered how tactical Mark really was. He couldn't even complete the reading assignments I gave him, much less other special projects I normally assign my clients. He was unwilling to make time for anything that took more than the hour we spent together twice a month.

The reasons Mark couldn't make time were many and varied. He was short on staff, had an underperforming regional vice president, had customer complaints that needed immediate attention, was in stalled negotiations with a key supplier, had outstanding requests from his boss, was missing his administrative assistant who had health problems, and had health challenges himself. Mark's mode of operation left him with no time to take on anything else.

After a couple of meetings with Mark, I told him that if he couldn't accept the assignments I gave him and complete the incremental actions we developed, he was wasting his time and money. After a candid discussion, we struck a deal. We would first work on actions to free up his time, so that the net impact of our coaching engagement on his time was neutral.

We concentrated on areas where Mark could be more productive and delegate more. We created priorities and identified areas where he should say "no." That freed enough time and energy for him to learn and practice the new behaviors he needed in order to think more strategically.

Mark's journey took him almost two years, but in that time his mode of operation completely transformed. Rather than applying himself to tactical activities, he spent most of his time guiding his company around uncertainties in the industry and in other more valuable activities. He led a training initiative through which he transferred much of his operational knowledge to other managers. He focused his attention on the company's systems and processes, making strategic improvements that dramatically reduced the number of operational issues they faced.

Mark multiplied his value by teaching others how to perform his tactical role while simultaneously allowing himself to take on a more strategic one. This was possible only because he created the time and energy needed to learn and change.

In a study of historic trends in the use of time outlined in Robert Fogel's book, *The Fourth Great Awakening and the Future of Egalitarianism*, researchers estimated that the average head-of-household's work week declined by nearly half between 1880 and 1995. This occurred through a combination of technological improvement, economic growth, and labor legislation. The decline in the number of hours at work allowed time for non-essential activities to triple from less than two hours a day to six. In our contemporary society, we are still busy, but we're doing things we want to do rather than those we have to do.

Nonetheless, the "not enough time" excuse, along with the "I'm too tired" excuse, are very real obstacles to self-improvement. Whether real or perceived, lack of time and energy keeps people from starting and sustaining their desired pursuits. For a plan to be reliably executed, it must take into consideration the time and energy it requires. Just as you budget money, you must budget time and energy. In fact, for many endeavors, time is more precious than money. Unlike other resources, time is fixed and limited. You can't order more, buy more, earn more, or create more. You have to work with what you have. To be successful you have to take the precious, finite resources of time and energy into consideration.

Unlike other resources, time is fixed and limited. You can't order more, buy more, earn more, or create more.

When you plan actions that take up your time, common sense suggests you have to give up something in exchange, but people routinely commit to things for which they don't have time. In their desire to achieve their goal, they ignore the obvious. Those that do think about it assume that they'll squeeze their actions into their schedule somewhere or find the time in some other yet-unknown way. This puts most action plans at a high risk of failure.

For people without much spare time, executing an action plan means they have to either do less of something they currently do or do it more productively. A realistic action plan includes elements of at least one, if not both.

Energy is a little different. The energy you can put toward something does have limits, but you can create more. The options are either to stop doing something to preserve your energy or to do things that produce more energy.

This chapter contains a variety of how-to methods to free up time and energy for your journey. As you find methods that will work for you, add them to your plan of incremental steps.

Energize

Performance experts Jim Loehr and Tony Schwartz, in their book *The Power of Full Engagement,* suggest that energy is more precious than time: "We have far more control over our energy than we ordinarily realize. The number of hours in a day is fixed, but the quantity and quality of energy available to us is not. It is our most precious resource. The more we take responsibility for the energy we bring to the world, the more empowered and productive we become."

Context determines which is more important, but most pursuits require both time and energy. If you are working on a goal that requires physical activity, getting out of your comfort zone, or periods of serious mental concentration, you undoubtedly need additional energy. If you are a manager and your objective is to delegate more, you need energy for a number of tasks: self-control to resist the urge to do the work yourself, coaching to help your employees learn how to do the work, and patience while they learn. Delegating tasks to others requires lots of energy, at least initially, when the workload can temporarily go up.

We need both mental and physical energy. In learning to delegate, the manager's patience, self-control, and concentration require mental energy. However, mental activity depends on physical energy; thinking is a resource hog. Our brains, on average, represent only 2 percent of our body weight, but use up 25 percent of our oxygen intake. Using our mind doesn't seem like a physical act, but it is. What we do mentally and physically is connected. Both take physical resources, and both make us tired. Consider how physically tired you feel after a long day at the office in back-to-back meetings or a day of phone calls dealing with problems. Most phone calls and meetings aren't very physical, but don't try to tell your body that. They make you physically tired.

Our brains, on average, represent only
2 percent of our body weight, but use up to 25
percent of our oxygen intake.

If you are the mother of young children and your goal is to become more patient or lenient, you will need more energy as you spend more time on the playground and afterwards when carrying them home. Your primary energy need will be physical, although chasing your kids around will be a mental drain as well. At the end of the day, it really doesn't matter—both physical and mental activity depletes energy.

You can build up your mental and physical energy levels through a variety of methods, and, in most cases, the same method recharges both. The first method is to find some downtime. You need free time that doesn't use up any mental or physical energy, blocks of time when you step out of the whirlwind of life and simply relax. Such time takes your mind off your problems, opportunities, to-do lists, and responsibilities and lets your mind slow down.

Downtime doesn't necessarily mean doing nothing. It doesn't mean sleeping, although getting enough sleep is also important. Downtime is sipping a glass of wine with your spouse. It is meditating, taking a steam bath, listening to soothing music, reading a book, or watching a movie, although the content and intensity level of many movies are not conducive to relaxation. Enjoying simple activities that free your mind allow you to recharge.

If you find yourself in a relaxing setting and you still think about your problems at work, you are not relaxing. If you're listening to soft music, yet thinking about your response to a neighbor who has angered you, you are not relaxing. Watching the sun set while running through all your tasks for the next day is not relaxing. Watching the news and getting upset about the state of the economy is not relaxing. You have to relax in the present moment. If you focus your thoughts on anything, it has to be the spectrum of colors in the sunset, the flavors of the wine on your palate, or the individual notes of the piano. Let go of the rest of your world and allow your brain and body to take a break.

If relaxation escapes you, block out free time in your schedule to relax. Plan calming activities that don't require concentration or physical exertion to allow your stress levels to return to normal. Spend time with others who enjoy relaxing and can escape to the present moment with you. If you're trying to relax but the people around you aren't, it doesn't work.

Build into your action plan downtime that allows you to free your mind. If you are the type who likes to be busy all of the time, put a special emphasis on slowing down for short periods. You may think you have enough energy for your journey, but the reality is that if your battery isn't charged, you don't. Like stress, low energy levels can become so chronic you become accustomed to them. Many people have no idea they are stressed or tired until they start to make mistakes or others bring their fatigue to their attention. The reason people get their best ideas in the shower or on a walk is because their stress is lowered and their mind is free to wander.

Deplete Your Battery to Increase Its Capacity

Another way to build your energy reserves is to exercise. This is counterintuitive, as exercise is the complete opposite of relaxation, but it has been well researched and proven by many studies of thousands of people. Physical exercise builds energy and reduces fatigue. Interspersing periods of relaxation with those of intense physical activity increases your energy capacity. Loehr and Schwartz liken energy reserves to a battery. To get the most out of a typical rechargeable battery, you first use up all its available power and then recharge it, allowing for the fullest recovery of power. In the same way, exercise depletes your energy supply so your body can fully recharge.

Exercise helps in several ways. It tears down muscle tissue by creating minute tears which, when the tissue regenerates, increases your physical capacity. Weight lifters gradually gain strength and muscle tone through this process. Exercising burns body fat, lightening the load you carry. Exercise increases the levels of energy-promoting neurotransmitters such as dopamine and norepinephrine.

Being in good physical condition increases your capacity to cope with stress. It gives you the energy to come out of your comfort zone. It enables you to deal with the challenges you encounter in your journey.

To maintain your physical condition, the Cooper Aerobics Center in Dallas, Texas, recommends exercising for twenty minutes four times a week or for thirty minutes three times a week, within your personal target heart-rate range. During exercise, your target heart rate is 75 percent of your maximum heart rate, which is 220 minus your age. If you are 40 years old, subtract 40 from 220 to get 180 for your maximum heart rate. Your target heart rate is then 75 percent of 180, or 135 beats per minute. Allowing yourself 10 beats per minute either side of your target, your ideal heart-rate range at 40 years old is between 125 and 145 beats per minute for the length of your exercise. Of course there are other factors and medical conditions that should be considered, so ask your doctor for advice before assuming this approach is the best fit for you.

In my own exercise routine, I rotate daily between cardio exercise and strength training. This gives me the suggested three cardio exercises per week and helps me maintain muscle strength. When I started my fitness program, I began with thirty-minute workouts. I currently work out for sixty minutes on days when I'm not traveling—sometimes less when I do travel.

Make physical exercise a part of your journey. Adding exercise to your plan will raise your energy level, help maintain your mental sharpness, increase your confidence, and improve your overall health. If your endeavor requires lots of energy, particularly mental energy, regular exercise is a must. The extra time you spend exercising is more than offset by the boost you get in your energy level.

Optimize Your Fuel

What and how much you eat have a great deal to do with your energy level. Just as an engine requires fuel, so do you. The quantity and quality of that fuel is vitally important. It affects how well you feel and how alert you are. That effect is obvious when you consider how you feel after eating a large lunch, like a full plate of pasta, high in carbohydrates. Back at work, sitting in a meeting, you find staying awake almost impossible. Eating too much diverts your body's energy to the task of digestion, making less energy available to your mind and body. Instead of focusing on work, you struggle to stay awake.

Eating too much diverts your body's energy to the task of digestion, making less energy available to your mind and body.

Many people are naive about nutrition. They unknowingly poison their bodies daily, reducing not only their energy, but also their longevity. For example, people regularly eat a candy bar for a quick shot of energy, but don't realize that, shortly afterwards, their blood sugar drops and they feel more fatigued than before.

What and how much you eat affect your health. Organizations pay for employee diet and nutrition programs because they reduce sick time and increase productivity. The less you eat of something like sugar, for example, the fewer illnesses you will have, the more energy you will have, and the more productive you will be.

Studies show that eating sugar raises your insulin levels, which inhibits the release of growth hormones and depresses your immune system. Excess sugar intake has been linked to over a hundred health issues, including cardiovascular disease and cancer. In the late 1800s, when people consumed on average five pounds of sugar a year, there was virtually no cardiovascular disease or cancer. In 1900, heart disease accounted for less than 10 percent of deaths. In 2003, the average annual sugar intake in the United States went up to 142 pounds per person, and cardiovascular disease accounted for over 40 percent of deaths, with cancer accounting for another 20 percent. While clearly not scientific proof of cause and effect, the data suggests the two could be connected.

What is proven is that eating the right foods strengthens your immune system. Diets low in saturated fat and cholesterol increase production of white blood cells, which defend your body from infection by destroying and neutralizing foreign materials such as bacteria and viruses. A diet rich in green leafy vegetables, fruit, and other nutrient-rich foods such as fish, carrots, and tomatoes is essential to maintaining good health.

Quantity is also important. Reduced caloric intake promotes improved health and extends life expectancy. It helps drive your body to repair and replace damaged cells and rogue cancer cells. The United States Department of Agriculture Dietary Guidelines offer personalized recommendations on caloric intake. The number of calories varies based on your age, gender, and level of physical activity, but for a forty-seven-year-old male, the recommended amount is 2,400 calories per day. This may not sound like a lot, especially knowing you could get this amount from one trip to a buffet restaurant, but it works fine if you spread your eating out over the course of a day.

I eat breakfast at 7:00 a.m., a snack at 11:00 a.m., a light lunch at 1:00 p.m., another snack at 4:00 p.m., and dinner at 7:00 p.m. This regimen keeps me from getting famished, which has always been my downfall. As a result, I maintain an optimum weight and a steady energy level.

Supplemental vitamins and minerals help many people maintain higher energy levels. I'm not a doctor and not qualified to recommend what you should take, but from my own experience, supplements work. They make me feel better and help me maintain a steady pace throughout the day. If I stop taking my supplements, I begin to feel lethargic and lose my mental sharpness within two days. I find supplements are especially important when exercising daily, as they help me recover my energy more quickly. Supplements are also reported to speed up metabolism, giving you extra help in losing and maintaining your weight.

Look into your eating habits and how they might be affecting your energy. See your doctor about taking supplements and getting the proper nutrition. Investigate how the right type and number of calories might keep you healthier. Find the dietary intake that is right for you.

Get Enough Good Sleep

Another factor in maintaining your energy level is getting adequate, restful, and consistent sleep which induces processes in your body that rejuvenate you. Sleep slows your heart rate, rebalances body chemistry, repairs muscle tissue, produces essential hormones, and regulates organ systems. Without proper sleep, your body doesn't fully rejuvenate. Irregular sleeping patterns interrupt your body's normal biological rhythm. The result is that your mind and body have more work to do and less energy to do it with.

Sleep requirements depend on age, gender, physical activity, and stress levels. Current research suggests that most adults need seven and a half to eight hours of uninterrupted, restful sleep each night. In my case, I've found six to seven hours to be ideal. Much more or less, and I feel tired late in the day.

Sleep disorders such as insomnia, restless leg syndrome, and sleep apnea prevent people from getting the sleep their bodies need. Night-shift work and dynamic schedules like those required by international travel also degrade the quality of sleep, draining energy levels. When I travel internationally, I need two good nights of rest to readjust before I get back to a normal energy level.

As much as your work and family environment will allow, create consistency in your sleeping pattern. Try to go to sleep and wake up about the same time each day. I watch the 10:00 p.m. news, then read and go to sleep by 11:00 p.m. I wake up at 5:20 a.m. This gives me the sleep I need to replenish my energy for the day.

A comfortable mattress and a comfortable bedroom are important for restful sleep. Up to one-third of your life is spent in bed. A good mattress is not cheap, but given the value of a restful sleep and the amount of time you spend on it, it's an excellent investment. Your sleeping room should be quiet, dark, and at a comfortable temperature. Curtains, fans, air conditioners, heaters, and soundproof wall insulation are items to consider.

What you do before you go to bed is also important. Eating more than a light snack, drinking alcohol, engaging in intense physical activity, consuming caffeine, or taking in nicotine all affect the quality of your sleep. Experts say to avoid these things in the two to three hours before going to bed. Certain medications can also spoil your sleep.

If you have trouble sleeping and these simple suggestions don't help, seek help from a sleep specialist. Even if you think you're getting plenty of sleep, conditions like sleep apnea prevent your sleep from being restful. A quick trip to the specialist and a proper diagnosis could be all it takes to gain the energy boost you need.

Sleep, nutrition, exercise, and relaxation are all important for maintaining your energy level. Consider adding daily exercise, taking supplements, improving your sleeping habits, replacing an old mattress, and scheduling time to relax. Write on your road map page titled "My Time and Energy" any incremental steps or actions you need to take to ensure you take advantage of these energy producers.

Free Up Time

Based on statistics gathered by the United States Department of Labor in 2008, the average adult has 5.2 hours per day for discretionary activity after subtracting their time spent at work, sleeping, performing household activities, and personal care. When you consider that many professionals and home caretakers work more than the normal eight hour day, the amount of time left is often less than five hours. Involvement in civic organizations, religious activities, family interests, and personal business further limit our free time. There may be twenty-four hours in a day, but they boil down to less than five that we can reasonably use.

To free up what little time you have, you have two options—do less or be more productive. You can either do what you currently do more efficiently, or you can give up some of it. But before we get into the best ways to do both, you will want to estimate how much time you need to free. Needing a couple of hours a week is one thing; needing twenty is totally different.

If your goal involves going to school and doing homework, estimating is pretty straightforward. Record the time involved in your commute to school, the time you spend at school, and the time you spend doing homework. If the commute is thirty minutes each way, your class lasts two hours, and you plan to do two hours of homework each day, your total time commitment is five hours a day.

If your incremental steps are less tangible, your estimate will be less scientific, but make an estimate nonetheless. If your action steps include conducting online research in your self-development area, participating in a couple of self-assessments, reading a book, and further refining your action plan, estimate something on the order of an hour a day for three weeks. This gives you a starting point in identifying how much time you need to take from your normal schedule in order to pursue your initiative. You can come back and refine it later if needed.

Elements of achieving your goal may also have an impact on your efficiency. Take into consideration any net time savings that your new skill or competency might give you when determining the time you need. If your self-development goal is to create a more positive attitude, you can eliminate the time-wasting rituals you won't be doing anymore, like complaining to co-workers at the water cooler. If you are improving your sales skills and closing sales in two months instead of three, you gain a sizable amount of time back by shortening your sales cycle. You won't get the whole month because you'll use the time to obtain more sales, but you could claim a percentage of it at some point after you start developing those skills.

Once you have an estimate of the time you need, the time savings your new behaviors give you, and the net difference, you are ready to decide which time saving methods are most suitable for you.

Increase Your Efficiency

Look for efficiency gains where you spend most of your time. It won't help you much to improve your efficiency by 50 percent in an area where you spend only five minutes a day. Instead, consider the areas where you spend an hour or more. Think about how you might do those things more efficiently. Studies on time management show that if people cut out the time they waste, they can improve their productivity by as much as 75 percent.

Here are my top tips on how to be more productive:

1. **Focus**—Constant interruptions, such as e-mails popping up on your screen, phone calls, co-worker chit-chat, and so on turn an hour-long activity into a half-day activity. Turn off your e-mail, forward your phone, close your door, or do whatever you can to concentrate on the task at hand. Make a daily to-do list and focus on activities you need to get done that day. Be sure that your to-do list identifies next steps, not merely outcomes. Defer any interruptions to a period of the day you reserve for that purpose. Don't let the urgent, easiest, or most convenient displace the important.

2. **Meetings**—Conference calls and meetings occupy up to 75 percent of a normal work day for many professionals. Research indicates up to two-thirds of a person's time spent in meetings adds no value to the organization, and many meetings actually take value away. Make meeting productivity a high priority if

you often find yourself in unproductive meetings or conference calls. Require people who schedule them to follow meeting best practices, including providing a meeting objective, agenda, and background sheet before every meeting. This helps ensure that you don't attend unnecessary meetings and that the ones you do attend don't waste the first thirty minutes sorting out background information.

3. **Root Causes**—Many day-to-day problems that take up your valuable time are recurring problems that are either routinely ignored or temporarily resolved with quick fixes. Rather than treating symptoms and sidestepping persistent core issues, deal with the causes properly to resolve them once and for all.

4. **Automation**—Repetitive tasks are good candidates for automation. Computer applications, paper-based templates, and tools can dramatically speed up otherwise labor-intensive tasks. Look for automation opportunities. Where you find substantive rework, redundancy, or repeated manual tasks, there is an opportunity for automation. Identify tasks that could be automated, seek out possible solutions, do the cost/benefit analysis, perform a trial run, and, where justified, recommend a permanent implementation.

5. **One Touch**—Touch e-mails, voice mails, paper mail, and other documents only once. Avoid the practice of reading them, setting them aside, reviewing them again later, and then touching them a third time to deal finally with them. If a task takes five minutes or less to complete, do it immediately rather than file it away to do later. Use the "do, delete, delegate, or file" rule for as much of your inbound correspondence as possible. If you can delete it, do so; if you need it for future reference, file it. Parking and

intermixing your correspondence, reference files, and to-dos in stacks around your work area is not productive.

6. **Communication**—Communication, or the lack of it, causes more problems and misdirection than any other activity. Be clear in your expectations. Communicate assignments and information early, clearly, and frequently. Write and speak in specific terms, not in generalities, and don't assume that others around you know what you are doing or what is expected of them. Communication also includes listening. Many problems originate from poor listening, so listen attentively when discussing important matters.

7. **Notes**—Make a habit of taking notes. Note taking helps reinforce what you hear or read and creates a source for future reference. Notes help you solidify your thoughts and retain what you have heard or read. In meetings and on conference calls, take notes. When you talk to your automobile mechanic, take notes. When you see your doctor, take notes. You will greatly improve your comprehension and retention, saving hours of lost productivity.

8. **Filing and Organizing**—Many people spend hours a day looking for their notes, articles, receipts, or documents. It may only be a minute here and there, but by the end of the day, this time adds up significantly. Set up an efficient filing system for your hard-copy materials and computer files. If possible, align the two so that you always know where to look. The same goes for your tools or whatever other resources you use in your trade. If you have papers scattered all over your office, materials all around your workspace, or tools all over your work desk, you are wasting time.

9. **Start**—Start your work even if you can't finish it—unless, of course, you're a surgeon or in some other profession where that isn't possible. Many people don't have enough continuous time to start and finish an entire job at once, so break your activities down into subcomponents and get started. The only caveat is that you should stop your work at a point where is easy to come back. Restarting an activity at a point of impasse prevents many people from coming back to it, at least until they have no choice.

10. **Audio Books**—Most self-development endeavors require reading. Even if yours doesn't, reading is one of the best ways to increase your knowledge and performance. A study revealed that high-income individuals read, on average, nineteen books a year, while the average person reads only two. Ben Franklin, Thomas Edison, and countless other successful people attribute a large part of their success to their habit of reading. Rather than limiting your reading to the rare moments when you can grab some quiet time at home, buy your books on audio media. Listen to them during your commute to work or while exercising. If you like the book and want a hard copy, you can always buy it later.

This is not meant to be an exhaustive list of productivity-improvement areas. It is meant to get you thinking. Depending on your lifestyle, work environment, and other responsibilities, there will be others that are more relevant. If needed, record an action in your plan to do more research on improving your productivity. There are countless online articles and books you can read on time management, getting organized, and being more efficient. The time you free can be the difference maker in achieving your goal.

Say No

Doing less starts with learning to say no. If you hate disappointing others and generally say yes to most requests, this will be your best opportunity to free up time. Even if you don't have the typical "helper" personality, doing less may be your best opportunity. This includes saying no to things that you enjoy, as well as things you don't. I have confronted this in my own life. In the few discretionary hours a day I had when my children were young, I found myself at parent-teacher meetings, church ice cream socials, home-owner association meetings, youth sporting events, and charity events. They were all important to me, but the reality was that I couldn't do them all. Over and over, I would arrive late, leave early, and compromise my schedule. I had to learn to pick the most important events and activities, let the others go, and learn to say no to family, friends, co-workers, and neighbors.

You can't satisfy everyone. As much as you might want to be liked or make others happy, there comes a point where you can't do it all. When you say yes to everything, you end up setting expectations you can't meet and disappointing people anyway.

You can't satisfy everyone. As much as you might want to be liked or make others happy, there comes a point where you can't do it all.

Learn to set your own standards. Instead of blindly following others or doing what they expect of you, decide for yourself how to spend your time. Saying no is deciding your own priorities and choosing what is important to you rather than what others think should be important to you. If you are waiting for the restaurant owner to take charge for you and serve you less or for your credit card company to quit sending you invitations for more credit, you will wait a long time. Many, if not most, of the influences around you are not in your best interest. They are cleverly worded and designed to entice you but are for the benefit of others. If you want to be successful, spend your time, energy, and money on what you deem important. Think and act for yourself.

Some say understanding what is important to someone is as simple as looking at their daily schedule and expense history. The point is that where we spend our time and money shows what is most important to us. Reality is not that simple. Where we spend our time and money is a combination of what's important to us and what's important to others. In fact, for many people stuck in the hamster wheel of "life as defined by others," most of their time and money goes to areas that are important to others, not themselves. As the nineteenth-century Irish playwright and poet Oscar Wilde said, "Most people are other people. Their thoughts are someone else's opinions, their lives a mimicry, their passions a quotation."

If you are a parent, you likely enjoy attending your children's activities, but that doesn't mean you have to go to every scheduled school function. If the mother of one of your children's friends schedules a school party, you don't have to attend. If a well-meaning member of your church schedules a potluck dinner or a Bible study, you don't have to attend.

Our modern society, with its myriad of social opportunities, convenient travel options, and efficient communications, offers boundless learning, entertainment, and social opportunities. This means there is more to do than time allows. You have to be selective; you must be intentional. You can't let society or others drive your decision making, or you will never have time for your own self-development. You will never find the hamster wheel's off-ramp. Decide for yourself what you will and won't do. When you're invited to attend a meeting at work, a civic gathering, or a family event, set your own standards and decide for yourself. Putting time into your goal, at least for now, can be a much more important use of your precious time.

Do Less

In my consulting work, I frequently deal with teams who lack focus. They get into the trap of *busyness as usual*. They slow down long enough to conceive a new idea, but as soon as they adjourn their meeting, they're back to their busyness. Whatever justified the meeting—and what all in attendance agreed to—fades into the background, and the urgent or usual takes over the foreground.

Important new ideas regularly languish because people don't agree on what they should stop in order to make time for what they want to start. Their ideas bounce from meeting to meeting, adding to their distractions, until they are adopted by someone else, pushed off indefinitely, or replaced by another idea that will probably suffer the same fate.

Too many great ideas that could save significant money, improve customer service, make people's lives better and increase sales, never get off the ground. When you can't stop what you're doing long enough to improve it, you will never stop what you are doing.

When you can't stop what you're
doing long enough to improve it, you will
never stop what you are doing.

If you are already at your full capacity and plan to start doing something new, you have to stop doing something old to make time for it. If you aren't willing to make a "to-not-do" list, you are setting yourself up for failure. Decide what is less important and shut it down, at least temporarily. It may be something you enjoy or that somehow adds value to your current activity, but if it's not as important as your goal, move it down on your priority list.

In 2008, Americans spent, on average, four and a half hours every day watching TV. That's just under the total discretionary time of five hours each day that most people have. To put that in perspective, 4.5 hours per day works out to be thirty-one hours per week, five days and sixteen hours per month, sixty-eight days per year, and fourteen years over a seventy-five-year lifetime. Unless your goal is to become a television critic, some TV time could surely be better spent on reaching your goals. The same goes for the plethora of other entertainment activities that occupy precious time.

Owning less is another way to do less. "Stuff" takes up time. Cars, houses, motorcycles, boats, bicycles, clothes, collections, and other material possessions require maintenance. The more you have, the more time you spend taking care of what you have. If much of your time is spent tracking, protecting, cleaning, organizing, counting, managing, repairing, maintaining, or dealing with your stuff, consider selling it or giving it away.

Think about how you spend your time and what you could defer or eliminate, at least temporarily. Look at your last few months' schedule and ask yourself which events or activities you didn't need to attend. Look at where you spend your money and where you could cut back, saving both money and time. Consider what you might sell or give away. Ask yourself how much of what you currently do is more important than your goal.

Delegate

Another approach to freeing your time is to use other resources. Delegating to others activities you can't quit altogether or that you can't do more efficiently is your next option.

Delegation is difficult for many people. If you have many interests, if you like to be in control, are handy around the home, and are technically inclined, you fit the profile of a non-delegator. Your varied interests and self-sufficiency lead you to take on too many projects. You try to control your surroundings and maintain direct involvement in, if not direct ownership of, most of your interests. You are used to solving your own problems, and you feel that delegating tasks is foolish.

If you're a non-delegator, you are a good candidate for doing less through delegation. You could free up your time best by handing over some of your responsibilities, problems, and opportunities to others and becoming more flexible about how things get done. When you trust others more and learn to let go, you discover a whole different world that has time for higher-value pursuits, not to mention a little recreation and relaxation.

A common mistake people make is doing another person's work for them. Many well-intending parents and managers have done it for so long, they are unaware that they do it. Perfectionist parents do their children's homework. Emotionally needy parents resist their children's independence and run their errands for them. Managers who don't know how to lead do their employees' work for them. Distrusting managers withhold empowerment from their teams. The result of non-delegation is overcontrol, overdependency, underdevelopment, and less time.

If you are a parent or manager, think about what you currently do that your children or employees could do. Empower them. Let them do what they, not you, should be doing. In the case of employees, let them do what they were hired to do. You can still keep up with what's going on; just don't do the work yourself.

Empowering and delegating work to others may initially take up a little more of your time than doing it yourself. You have to instruct them and show them how you normally do the task. But be patient. Delegating will quickly turn into a time saver for you and a development experience for them. They will become more proficient and self-sufficient, and before you know it, things you used to do yourself are being done as well or better by others.

If you attend many informational meetings or conference calls, consider which ones you could depend on others to attend in your place. If you normally attend a particular industry conference, arrange for a proxy to represent your interests and give you a concise debriefing afterward. If you are mired in detailed work that someone else could do, hire an expert to do it. Instead of trying to repair your own leaky faucet or faulty icemaker, hire a repairman. If you are your children's personal maid, quit. They made the mess; teach them to clean up after themselves. The responsibility is good for them, and the relief is good for you.

If you are your children's personal maid, quit. They made the mess; teach them to clean up after themselves.

Recall the importance and benefits of your goal. Compare the expected value of achieving it to the discomfort, cost, or hassle of delegating to others. Remember that delegation is as much a self-development opportunity for them as it is a time-freeing opportunity for you. Think about what you *can't* do because of what you *do* do and about what you can delegate to others. You may be missing one of the most important opportunities of your life simply because you can't hand over tasks to others.

Reduce Your Distractions

If you are easily distracted or regularly interrupted, reducing distractions is a good place to free up time. You may have an ill parent, a high-maintenance employee, a gossiping friend, or a home-remodeling project that keeps you perpetually disengaged from your own goals. You may have e-mails popping up on your screen, television noise coming from the next room, or kids yelling down the hall. When you work or live in an environment full of distractions, your productivity, as well as your energy, takes a big hit.

Think about what diverts your attention. Consider how you can reduce or eliminate your distractions. Try turning off your phone, television, and e-mail for a few hours. Close your door. Change to a quieter place where you do work that requires concentration. Ask the interrupters around you to be more considerate of your need for peace and quiet.

You might be a good candidate to exchange some of your night for some of your day. You might find it less distracting to work when others are asleep or gone. Try going to bed earlier and getting up earlier. Exchange an hour or two of being awake at night for an hour or two of being awake in the morning when there are fewer distractions. You can concentrate better when it's quiet, and since your mind is sharper in the morning after a restful sleep, you can work faster and at a higher level of quality.

Activating Your Ambition

Lack of time can completely obstruct self-development. Your intent, awareness, motivation, belief, desire, and plan of small steps may be in place, but if you lack the time or energy, you will merely frustrate yourself.

On the page of your road map titled "Activating Your Ambition Scorecard," score how well you currently do in applying the concepts of time and energy. In your road map page entitled "My Time and Energy," estimate how long it will take to reach your goal. Review your incremental steps and identify how much more time will be required. Consider how you might free that time by being more productive, setting your own standards, doing less, delegating, getting rid of unnecessary stuff, and reducing your distractions. Note actions you can take that will recharge your batteries and give you the extra energy you need.

9

Initiate Your Launch

I think there is something more important than
believing: Action! The world is full of dreamers, there
aren't enough who will move ahead and begin to take
concrete steps to actualize their vision.

                                        –W. Clement Stone

Ken was an intellectual and the president of a small U.K.-based
software company. He had an undergraduate degree in political science
and master's degrees in psychology and business administration. He
loved the pursuit of knowledge. He was an avid reader and always one
of the first to read the latest nonfiction books on business and self-
help. He was an introvert who stayed away from most large gatherings,
although he enjoyed rigorous intellectual debates with close friends
and colleagues.

Ken contacted me to help him improve his company's sales
approach. Lagging sales, however, turned out to be a symptom of a

more problematic root cause. After spending some time with him assessing his company's sales approach, sales team's skills, and past sales training programs, a pattern emerged. Over the past years, Ken's company had launched a number of initiatives that they had not sustained. The company introduced new products, installed new internal systems, established new sales processes, created new strategic plans, and hired consultants, all of which had initially held great promise, but gradually faded into irrelevance. Some initiatives were never fully implemented, while others were adopted by only a few of the potential stakeholders.

As Ken went through his explanation for each failed initiative, it became apparent that Ken himself was the source of the problem. His passion was innovation, not execution; thus, he was more interested in generating new ideas than in implementing them. He valued the academic more than the practical. Being the president and having hired many people just like himself, he had created an organizational culture that emphasized strategic thinking and creativity over execution. They had lots of ideas, but little implementation.

What had started as a business-intervention consulting engagement turned into a coaching engagement. I proposed a plan that focused on achieving better business results through operational excellence. He agreed and, given his intellect, we quickly crafted one of the best coaching plans I'd ever seen. It was complete with specific on-the-job assignments, projects for his employees to complete, books to read, and frequent milestones to track his progress. All seemed to be on track.

After two meetings with Ken to review how he was doing in his on-the-job assignments, he confessed that he had yet to begin them. He was stuck in the conceptual aspects of coaching, just as he was in his business, and he couldn't move into action. He didn't mind the planning, learning, and intellectual discussions, but actually putting the plan to work was beyond him. Whenever he was about to start a new project, he got sidetracked with an even newer idea.

We regrouped and worked on Ken's ability to start and sustain a project. We redefined his incremental steps so that they were more aligned to his style of learning. We made sure the timing was right so there were no convenient excuses to sidetrack him. We picked specific dates to implement his incremental steps and put controls and resources in place to ensure that other, flashier projects wouldn't hijack his plan. As a result, we finally crossed the canyon between the conceptual and the practical, and Ken learned a new paradigm—execution.

Thinking and planning are one thing; taking action is another. As Johann Wolfgang von Goethe, eighteenth-century German playwright, poet, and novelist said, "Knowing is not enough; we must apply. Willing is not enough; we must do." Preparation is great, but to win, you have to show up and play the game. You can have a clear *goal*, establish an accurate *awareness* of what you need to accomplish, find the *motivation* to sustain the journey, hold an unwavering *belief* that you can overcome any obstacle, have a plan of *incremental* steps ready to engage, have the *time* available, and yet still not act. Your boat is ready to leave the port, your bags are packed, you have a map to your desired destination, and you know how to sail, but you just can't manage to untie the rope from the dock.

Initiation is moving from the theoretical to the practical—crossing the boundary from thinking and watching to doing. It is launching your initiative and following through, leaving the spectator seats, putting on your gear, and getting into the game. If you have ever gone on a serious diet, started an exercise program, or quit an addiction like tobacco or alcohol, you know how hard crossing the line from thinking to doing can be. Initiation is saying good-bye to your routine, going into the unknown, exposing yourself to risks, and giving up the comfort of your comfort zone. It can be like leaving a longtime friend.

Many people find the transfer from planning to execution difficult; some find it overwhelming. The thought of actually doing instead of thinking moves people quickly back into the safety of their comfort zone. You hear, "Oh, you actually want to get started. . . . Um, how about we do a little more planning?" or "I still don't think I'm quite ready," or "Let's wait until . . ." You can work with someone for weeks or months and never hear a single objection until it's time to write the check, let go of the rope, make the jump, confront the adversary, or dial the phone number. Then the excuses pour out like a fire hose.

If you or anyone you know has tried to overcome an addiction, you've no doubt heard the excuses. They are many, but when stripped down to the core, none is more likely to be a showstopper than lacking the mind-set and commitment to cross the line from planning and thinking to actually doing. People procrastinate, make excuses, avoid commitment, and perpetually postpone putting their objectives into action. There is a huge difference between knowing what to do and doing it.

Have you ever attended a seminar and thought that you could present the material as well as the presenter? Have you read a book and thought you could have written it as well or better than the author? Has it occurred to you that you could paint, sing, run, ski, bike, diet, exercise, coach, mentor, or perform countless other activities better than someone else? Maybe you could, but so what? What matters is not what you can do but what you actually *do*.

Once you initiate and start executing your incremental steps, the clock of progress finally starts.

When you initiate, you are no longer thinking about change, but actually changing. Instead of wishing you were making progress, you *are* making progress. Instead of watching the days pass and time mount against you, you are taking action and putting time back on your side. Once you initiate and start executing your incremental steps, the clock of progress finally starts. Each day from that point forward moves you closer to achieving your goal.

Initiation is about starting right and ensuring that the timing of your launch is appropriate, so your journey will be as straightforward and obstacle free as possible.

Watch Out for the Causes of Initiation Failure

People postpone getting started for many reasons. For one, the timing can be wrong. A current event might make initiation problematic, a big project at work may leave no time or energy, or an imminent reorganization may have all budgets on hold. The need to help carpool to youth sports practice could delay you until the season is over, or an upcoming family reunion full of your aunt's home cooking could make starting a diet frustrating and foolish. Quarter endings, customer deadlines, and project kickoffs can all be obstacles to vacations, much less starting a new initiative.

If an impending event at work or a temporary situation in your life could significantly affect your journey, you'd be unwise to ignore it, but you can plan for it. Put the affected part of your plan on hold if necessary and work on other parts of your plan that don't depend on the outcome of the event, or work around the situation. If you can detour around it instead of confronting it, take the detour. Going straight through a roadblock is normally not the best path. If your goal is to sell a new product and you know a certain individual in your account will block your idea, don't take it to that person. Find a different person to be your sponsor.

Don't ignore events, circumstances, and situations that truly lower your odds of success. Be patient, do what you can, go around roadblocks where possible, and look for opportunities to initiate fully later, when it is wiser to do so.

Another reason initiation is difficult is risk. Anticipating that one of your identified risks, obstacles, or temptations will crop up can easily keep you from leaving the starting gate. It makes sense, knowing that if certain risks come to fruition, you could actually end up in worse shape than you are in now. Say, for example, you want to be a better spouse; specifically, you want to argue more constructively. You could find yourself reexamining old issues with your spouse that could create even bigger arguments. Or if your goal requires investment of your limited finances, you may run the risk of losing your money.

Risks are valid concerns and should be mitigated to the fullest extent possible. If your holdup is risk, go back to your awareness-building phase and look for other ways to reach your goal without exposing yourself to as much risk. To make sure the reward is still greater than the risk, go back to the chapter on *motivation* and reassess the assumptions you used to determine your return on investment. Revisit your contingency plans in the chapter on *belief* and adjust them until you're confident they are failsafe and can handle the potential risk. Or scale back your commitment and perform a trial run until circumstances change.

Risk and timing concerns confront every initiative, but they don't have to be showstoppers. Don't use them as convenient excuses. You might legitimately expect reorganization at work, but if it doesn't prevent you from starting your plan, it's just an excuse for putting it off.

If you find yourself looking for excuses not to begin, see if fear is holding you back. You could be afraid of looking foolish, making a commitment, the unknown, or something else. If fear still has a grip on you, reread the section on fear at the end of chapter two. Read other books and talk to people. Identify the unknowns that are holding you back and turn them into knowns. Create plans to deal with the worst possible outcomes. Build your courage. Don't give in to insecurity or let false evidence prevent you from initiating your journey.

Another obstacle to initiation is simple laziness. If plenty of benefits are to be had by pursuing your goal, resources are abundant, time is available, no physical conditions prevent start-up, and no unreasonable risks or fears are present, you have nothing to blame but your own laziness. If you'd rather be a couch potato and do nothing, you will probably do nothing.

You may think that you've paid your dues and it's your time to cruise on easy street. You might feel that you've been victimized and can do nothing about it. Just realize that the world is not standing still. No matter how satisfied you might be today, it won't last. Consider, too, that you're probably driving those around you crazy.

Laziness causes health problems, both mental and physical. If these are your goals, keep slacking.

Laziness breeds trouble. It is unrewarding and unfulfilling. It leads to poverty, dependence, isolation, and regrets. Laziness causes health problems, both mental and physical. If these are your goals, keep slacking.

Know How You Learn

Learning styles play a part in the reluctance to initiate action. There are three basic learning styles. People prefer to learn by watching, doing, or analyzing. When faced with the task of assembling a new barbecue grill, if you are a "watcher," you prefer to watch a neighbor or someone at the store put one together first. Watchers prefer to learn from observing others. If you are a "doer," you prefer to buy the grill, bring it home, and begin assembling it with little regard for the directions. Doers prefer to dive in and figure it out as they go along. If you are an "analyzer," you prefer to read the instructions, probably including the fine print, or listen to others who have done it themselves before putting a single piece together. Analyzers prefer to be prepared with the fullest knowledge possible before getting started

Which one are you? If you are a watcher or an analyzer, you probably have the greatest success at assembling a grill to the manufacturer's specifications. However, you'll be the last one to get started.

Natural doers have an advantage when it comes to initiation. Instead of "ready, aim, fire," they are more likely to "ready, fire, aim." This method has its disadvantages, but getting started isn't one of them. Doers often have problems as a result of jumping in unprepared, but they don't mind the jump. Initiating action is easy for them.

If you are a watcher or an analyzer, you may need extra insight to get started—a little extra research or a chance to shadow someone else who's already achieved what you're about to pursue—before you feel comfortable starting on your own. You may need someone to start with you or to talk with before you begin—someone who completed a similar journey before. Or you may need to accept that no amount of planning, watching, or researching will ever be enough; simply accept the perceived risk, and get started. By all means, consider the eight principles of *Activating Your Ambition* before you jump into your endeavor, but at some point you have to take action, and that point may be sooner than you are comfortable with.

If you are a parent or manager, recall a situation where you gave your employees or children tasks to complete—a report that you asked to have completed by the end of the day, or an entertainment center to be assembled by the end of the weekend—but the report was nowhere to be found and the entertainment center stayed in its box. The failure could have been blamed on an infinite number of reasons, but consider that they might have had trouble beginning because you were a doer and they weren't. You gave them a "just do it" assignment, and it was too far outside their comfort zone.

Had you given them a little more instruction or observation, and helped them get started, they might have completed their assignments right away. The same could be said for a watcher or analyzer giving a project to doers. If the start of the project required reading a hundred-page policy manual or a twenty-page instruction manual, a doer would struggle too.

Accommodate your preferred learning style the best you can. Add incremental steps that support your learning style to your road map. If you are a watcher, add a step that involves shadowing someone who has the skills you want to develop. If you are an analyzer, add a step to do more research and know more about your endeavor before you launch.

If you are a doer, don't be too quick to throw out the assembly instructions; a little instruction and planning up front could save you time in the long-term. Think about what you might do to mitigate your risks. Get out of your comfort zone and plan.

Spot Your Opportunity

Some endeavors are best begun in tandem with another event. If you are planning to buy a new home, you may need to wait until mortgage interest rates fall to a level you can afford. If you are working on public speaking, you may need to wait until a speaking opportunity comes up to apply your newfound skill. If you plan to start your own business, it might be best to wait until you secure a customer. If you want to learn how to play the piano, it might be wise to wait until summer is over and the kids are back in school. If you want to write a book, it may be best to wait to write your manuscript until your sister, the language arts major, comes to visit. If your manager doesn't support your attending a leadership program, you may need to wait for a skip-level discussion with your boss's boss for a better chance of getting the go-ahead. Note: I'm not advocating that you bypass your manager, but under certain circumstances, especially when it is your professional development at stake, you may need to.

Corporate strategists are constantly on the lookout for these *opportunity triggers*—events or situations that trigger a need to take action. Organizations wait for key changes in their competitive landscape to trigger action. When certain events happen or conditions are met, it signals them to build a new product, reduce prices, enter a new market, or make an acquisition. In the same way, there may be opportunity triggers you can take advantage of—specific opportunities or events that you can use to initiate or advance your objective.

There may be opportunity triggers you can take advantage of—specific opportunities or events that you can use to initiate or advance your objective.

Consider the ideal circumstances for initiating your plan. Is a season, quarter, month, or specific day of the year the best time to initiate your plan, or is there a period or event at work that would be most conducive to your launch? Look for an event to get you off to a great start. Identify any triggers in your environment or a condition which, when met, would be a great starting point.

It may require that you put a scanning mechanism in place so you know when your ideal opportunities occur. If it would help to meet with a certain executive, place a standing request with the assistant to alert you if he happens to come through your town. If your journey depends on a certain transaction, find where those transactions are tracked and become a subscriber. Figure out how you can best scan for your opportunity triggers and be ready to act on them once the trigger is activated. Online resources are available to track just about every event that occurs in the public domain—sales, purchases, deaths, births, legal proceedings, promotions, patent issues, and many other events—to give you just the information you may need.

If you can't identify an opportunity trigger for your particular endeavor but you still need some initiating trigger, there is always the calendar. The beginning of a week, a month, a quarter, or a year might be your best cue to make a start. By far the most common trigger for self-initiated behavior change is New Year's Day. Nine out of ten people make a New Year's resolution. That doesn't make much sense when you think about it; January 1 isn't materially different from December 31. Maybe that's the reason New Year's resolutions are so short-lived. Only one in nine people keep their resolution.

If you are planning to start your endeavor as a New Year's resolution, make sure that you have more going for you than the start of a new year. Ensure you are fully application-ready and the eight principles of *Activating Your Ambition* are in place before the New Year arrives.

Take Responsibility

If you blame others or your circumstances for your situation, you're not taking responsibility, and stepping up to any needed change will be very hard. If you believe the actions of others control your destiny, initiating any self-development will seem a waste of time. If you believe the locus of control in your life is outside yourself, you accept the results you get, rather than doing something about them. Instead of operating intentionally, you operate reactively.

If you think you don't have much control of your life, you watch opportunities come and go without taking action on them. You defer responsibility to others, allow others to control you, and put off taking action because of your circumstances. You consider yourself a victim.

A victim mentality is as inconspicuous as believing you work for an organization that doesn't want you to succeed. It is thinking nothing you do will ever improve your marriage, blaming a professor because you didn't finish college, or holding your parents responsible for not teaching you something. It is blaming your boss for not giving you a raise or a promotion, blaming your current circumstances on the government for not taking better care of you, or blaming a concerned citizen for reporting you for breaking the law. It is watching opportunities for initiating change in your life go by instead of acting on them. It is choosing to stay in the blame game by thinking that the problem is the other person's or the situation's fault, not yours.

No one escapes the trials and tribulations of life. We all deal with problems, have setbacks, and fail at something. With few exceptions, we lose our jobs, struggle to pay our bills at some point, and postpone expenditures because we can't afford them. We encounter conflict, have arguments, mess up valued relationships, and lose loved ones. We suffer neglect, abuse, or prejudice against our age, sex, nationality, race, religion, values, or opinions. We all get ill, have some sort of medical condition, and experience strange sensations. We have low moods, think things we shouldn't, are tempted by things that are bad for us, and struggle to stay in control of ourselves. As much as everyone else might look like they have it all together, they don't. No one lives a life of perfection. No one is normal. There is no "normal."

No one has more justification to feel victimized or to feel self pity than anyone else. No one has more justification than anyone else to blame their lack of success on something or someone else. We all deal with adversity, and we all choose to make it an excuse or to put it in its proper place in our past. If you are like me and most others, you have been the unfortunate victim of someone or something, yet you have moved on. You've accepted it, learned from it, put it in your past, and decided to focus on the present and the future. If not, do it now.

No one has more justification than anyone else to blame their lack of success on something or someone else.

You can put even verbal, physical, and sexual abuse from childhood in your past and move on. Dr. Martin E. P. Seligman, who has studied what people can realistically expect to change, has investigated the effects of adversity and traumatic childhood events. His findings reveal that the traumas of childhood do not mandate adult troubles.

There is no logic in blaming your adult depression, anxiety, bad marriage, drug use, sexual dysfunction, unemployment, abuse of your children, alcoholism, or anger on what happened to you as a child. Any blame you place for your current condition is of your own choosing and to make yourself feel better. It is not a rational or necessary thought process. You choose to dwell on your past or present adversity. Your entrapment is imaginary. If you feel like a prisoner, it is because you won't use your own key to let yourself out of your cell.

Dwelling on the positive experiences in your life is just as possible as dwelling on the negative, and you can just as easily dwell on the future or the present as on the past. Unless you are physically or mentally disabled, legally restricted in some way, or live in a Third World country, the opportunity to take action is within your control.

If you dropped out of high school, you may not qualify for certain jobs, but that doesn't mean you can't do something to improve your prospects. You can start by completing your General Equivalency Diploma. A lack of formal education doesn't mean you can't start your own business or pursue other jobs that depend more on experience or a willingness to learn. You control these decisions. You decide whether or not to let your current circumstances hold you back.

Everyone is disadvantaged. I grew up in a divorced household and never witnessed a happy marriage. Should I complain about it and let it prevent me from trying to be a better spouse? Should I complain that I'm not six feet six inches tall, so I can't play in the National Basketball Association? Should I complain because I'm not the son of a U.S. president?

If you choose to think in terms of what you don't have, you will always be a victim of circumstances. Nobody ever has a purely unobstructed road to success. You will always deal with differences, biases, inequalities, and unfairness, no matter what you do. Things won't always go your way. Accidents will happen. Mistakes will thwart your progress. Failures will set you back. Bad decisions will be made. Sooner or later, you'll find yourself in a situation you don't want to be in. But except for events that cause you permanent physical or mental damage or a criminal record, all of these circumstances can be overcome. Your circumstances and situations may affect you, but they don't have to control you.

Victor Frankl was a respected Viennese doctor. In 1942, the Nazis deported him and his family to a concentration camp in Terezin, Germany, where his family was murdered and Frankl was ridiculed, beaten, and starved. He endured horrific treatment and humiliation that would leave most people with no sense of dignity or self-worth. Yet as he recounted in his book, *Man's Search for Meaning*, Frankl learned there was one thing the Nazis couldn't take from him—his freedom to choose his own attitude. They couldn't deprive him of the choice of how he would react to his circumstances.

Like Frankl, you have a choice in how you respond to your circumstances. If you want your own personal freedom, choose to take responsibility for it. Don't blame others. Don't let others control your destiny. Don't let others—or circumstances—prevent you from pursuing your goal. Take responsibility for what you do control, and recognize that you can act to improve yourself.

Don't let failures or any other circumstances control your attitude. If you fail at something, learn from it and move on. Let it boost your confidence, since now you're smarter than you were before. Thomas Edison was asked why he didn't view himself as a failure. The question was reasonable given that he'd tried and failed so many times to perfect the incandescent lightbulb. He responded, "I have not failed. I've just found ten thousand ways that won't work." Choose to view your past in terms of the learning it has given. Take ownership for your past. Be glad for it; you're better because of it. If you regret it or hold someone else responsible for it, you're missing its true value.

Learn from your experiences, but don't concentrate on them. Choose to move on. Choose to improve and make your future better than your past. Don't wait for forces outside your control to do it for you. The more you let others dictate what you can and can't do, the more likely the terms won't be in your best interest.

If fear, risk, or a victim mentality is holding you back from pursuing your dreams, create a plan to overcome them. You will then be free to pursue your dreams.

Remove Your Fallback Option

To test your readiness to launch, consider removing your fallback options. While you may have few doubts now that you can steer clear of temptations, avoid procrastination, or overcome other obstacles, your reality may be different when you are scared, hungry, tired, angry, or aroused in some other way. Thinking about self-control is much easier than practicing it, especially when conditions are ripe to fall back into old habits.

Where you can remove the need for self-control, do so. When you have no option but to control yourself, your chances of success significantly increase. For example, don't go to a pizza restaurant offering a buffet lunch thinking you will limit yourself to the salad bar. Don't take your checkbook or credit card with you when just looking at new cars. Instead of relying on your self-control to put part of each paycheck into savings, have your deposits toward your down payment for a new house automatically deducted from your paycheck. Put only twenty dollars in your purse when you go shopping with a plan to spend only twenty dollars.

You are much more likely to persevere through the frustration of learning a new software application if the old one is no longer available. You are much more likely to learn to drive a car with a manual transmission if one with an automatic transmission is no longer around as a backup.

Don't do something stupid like removing your reserve parachute from your backpack, but where the consequences are not so dire, consider how you can remove the possibility of retreating to the comfort of your old habits. You may need to perform a trial run first, but when you fully launch your initiative, do it once and for all by removing your fallback option.

Don't Let This Be an Academic Exercise

The problem with initiation and execution for many people is that they unconsciously confuse what they know with what they do. They think, "I know how to quit smoking and can do it when I'm ready," or "I know I interrupt others when they speak, but I know how to control it and will when I want to."

The problem with initiation and execution for many people is that they unconsciously confuse what they know with what they do.

The truth is that the person who quits smoking is the one who throws away his cigarettes and deals with the withdrawal, not the person who thinks he knows how to do it. The person who becomes an effective listener is the one who controls his interrupting habit, not the one who knows how to do it. The person who overcomes fear is the one who confronts it, not the person who thinks about it. It's not what you know, but what you *do* with what you know that counts.

Knowledge and plans don't produce results, application does. Don't leave your knowledge unapplied. Putting your plan into action is the only way to reach your desired destination. Confucius said, "A journey of a thousand miles begins with a single step." No matter how hard or how long your journey might seem, you can complete it. You just need to take the first step—and then another, and then another. Don't let the complexity or duration or the magnitude of your goal overwhelm you. Just focus on the next step.

Now is the time to activate your ambition. Don't wait for the day when everything is perfect to launch your initiative. That day will never come. Declare your date now, or decide what opportunity trigger will enable you to take the next step. It may be the day you actually start your diet, the day you try a new approach to managing people, or the day you start putting money in savings for the down payment on your new house. Set the date, and when it comes, stick with it. The sooner you start, the sooner you will reap the rewards. As fast as time goes by, it won't be long until you're looking back on your achievement and feeling the satisfaction that you took action.

Activating Your Ambition

You should now be ready to initiate your journey. The two remaining principles of *Activating Your Ambition* are designed to help you sustain your journey. If you don't feel confident in initiating action, review the six principles we've covered thus far. Determine where you need additional focus.

On the page of your road map titled "Activating Your Ambition Scorecard," score how well you currently do in applying the concepts of *initiation*. On the "My Initiation" page of your road map, list any issues you face in taking action and beginning your journey. List any uncontained risks or unresolved fears that might prevent you from initiating your plan. Add actions that accommodate your learning style. Identify any relevant areas where you have allowed others or your circumstances to control you and prevent you from taking action. Add to your action plan any new incremental steps needed to contend with these obstacles. Set a start date for the execution of your plan.

When you start your journey, note it in your road map. Contact your coach, your support group, or whoever is supporting you during your journey and let them know too. I would also like to know. E-mail me at ambition@alpinelink.com.

10

Involve Others

We don't accomplish anything in this world alone . . .
And whatever happens is the result of the whole tapestry
of one's life and all the weavings of individual threads
from one to another that creates something.

–Sandra Day O'Connor

Lori could best be described as "high energy." For a woman in her mid-forties, she had the stamina of a twentysomething. She was involved in numerous task forces at her nonprofit employer, volunteered at church, and helped out at the school her two children attended. She was full of vitality and applied it nonstop from sunup to sundown every day of the week. When I met Lori, she seemed to have everything together. She was successful at work, had a large social network, belonged to a great family, exuded confidence, and radiated a positive attitude. The problem was she didn't listen.

Lori had been told more than once that she tended to talk over people. She rarely let someone finish speaking before she started talking. Even when she wasn't talking, she thought about what she wanted to say next instead of listening to others. In her busyness, she unconsciously pushed people to say what they had to say quickly or they couldn't finish. The result was that her communications were either one-sided or disconnected, and they were rarely a pleasant experience for the other party.

Clearly, Lori needed to develop better listening skills. We created a plan to raise her awareness of her own actions and then to learn the "whys" and "hows" of good communications. Since communication requires another party, we added to her coaching plan the task of telling everyone she communicated with that she was working to improve her listening and that she wanted their honest feedback whenever they noticed her failing to listen.

Right from the beginning, everyone did a good job of constructively pointing out her listening offenses. Because of the volume of feedback, she sometimes felt she would be better off not talking with anyone, but as days turned into weeks, the number of offenses decreased. Over time, she slowed down and started listening to what others had to say. She discovered a new world as she truly heard and understood what people were telling her.

As Lori made progress, the feedback turned from criticism to praise. As she became a better listener, those around her affirmed her progress and let her know how much they appreciated her improvements. The feedback encouraged her to continue to improve. The result was that her listening became top-notch, as did her relationships with friends, family, and co-workers. The help of others had made it possible.

Others give feedback, encouragement, support, and resources that are critical to self-development. Few people are successful without others. Some claim to be "self-made" or "self-taught," but the pathway to sustainable success is lined with the help of others.

You may have a clear *goal*, a rock-solid *awareness* of what you need to do, the *motivation* and *belief* you can achieve your objective, a cogent plan of *incremental* steps, and the *time* and *energy* to devote to your plan; and you may have invested in the *initiation* of your endeavor. But unless you have the involvement and support of *others*, your accomplishment will be constrained. To be successful in any self-development initiative, you need other people.

Tiger Woods, perhaps the best golfer ever, couldn't have succeeded without the help of his father, Earl Woods. Pablo Picasso couldn't have become a world-renowned painter without the help of his collaborator, Georges Braque. St. Paul of Tarsus benefited from the help of fellow teacher Barnabas. Bill Gates, one of the richest men in the world, had the help of his mother, Mary, in establishing Microsoft's critical partnership with IBM through her United Way board relationship with John Akers, then an executive in IBM's personal-computer division. No one, including the greatest, succeeds alone.

You need others before you begin your journey, throughout your journey, and when the journey is complete. You need friends, family, and co-workers to give you feedback, wise counsel, encouragement, and resources. You need others to join you in celebrating your successes. Others are critical every step of the way.

Engage Your Feelings

Behavioral change involves reasoning and feeling. It involves application of the logical-thinking left side of your brain as well as the feeling-oriented right side of your brain. Building awareness, understanding benefits, identifying incremental steps, and freeing your time and energy are all left-brain cognitive approaches to effecting change. They primarily rely on your thinking and reasoning capabilities, whereas securing your motivation, visualizing, solidifying your belief, and initiating your pursuit engage more of the feeling-oriented right side of your brain.

The most reliable approach to self-improvement uses both thinking and feeling. The reasoning part of your brain helps you understand the facts, follow the structure of a plan, and make logical decisions. The feeling part taps into your creativity, makes you excited, pushes you to be compassionate, and gives you a sense of accomplishment. Together, thinking and feeling create a healthy balance.

When you overly rely on either thinking or feeling, the healthy balance goes away. Without tapping into your feelings, you are less likely to be considerate of others and more likely to ignore your own stressors. When you don't follow your logic, you are more likely to base a decision on emotional impulse and regret it later. Planning your self-development journey is a mostly logical process, but executing it depends more on feelings. Your feelings move you to action and give insight into your thinking. Engaging and acknowledging your feelings is critical to sticking with your journey and reaching your goal.

One important reason to involve others is to tap the power of feelings that come through relationships and open communication. Talking and listening bring emotions to light. Whether you know them or not, you have feelings, and they are affecting your pursuit. Understanding them permits you to reinforce the positive ones and eliminate the negative ones.

Whether you know them or not, you have feelings, and they are affecting your pursuit.

If this talk of feelings and engaging others makes you uncomfortable, take comfort in knowing you're not alone. I too habitually stifled my feelings instead of expressing them. Many people, especially men, equate feelings with weakness. We build barriers to engaging our emotions and expressing ourselves. I've coached many men who would do almost anything to avoid talking about their feelings. They don't realize that the disclosure and engagement of their feelings gives them an enormous opportunity to grow. Feelings reveal our thoughts, giving great insight into what we are thinking. They also move us to action.

As logical as we may appear, many of the decisions we make in life are based on feelings. Even major corporate initiatives, like implementing a new computer system or making a company acquisition, often come down to how the decision makers feel. Prestige, relationships, security, fear, revenge, anger, and guilt weigh heavier in our minds than do facts or return-on-investment calculations.

Memories created by our feelings are stronger than those that come from our logic. How a situation or person made you feel is more likely to make a lasting impression on you than what they said. Think about the many situations in which you forgot what was said, but have a distinct memory of being happy or joyful or energized. You probably remember teachers or bosses in your distant past as being kind or cruel because of how they made you feel. On the other hand, you probably can't recall if you agreed with their logic or not. Great speakers, trainers, leaders, parents, and salespeople know this. They tap into your emotions while trying to inform, entertain, and influence you. Emotions and feelings are powerful and can't be ignored if you are to grow and develop to your highest potential.

Seek out relationships with others who are emotionally stable. Talk frankly with them about your feelings. Even if you are not emotionally inclined, don't neglect the power and impact of your feelings. Give the idea a chance. Identify a couple of people you trust and talk transparently with them about your pursuit. Explain to them how you feel about your risks, benefits, incremental steps, and so on. The process will be a huge boost to the overall success of your initiative.

Obtain Different Perspectives

In my leadership development work, I regularly have clients complete a personality assessment such as the Myers-Briggs Type Indicator. During the assessment interpretation, clients always gain valuable insight into their personality preferences. The findings explain many of their behaviors and provide insight into their unknown biases.

Personality biases are often blind spots, unique traits of your personality that are unknown to you. These traits affect how you take in information and how you make decisions. Uncovering your blind spots exposes predictable errors in judgment. The stronger your preferences, the stronger your biases; the stronger your biases, the more likely you are to use them unconsciously; the more likely you are to use them, the more predictable are your errors in judgment. Unknown to you, your biases filter what you hear and read. They direct how you think, make decisions, and behave. You might think you see, feel, and reason without bias, but you don't.

The more you use one quality or personality trait, the more you ignore another. Strong preferences result in strong deficits. A strong preference for extroversion results in a significant lack of introversion. A strong preference for using logic results in a significant neglect in using your feelings.

In my case, I naturally prefer to take in only enough information to satisfy my basic curiosity and then apply logic to it to make a decision.

Before I knew I had this tendency, it was my blind spot. I didn't recognize that through more discussion better ideas and the feelings of others would come out and help me to make better decisions.

To counteract this tendency, I make an effort to be more open to ideas and information before making judgment. I still have a natural tendency to make quick decisions, but through focused attention, I comfortably resist the tendency. I've learned to leave my mental data aperture open longer and take in more information before coming to a conclusion. I can't count the times I've resisted the urge to declare an idea a waste of time and been glad I resisted. I've learned people are more likely to judge a book, a person, or anything else more correctly if they wait until they've taken in a more detailed perspective.

Unless your personality is uniquely balanced or, through self-development, you have overcome your natural preferences, you too have blind spots. To expose your blind spots and ensure your perspective is broad, seek involvement with others who offer different viewpoints. They help you more accurately establish your self-awareness, interpret your research, and decide which approach to pursue. They give you different ideas as you design your incremental steps and help you compare your options in freeing up spare time. In every facet of your pursuit, other perspectives are helpful. Involving others ensures that your understanding of yourself and your self-development program is less biased and more accurate. Others balance out your decision-making biases.

To expose your blind spots and ensure your perspective is broad, seek involvement from others who can offer different viewpoints.

Your objective might be to build a new house. You may believe you've spent so much time in your laundry room over the past twenty years that you know every important laundry-room feature to include in your new house. You want the laundry room a little larger with a built-in ironing board, multiple clothes rods, and a set of drawers for miscellaneous items.

As well as you may think you know what you want, the reality is that if you solicit the advice of others, you will uncover additional uses and features that you never imagined. You could discover that a floor-level wash basin is helpful for cleaning mops and washing pets, an extra-long cabinet allows you to store rolls of gift wrapping paper, a foldout table added onto the built-in ironing board facilitates easier gift wrapping, new washer-dryer technologies use less water and don't exhaust lint, laundry-separator bins organize wash loads for you, laundry chutes bring dirty clothes to you, recycling bins take the hassle out of recycling, automated pet feeders take care of your pets, pet-passage doors give pets access to an area without you having to open doors for them, and the list goes on. On your own, you would not have thought of many of these valuable time-saving features.

Because of your biases, blind spots, or limited experience, you will always benefit from the different perspectives of others. Others' strengths compensate for your weaknesses, as do people with different backgrounds and experiences. You would be irresponsible to exclude others. When you go it alone, you don't establish an accurate awareness of yourself, you miss out on innovative incremental steps, and biases you didn't know you had affect your decisions. The result is predictable errors in judgment that others may see but you don't.

One of my goals is to develop my right-brain ability and to better understand feelings. As an off-the-charts logical thinker, I recognize that engaging and valuing feelings are my blind spots. While I've made considerable improvement, I'm not where I want to be. To help me bridge the gap, I look for and engage others who have a more developed right brain than I. Gaining their insight about feelings helps fill in my blind spots.

Request Feedback and Reinforcement

During your initial planning and awareness-building phase, other people can give you feedback to help you build an accurate baseline of self-awareness. They see things you can't. There are several ways to get feedback. In a work setting, many organizations conduct an annual, documented employee evaluation as part of a performance appraisal. It can include feedback from bosses, peers, employees, and customers. This type of formal feedback is generally given thoughtfully, although less frequently. Because it is part of a performance appraisal, it is also subject to some limitations. In terms of other formal sources of feedback, some organizations capture feedback through satisfaction surveys and other means. These can all be valuable sources of information that you can use in your development.

Where feedback processes are not in place or where feedback is not provided on a regular basis or is not geared toward self-improvement, request feedback on your own. Periodically ask your stakeholders for feedback through a simple e-mail request. Or simply ask others to give you on-the-spot feedback; establish an "if you see it, say it" principle. Or invite them occasionally to give you feedback over coffee at a local coffee shop.

When you solicit feedback, give your feedback providers a reference point. Ask them how they perceive you are doing in relation to your objective or in a specific area. Let them know what you are working on so they have a reference to measure against. Have them point out where they believe you're making progress and where you're lagging. Ask for specific examples. You can ask for broad feedback, but you're likely to get unhelpfully general or vague responses. Just asking, "How am I doing?" usually results in feedback that is too general to be very helpful.

Just asking, "How am I doing?" usually results in feedback that is too general to be very helpful.

When you start building a competency, your first concern is getting the basics right. If you're taking up golf, learning how to grip your club, where to place the ball in your stance, and how to swing the club are critical. You don't want to develop your golf skills using the wrong stance, swing path, or grip. The same is true for improving or building other competencies. Whether you are learning to listen, control your temper, coach your employees, or play a sport, ensure that your early development receives plenty of feedback. Adjustments are most easily made during early development. Once a skill or idea is engrained in your mind, adjustments become much tougher to make.

As you make steady progress, continue to seek feedback. Continued attention from others helps keep you engaged, makes you feel good about your progress, and keeps you going in the right direction. Without feedback, you are less accountable, less accurate in tracking your progress, and less likely to recognize or make needed adjustments.

Establish a feedback-rich environment around you. Involve your colleagues, family, and friends early in the planning phase as well as during the journey itself. The more others are involved, the more they will know how best to help you and the better the help you will get.

Lastly, don't forget to show your gratitude. Thank people for their feedback. Resist any temptation to be defensive. Don't "shoot the messenger." Without their help, your journey would be much more difficult.

Seek Expertise

Wise people seek wise counsel. They know that they don't know everything. Even if you are an expert in your field, there is always someone else who can give you new insight and knowledge. The moment you believe you know it all, be careful; that's the moment you become stupid. Even if it were possible to know everything, that moment would be brief. Our world is constantly changing.

You can work for a restaurant for ten years as a waitress, but because of your limited waitstaff perspective, you'd know only a fraction of what it takes to run the business. You can be a salesman for twenty years but know very little about brand marketing, advertising, and channel optimization. You can be in mid-level management for most of your career, but know virtually nothing about contemporary leadership theory or corporate strategy. There is always something new to learn.

Increase your knowledge in the area of your pursuit by seeking wise counsel, and avoid the costly mistakes that ignorance causes. Resist any temptation to be your own and only expert. Seek out the experience, knowledge, and wisdom of others, particularly the experts in the area of your endeavor. Talk to people who have been through similar endeavors. Read the books and attend the seminars of experts in your subject. Take advantage of the knowledge and experience of others.

Join Others on a Similar Journey

A prime reason Alcoholics Anonymous is so powerful in helping people deal with their alcoholism is that the organization forms a stable peer-support group. You gain confidence from others who have accomplished what you seek to accomplish and can be comforted by the companionship of others like yourself. You feel more secure and confident when you're not alone. You relate more to people who have been through or are going through the same difficulties that you are. They have a better understanding of what you are going through. Whether quitting an addiction, building a new professional skill, or learning a hobby, the involvement, support, and encouragement of others on a similar journey makes a tremendous difference.

If you plan to diet, recruit one or more co-workers to diet with you. Many organizations promote diet-support groups and contests that engage entire departments. These promotions are not only a great source of support, but make the process more fun. If you're working on building your leadership skills, pull together a group of like-minded managers to start a leadership book club. You could get together once a week to review the prior week's reading assignment and discuss what you learned. If you plan to write a book on your family history, find a few neighbors or friends with similar aspirations to write their books with you. You could share each other's ideas and gain valuable insight as you write.

A key benefit of being in a group with similar objectives is accountability. If you are accountable only to yourself, you disappoint only one person—albeit an important one—if you fall behind. If you are part of a support group, however, there are more people to disappoint, which strengthens your motivation to stick with your plan. The more people who are supporting you, the more motive you have not to disappoint.

If you are building your cycling skills and preparing for a bike race, your disappointment for not making it up a certain hill or through a difficult section quickly enough is less if you're on your own. When riding with a group, the disappointment is multiplied, so the pressure to succeed is greater. In my own mountain biking excursions, my ride times are much faster when I ride with others of similar ability than when I ride by myself, and it happens without my knowing it. The pressure is in my subconscious. It doesn't seem as if I ride any faster, but I do.

Like accountability, encouragement has a greater impact when it comes from others. If you are the only person involved in your pursuit, you are limited to your own encouragement. You might be able to pat yourself on the back, but it isn't the same as if somebody else did it. If you make it up a difficult hill climb on your bike on your own, you feel good. But when you're in a group that gives you high-fives and celebrates your achievement, the successful climb leaves you with an even larger and longer-lasting impression.

Like accountability, encouragement has a greater impact when it comes from others.

Celebrating your milestone achievements with others is important for both you and them. The more others are involved in your journey, the more they need a sense of accomplishment too. Don't let their investment in time and energy go unrewarded. Allow those who've given you feedback, advice, and support to join you when you celebrate your successes. When you reach a milestone, share the moment and show your appreciation. Not only your support group, but any family, friends, and co-workers who played a role in your journey will feel good knowing that they've contributed. Most people get much less praise than they deserve or would like.

Offering your support and encouragement to someone else in exchange for theirs is another way to form a support group. A buddy system allows you to help them while they help you. If a smaller support group is more appropriate for your journey, ask one or two people to become your key allies and offer reciprocal support to them. They could be on a similar journey or on a completely different one. If they are weak in an area where you are strong, and vice versa, you have an ideal match. You help each other not only with feedback and encouragement, but also with expertise and coaching.

You gain strength, confidence, courage, and comfort from others. Find or create a support group. Seek relationships with others who can be part of your buddy system.

As a point of caution, you can have a support group that is beneficial to you in one area but is destructive to you in another. If you find yourself gaining in one area but losing ground in another, find a different support group. If you want to quit drinking but think the only way you can bear your boss's wrath is by meeting with your co-workers who go out for a few drinks after work, find a different meeting place or a different support group. If you consider a close group of friends to be your family, yet their negativity pulls you down, find new family. If you are part of a group that makes your self-improvement harder instead of easier, it's not a support system; it's an opposition system. Get out of it and develop a new one.

Find a Mentor or Coach

A formal mentor or coach can be a priceless resource while you pursue your goal. If you know more senior or more experienced people in your area of interest, talk with them and get to know them. Ask for their advice and counsel. If they seem willing to help, ask if they'll remain accessible during your journey. If appropriate, ask them to be your mentors. Let them know you would greatly value their ongoing input, and offer to help them in some way in return. They may only need the assurance that their time won't be wasted or that you will mentor someone else in the future, but running an occasional errand for them or offering to do a small part of their work could help too.

If a mentoring relationship is not a good option for you, consider a coach. Unlike a mentor, you pay a coach, but the added experience and structure could be well worth it. If you are working on being more social and outgoing, a coach who has consistently helped others with similar objectives is invaluable. If you're building your sales skills, a seasoned coach with sales experience and the know-how of coaching can help you learn valuable selling principles while helping you improve your sales. An experienced coach helps you not only get to your desired destination but get there quicker.

A good coach helps you stay focused. She aids you in getting through roadblocks and challenges. She gives you ideas and assignments to help you grow. She gets to know you and works with your individual strengths, weaknesses, and values. She encourages you and helps you measure progress. She holds you accountable and helps you sustain your progress. An investment in a seasoned coach in the area of your endeavor can provide a substantial payoff.

Only through full disclosure can your coach or mentor help you make real progress.

In either relationship, you must believe in your mentor or coach, and they in you. There must be trust so that your conversations can be candid and transparent. You must be comfortable in sharing your needs, obstacles, feelings, and desires. Only through full disclosure can your coach or mentor help you make real progress. Pick one you trust and with whom you can be fully open.

Road Test

Communicating and explaining your ideas to others clarifies them in your own mind. The more you communicate, the clearer things become. If you have an idea for an improvement at work, the more you talk about it with others, the clearer the solution becomes. If you have an idea on how to improve your relationship with a family member or friend, talking about it with others hones the idea and makes it better.

As soon as you have the basic outline of what you want to pursue, share it with others. The insight, validation, and suggestions for improvement are priceless. The process of explaining your idea pushes you to put it into words that are understandable, not only to the other person but also to yourself. You can have an idea or dream in your head for years, but until you share it repeatedly with others, it can be as vague as the first day you conceived it. Not until you share your thoughts do you realize how poorly or well thought-out an idea really is.

Get your dreams and ideas on the road to clarity. Find people with whom you can share and test your ideas. Find opportunities to describe your plans. Request feedback and incorporate the knowledge you gain into your plans. The process of explanation, answering questions, and reflecting on others' feedback turns vague concepts into actionable steps.

Partner

To take the concept of a support group or buddy system to the next level, find a partner. Unlike a support group that you meet with on occasion, a partner shares your goal. Unlike a buddy with whom you spend time in certain aspects of your pursuit, a partner is someone you work with constantly. You execute the incremental steps together. You have the same milestones. You share the desired destination.

When I decided to improve my physical condition, I developed a plan that included diet and exercise. I knew that if my family didn't share my dietary goals, I would find myself at the dinner table with too many temptations to resist. I also knew how difficult it would be to get up every morning to exercise by myself. To my delight, my wife agreed to pursue my objective with me. She developed the same desire to get in shape and eat a healthier diet.

Sharing my goal with my wife made the difference between success and failure. On those mornings I was too tired to exercise, she was there to pull out the exercise charts and get me started. On those evenings I was famished and wanted to overeat, she was there to stop me. She was the key to my success. I did the same for her, and I was the key to her success.

Look for others who may be in circumstances similar to your own. Talk with people who work, live, play, eat, relax, and visit the same places and in the same ways you do. Consider your family, friends, neighbors, and co-workers. Pay attention to the interests of new acquaintances. Seek out people who have similar objectives and interests to yours. Share your vision and goal with them. Listen to theirs. If you deem them trustworthy, ask them to partner with you. Create a shared goal and shared road map. Work on your objective together. If you can share the same resources, it can cut your costs in half.

Get Buy-In

Many initiatives fail because people don't get others who are affected by their endeavor to buy into it. When others are affected in some way, and especially if you need their resources or approval, their buy-in is critical. If you don't have it, your road to success will be much tougher, if not impossible.

If you expect to win someone's approval, start by getting them to buy into your plan. Buy-in comes *before* you ask their approval, request their resources, or inconvenience them. Gaining support is much easier if you establish trust well before you need help. People appreciate being involved, consulted, and given plenty of notice when they're needed. If you expect ongoing support and a smooth journey, don't charge ahead without getting the appropriate levels of buy-in and approval. Most people don't like surprises, good, bad, or indifferent.

If you expect to win someone's approval, start by getting them to buy into your plan.

Involve in your journey anyone that the journey will affect. Talk to them. Review your plan. Let them know how it will affect them. If the effects are positive, enjoy the opportunity to share the good news. If your objective is to create more balance in your career and personal life, sit down with your spouse and children, and let them know that you'll be working a little less and spending more time with them. Let them know what you're doing and how it will benefit them, and gain their support.

If your journey uses someone else's resources, requires their approval, or impacts them negatively, your conversation may be more difficult but no less important. Think about and prepare for these interactions carefully. Look for opportunities to offset any inconveniences or costs to them. If your endeavor will prevent you from attending meetings from time to time, offer the meeting sponsors your willingness to catch up on the details with other attendees. If your endeavor requires co-workers to give you more of their time, offer to help them in other areas. If your endeavor will take you out of work for any period of time, let your manager know how you'll get your work done. If you are a manager and your journey affects your subordinates, let them know how and come up with temporary work-arounds if needed. If your endeavor inconveniences your family, friends, or neighbors, let them know ahead of time and emphasize how the temporary nuisance will be offset by your future improvements.

Here are a few basic principles to follow in "selling" your plan. First, find a way to make your objective a win-win for you and them. If there isn't an element of value for them in your plan already, add an incremental step that provides it. Second, be honest about any burdens you will place on them. Prior warning makes inconveniences and bad news a bit easier to take. Third, involve them early so there are no surprises. When you wait until the eleventh hour, people feel like an afterthought. Fourth, emphasize the benefits, not the costs or inconveniences. What you emphasize will be what they give most consideration.

Your best sales pitch is one that creates value for everyone. The value doesn't have to be immediate, or even guaranteed, but it must represent something reasonable that the other person can benefit from, and it should be greater than the cost or inconvenience that it causes.

Communicate your plans and benefits in person. The convenience of e-mail, messaging, or voice mail may be tempting, but it's a poor substitute for direct communication. Imagine how you would feel if you received an impersonal e-mail requesting your help along with that of many others. You would not only be tempted to let the responsibility fall on the others, you would feel your contribution didn't matter much. Or think about how you feel when your manager relies on an annual survey instead of a face-to-face, real-time dialog to discuss your performance, or requires weekly forecasts and progress reports to the exclusion of candid exchanges of ideas and solutions. Don't let yourself fall into the same trap. Pick up the phone, walk down the hall, drive across town, or do whatever is reasonable in order to personalize your request for buy-in, support, and approval.

Don't underestimate the importance of having others buy in to your endeavor. Without their buy in, you could easily find yourself well down the road toward your goal only to hit an impenetrable wall of rejection and disapproval that could cost you dearly.

Consider Other Resources

Offering to compensate others, financially or otherwise, for any inconveniences you cause can help you gain their buy-in and support. If you are restoring an old car sitting in your garage and need to move it out on the grass you share with your neighbors' property, letting them know about it beforehand and offering to compensate them for it gives you a better chance of securing their support. You could offer to mow around the car while it's on the grass, replace any dead grass when you're finished, and pay them an amount equal to the rent of the piece of their property you hope to use. The gesture would be well received by most reasonable people.

Consider any remaining elements you need in order to achieve your objective. Do you need financial, information-technology, or administrative support? Do you need tangible assets like tools, a computer, software, special venues, transportation, books, reports, supplies, or other equipment? Where are they? Do you need to buy them, or can you rent or borrow them?

Initiatives frequently fail because they are underfunded or the required resources have not been allocated to them. If your goal is to exercise, secure the equipment, clothing, or fitness club membership dues required. If your goal to improve your working relationship with other people requires that you be nearer to them, include the resources required to move your work space closer. If you require regular feedback and expect to buy lots of coffee at the local coffee shop, add in the cost of six lattes per week. If you expect to increase your presentation skills, include in your list of needed supplies a video camera to record yourself.

Initiatives frequently fail because they are underfunded or the required resources have not been allocated to them.

Think about the resources you need and who might help you to obtain them. Think about who you might borrow them from if you can't buy them. If your goal will truly add value to you, your assets, or others, you can find people or institutions that will loan, rent, or give you what you need. You just need to find them and gain their buy-in. Add to your plan any incremental steps needed to secure your required additional resources.

Activating Your Ambition

Think about those in your circle of friends, family, co-workers, and neighbors whom you might engage in deep and meaningful conversations about the logic and emotions behind your goal. Find a support group. Find someone who has completed the same journey and ask for their counsel. Let others know what you're working on and ask them to give you feedback, help hold you accountable, and encourage you. Find a partner. Think about other resources you may need and how you will secure them.

On the page of your road map titled "Activating Your Ambition Scorecard," score how well you currently do in applying the concepts of *others*. On the page of your road map titled "My Others," list any people or resources you will need on your journey. Add any actions to your incremental steps needed to secure them.

11
Make It Normal

The chains of habit are too weak to be felt until
they are too strong to be broken.

            –Samuel Johnson

When people tell me they can't change, I look no farther than my own experiences for proof that they can. I've overcome a long list of dysfunctions and weaknesses related to mental, physical, social, and professional areas of my life. My changes include developing the abilities to maintain self-control, exhibit strong character, retain what I learn, inspire others, listen, build relationships, and deliver results. I've overcome addictions to tobacco, overeating, overspending, and material accumulation. I've gone from an overwhelming fear of public speaking to speaking in front of thousands of people, and from having no empathy to putting myself in the shoes of others. I've gone from having no faith to becoming a Bible education teacher and from a selfish "taker" to a considerate "giver" whose goal is to give much more than I receive.

I've learned to be accepting and forgiving. I learned how to work as a team player. I changed my career from engineering to business management to organizational development, and I've exchanged friends who were mostly focused on fun for friends mostly focused on making the world a better place. I developed from a terrible manager who was relieved of my first management position into a leader whom people respect and follow. I've given up my perfectionist and judgmental tendencies along with a desire to control everything. I have changed like I never knew was possible.

If there is one common denominator underpinning all these changes in my life, it is staying with something until it becomes *normal.* This takes practice, practice, and more practice. I've learned that to succeed in changing my behavior, I have to stay focused on my objective until it becomes an integral part of myself.

To do that, I've learned to endure discomfort until it's no longer uncomfortable. I stick with whatever I'm developing long enough to make it a habit. I ensure that the new habits replacing old habits are strong enough that any thinking required is unconscious. I practice and keep my mind focused on my desires long enough that my existing synaptic connections wither away from lack of use and are replaced with new, stronger synaptic connections.

Behaviorists and other experts who study success and human behavior find that the difference between those who succeed and those who don't is what they do repeatedly—their habits. If your habits are conducive to success, you'll succeed; if your habits are self-destructive, you'll self-destruct. Your thinking habits determine the extent of your positive attitude, your eating and exercise habits determine your bodily health, your social habits determine your friendships, and your work habits establish your professional image and salary. Your habits determine what you become.

The eighth, final, and most important principle in activating and achieving your ambition is making your endeavor part of your normal life—reaching *normalcy*. It is maintaining your journey long enough to reach competency and sticking with it until it becomes so natural it fades into your unconsciousness and enters your comfort zone. What might have been a chore at the beginning becomes a nonissue. In many cases, it becomes an activity you look forward to because you do it well. You reach normalcy when you've acclimated to your new surroundings and they seem native.

To reach normalcy, your new behavior must become as natural as reading the paper in the morning, watching the news in the evening, using a fork to put food in your mouth, or brushing your teeth after you eat—something you do without thinking. It must simply become you.

If your goal is to improve your physical condition, normalcy happens when your exercise and diet habits are no longer part of a weight-loss initiative, but part of your normal routine. If your goal is to get out and network within your professional community, normalcy is when you go to civic functions, invite dinner guests over, and attend Chamber of Commerce or Rotary Club meetings without any thought. If your goal is to be more organized, normalcy occurs when you find yourself putting things in their proper places, making to-do lists, and doing things more efficiently without consciously thinking about it. Normalcy means that behaviors that might initially have been difficult and out of your comfort zone are simple and well within your comfort zone.

Reaching normalcy is especially important when overcoming addictions like tobacco. According to the National Cancer Institute and Centers for Disease Control and Prevention, of the 17 million American smokers who try to quit each year, only 1.3 million are successful. In other words, less than 8 percent succeed. You can be aware of your need to change, be motivated to change, believe you can do it, create a clear plan of action, free up the required time and energy, initiate the journey, and enjoy the support of others, but until "not smoking" becomes a normal part of your lifestyle, the likelihood of reverting to old ways remains high. Until you reach normalcy, the temptation to go back into old habits is a daily struggle. Your desired behavior must become just as much a habit as your undesired behavior was before.

As you read this chapter, think about your habits and how they are moving you closer to or farther away from your goals.

Your desired behavior must become just as much a habit as your undesired behavior was before.

Stretch Daily

As long as your changed behavior, attitude, or surroundings remain outside your comfort zone, they will take extra energy, willpower, discipline, patience, and focus to maintain. But once your new behaviors become native to you, their maintenance is much easier, if not totally subconscious. The key to making a behavior normal is to apply it often and for extended periods of time.

The length of the time to *normalcy* depends on three factors—how long an old habit has been in place, the size of the gap you're bridging, and the extent to which your new behavior competes with your innate personality preferences. The third challenge is the most difficult and takes the longest to deal with.

In my executive coaching, I regularly stretch my clients beyond their natural personality preferences and comfort zones. That's usually the only way to enable their desired changes. For example, I regularly receive requests from operations, finance, and engineering executives who are naturally introverted yet want to be more extroverted. Being introverted, their natural preference is to seek seclusion, especially when they're tired or stressed. However, they know that to be successful leaders they must resist their desire for seclusion and create a habit of socializing and networking with others. Creating and sustaining a habit that goes against their natural preferences generally takes a couple of years of stretching before they can consistently leave their comfort zone without a great deal of mental effort.

Overcoming natural preferences is like overcoming an addiction. Recovering alcoholics still consider themselves alcoholics because their desire for alcohol never completely goes away. Their task is to learn to cope with the desire. The behaviors and attitudes they build to cope with their undesirable desires enable them to resist temptation. Any competency, behavior, or attitude you wish to change that goes against your natural preferences requires the same mentality. Your desired state may never be completely natural, but through frequent and consistent stretching outside your preference, it becomes normal. Normalcy isn't always the complete absence of a desire to revert back to an old habit. It is a discipline that allows you to resist the desire.

Reaching normalcy in some initiatives is less an event and more a process of steady progress. For competency-building endeavors like selling, coaching, speaking, and listening, normalcy is a long, continuous learning curve. "Normal" means always improving, refining, and continuously developing. The process itself becomes normal.

For your desired behavior, attitude, or skill to become part of your comfort zone, you must apply it frequently. For most behaviors to really become normal, you must use them daily. Stretch yourself daily and, like an elastic band, your comfort zone will stretch more and more easily each time. The more you stretch yourself, the more familiar the new behaviors become, the more competent you become, and the more natural they feel.

Don't let there be long pauses between your stretching or, like a rubber band, you will lose your elasticity. If you're on an exercise program and schedule a vacation, think ahead about how you will exercise while on vacation. If you're developing new project-management skills but expect to be away from your projects on a special assignment for a month, think of ways to apply your project management skills, at least partially, during your assignment.

The key to reaching normalcy is not stopping. Don't put yourself in a situation where you completely stop what you are developing. Stopping requires starting over, and starting is difficult. Every time you take a prolonged break, you have to reinitiate— rebuilding your desire and overcoming complacency, comfort, and convenience. Don't let special assignments, vacations, or other unique circumstances derail your progress. Plan for them and if, temporarily, you can't continue to improve, at least arrange to maintain your existing progress.

The key to reaching normalcy is not stopping. Don't put yourself in a situation where you completely stop what you are developing.

Achieve Unconscious Competence

The Conscious Competence Learning Model created by Gordon Training International employee Noel Burch in the early 1970s is one of many learning models widely used in education and training. The model is especially relevant to self-development endeavors and suggests that people go through four phases in their growth from incompetence to competence.

1. **Unconscious incompetence.** People are incompetent in many areas and, unless they are put in a situation where a specific competency is required or demanded of them, they're unconscious of their incompetence. Someone is in this stage when he reviews the 360-degree survey feedback from his co-workers and learns for the first time that they don't consider him a good listener. He has been unconsciously incompetent at listening.

2. **Conscious incompetence.** Being aware that you lack a certain skill like listening is the second phase of learning. Once you recognize your shortcoming, you are in position to start developing the competency.

3. **Conscious competence.** In the third phase of learning you consciously engage and develop your competency. This phase involves deliberate learning and application.

4. **Unconscious competence.** Once you've practiced a competency long enough that it's well established, it moves into your unconscious. The competency becomes second nature, and you use it unconsciously. This is when your competency becomes normal.

Early in my career, I set out to change from engineering to sales. When I did that, most of my engineering skills no longer applied. In effect, I started my career over. I developed new skills such as relationship building, sales-call planning, and presentation giving. The transition was difficult, and I felt overwhelmed. The hardest part was moving from a feeling of competence to incompetence. I know others who watched my progress felt the same way about me. I truly had no idea how to sell, but as I stuck with it and time passed, my incompetence turned to conscious competence. Then my conscious competence turned to unconscious competence, and those new skills became a normal part of who I am.

Your journey isn't complete until you reach unconscious competence. You will make great progress well before that, but only when you do what you do well and without much thought do you reach *normalcy*.

Practice

People who attain a high level of competency make their skill look effortless. Their apparent effortlessness leads others to believe that their mastery is a result of some natural ability. In reality, mastery comes through practice. Psychologist and Professor K. Anders Ericsson found that the level of performance attained by many experts—musicians, chess players, and athletes, for example—is more closely related to their amount of deliberate practice than to their natural ability. Anders found that the most accomplished musical soloists had spent ten thousand hours in solitary practice by the age of twenty. The less-accomplished expert musicians spent five thousand hours in solitary practice, and serious amateur pianists spent only two thousand hours in solitary practice. The correlation between practice and performance is strong. The more you practice, the higher your performance.

World-class athletes get to the top of their game through practice. They continuously try to improve by practicing their swing, throw, kick, jump, turn, or whatever their sport requires. Spectators who see them only in competition don't realize how they developed or continue to develop their skills. Tiger Woods, who has been consistently rated the top golfer in the world, practiced for fifteen years before his first championship win. To continue to develop his strength and skills, his daily practice regimen includes running, biking, weight lifting, and hitting thousands of balls over a period of three to four hours—in addition to actually playing a round of golf on most days.

Ricky Carmichael, motocross racing's most decorated rider, with hundreds of championships and victories, had an equivalent routine. Ricky's daily practice regimen went from 8:00 a.m. to 5:00 p.m. working with a full-time personal trainer on strength, cardio, and skill training. Activities included road cycling, mountain biking, swimming, weight lifting, and motocross riding. Many in the know considered Ricky's regimen and physical condition to be the highest of any professional athlete in any sport at the time, and it was also widely known to be the source of his amazing competitive advantage.

Warren Buffet, consistently one of the world's best stock pickers and richest people owes much of his success to his practice. He constantly reads and researches financial and business information. To stay on top of his holdings and spot new opportunities, he reads and researches financial statements, market reports, economic news, business articles, and other information for hours every day.

For competency-based goals, reaching normalcy and unconscious competence takes repeated application *and* practice. Application requires putting your new skill into productive use; practice is honing your skill in nonproductive settings, just as athletes apply their skills on game day and hone them the rest of the week on the practice field.

For competency-based goals, reaching normalcy and unconscious competence takes repeated application and practice.

Your brain's neural pathways hold your skills. The reason you can ride a bicycle after not being on one for twenty years is that you imprinted your riding skills into your brain's neural pathways in childhood. Those pathways stored the knowledge you built, including how to steer, how to pedal, and how to maintain balance. You might take a few minutes to feel comfortable on the bike again because the pathways aren't as strong as they once were, but they are there nonetheless.

To strengthen your pattern of neural pathways, you repeat what you do, say, or think over and over. As you repeat a behavior, you strengthen its associated mental blueprint and, at the same time, weaken the imprint of behaviors you are replacing. It is the same process used to memorize a presentation, a poem, a phone number, or most anything else.

Competency requires regular use. You can't become a great public speaker by speaking once a year; you can't stretch out of your introverted nature by engaging socially with others once a month; you can't become fluent in Spanish if you use it only once a week; and you can't become a great coach to your employees if you visit with them only during biannual reviews. Your journey must include the regular use of your desired competency. You must put yourself in situations where you can apply it often.

Like skill building, knowledge building requires repetition. Without repeated use, you don't retain what you know or learn. Without immediate and repeated use, what you learn in a seminar, in a book, or through casual discussion never makes it past your short-term memory. The information and your interpretation of it are not instantly encoded in your long-term memory. It takes repetitive recollection and use or it is quickly lost.

Unless you have a true, inborn talent in your area of interest, you will need to accept the initial awkwardness that comes with building a new competency. At first, you might not only feel uncomfortable, but outright awful, which amplifies challenges to development like the fear of looking foolish. This is an added reason to have the support and encouragement of others. It also requires that you not take yourself too seriously. You are just learning, and you can't depend quite yet on your new skill for your source of confidence. What doesn't come naturally does come with practice.

You need a place to practice where it is physically and emotionally safe to be awful. At first, you might only apply your growing competency when you are with your family or those who are helping you. Or you might practice on your own in front of the mirror or in situations you create solely for the purpose of developing your competency. If you are learning to weld, weld only on scrap metal until your welding bead is good enough for productive use. If you are learning to be a technical writer, write your first technical manuals on how to operate the appliances in your home. As when you learn to drive a car, don't let your first trip behind the wheel be in rush hour traffic on the freeway.

Rather than feeling incompetent early in their development, some people become over confident—foolishly confident—with their initial progress. While not worrying about failure or what others think can be healthy, it can leave you the loser in the end. Overconfidence prevents you from seeing the warning bumps along the road. Before you know it, you've taken too big of a step and made an error that will be very hard to reverse or overcome.

Don't let your first stand-up presentation be in front of your organization's president, your first singing audition be on television, or your first coaching session be with your toughest critic. If fearlessness is your natural tendency, control it by taking incremental steps. Look for practice opportunities where you can get by with being less than perfect. Look for environments where it is safe to fail.

As you practice and stick with it, learning gets easier. It's like building muscle tone. When you first start to lift weights, you feel a lot of pain, but as you continue, you build muscle and grow stronger. Your exercises become easier, your recoveries shorter. Your pain fades away. You ultimately achieve the tone and shape you want with what seems to be little effort. You still have to work out to maintain your fitness, but the effort flattens out to a manageable level. It becomes your normalcy.

When you reach your desired level of proficiency, kick your practice up a notch. Go further, faster, longer, deeper, or more than you normally need. Many athletes practice a level above their normal performance. Olympic athletes train at higher altitudes to make their performance at normal altitudes easier. Swimmers swim against a current to make swimming without one easier. If your goal is to become an expert in something, try teaching more advanced material than you normally use at a local college or seek opportunities to speak in front of a hundred people when you normally expect to speak in front of only twenty. If you are in school, study an extra hour, even though you believe you know all the material to be tested.

If you learn by "just doing it," be careful that you don't "overdo it." Steady application beats inconsistency and excess every time. Slow, nonstop progress and incremental steps are your best friends for reaching normalcy.

Winning athletes view practice as normalcy. If you want to achieve your goal, make repeated application part of your routine. Great athletes, financiers, musicians, leaders, and public speakers become great only by repeated application and a continuous honing of their skills.

Measure

Practice is best done against a metric or standard. Measurements provide you with meaningful feedback. If you practice without measurement, you don't know whether you improved or fell back compared to your last practice or your goal. You lose the correlation between your actions and your progress that explains your changes in performance. Without objective measures, you don't know if a technique or method actually helped you or hurt you.

Valid, objective measures give you clear direction on what adjustments you need to make to keep your natural tendency to deceive yourself in check. Without an objective measurement like weight, you can end an exercise routine and convince yourself you just lost five pounds when, in reality, you lost half of one.

Select something you can measure objectively. It should be aligned with your milestone and often is your milestone. Some metrics, like your weight, are straightforward, but others require more creativity. If you are learning a foreign language, you might keep track of the amount of time you can carry on a conversation in that language, or how long you can talk before someone asks you to repeat yourself. If you are working on being more intentional and less reactive, a measurement might be the time you work on your own initiatives versus those of others. Less tangible measures are not quite as scientific, but can still be effective in tracking your progress and helping you make adjustments to stay on track.

Take It One Day at a Time

To make your new behavior part of your normal ritual, you may need a level of willpower and self-control you haven't been able to muster before. If you are battling an addiction to food, alcohol, or tobacco, self-control will be your challenge. To keep from feeling overwhelmed, focus your attention on your nearest milestone. Focus on one day at a time. If you are avoiding alcohol or tobacco, set your goal to avoid it just for today. When you've made it through the day, celebrate and take pride in your accomplishment. When the next day comes, set the same goal, and continue taking it one day at a time. Thinking about staying off your addiction forever, or even for a week, seems completely impossible when you first start. It can produce more anxiety than you can handle, forcing you to eat the candy bar or light up the cigarette just to calm down. Instead, concern yourself only with getting through the day. Your plan will keep you on track and do the worrying about the future for you.

Self-control and confidence are mutually reinforcing.

Self-control and confidence are mutually reinforcing. As you make daily progress, your confidence grows and your temptations diminish. For each day you resist, your sense of accomplishment increases and reinforces your motivation, belief, and drive. Your willpower strengthens. On the other hand, a loss of control gives you a sense of defeat and erodes your confidence. Stay in control one day at a time, and watch your confidence grow. You may not see any way today to stay strong and reach your goal over the long-term, but don't worry about it. Just make it through the day. Before you know it, the days turn to weeks, which turn to months, which turn at last into a triumph you didn't think possible.

Discipline Your Thinking

If there's one word that's harder to get excited about than "practice," it's "discipline." Discipline just doesn't sound like fun. For many, it conjures up thoughts of control, restraint, and work. But discipline is a quality you must embed in your journey to keep you focused. Without it, you won't persevere through the temptations, and getting to the point where your pursuit becomes easy will be a struggle.

Lack of discipline is the same shortcoming found in organizations that plan but don't execute. Management consultant and author David Maister knows it well. As he says in his book *Strategy and the Fat Smoker*, success doesn't come from the quality of analysis or analytical insight, but in the level of resolve and discipline created to reach the goals. With discipline, plans get executed. Organizations and individuals who exercise discipline get things done.

Discipline is mental toughness—being dedicated, persistent, and in control. It gets you through those demanding moments in your journey, particularly at the front end when the journey feels far outside your comfort zone.

Discipline is a learned quality, a capability that comes from your thinking. Remember that your feelings and actions start with your thinking. You take in information from your surroundings, process and filter it through your biases, and then take action. To be disciplined, you must develop the right biases, care about the information you take in, and dwell on thoughts that reinforce the behavior you want. What you think—whether self-improving or self-defeating—reinforces your desires until you can no longer resist them.

In *You Can Be Happy No Matter What,* author Richard Carlson explains that thinking is ability, not reality. This seems obvious, but people frequently confuse their thinking with their reality. Two people can witness the same event but have completely different explanations of it. Each sees it clearly, believes he understands it, and is adamant that his version of the event is accurate. But because people interpret their environment differently, the same event can have many interpretations.

Our unique knowledge, experiences, and values cause us to interpret situations differently. What you might consider an indisputable fact takes on different meanings for different people. Our thoughts therefore represent only our interpretation of reality. In strengthening your discipline, use this to your advantage. Whatever the circumstances, you can interpret them however you want. All you need is to develop the right thinking habits and biases.

Dwell on the benefits your goal provides. Think positive thoughts to create positive biases. Focus on your positive self-improving behaviors, and replace any self-defeating mental pictures with pictures of yourself reaching your goal. Avoid negative people and reject their negative information. Plan responses to expected obstacles and temptations. When a temptation presents itself, respond appropriately and turn your attention to your confidence. Take pride in your mental toughness. Feel the satisfaction of being in control.

Challenge yourself to get tough—physically and mentally. Accept that you will face challenges and be ready for them. Learn the discipline of controlled thinking. Have a "bring it on" attitude. Be confident you will exercise self-control and resist any temptations to fall into old habits. The more you control your actions, the more confident you will become and the more your mental toughness will become a natural part of you.

Increase Your Retention

If your self-development plan involves learning, reaching normalcy will depend on how well you retain what you learn. Studies show that you lose much of what you learn if you don't put it immediately into practice. Within a few hours of receiving new information, your retention of that information rapidly diminishes. Fortunately, with a little extra effort, you can greatly increase your retention.

If your self-development plan involves learning, reaching normalcy will depend on how well you retain what you learn.

The following six methods progressively increase your information retention and help you get the most out of your learning:

1. **Invest**—Your investment in your goal is a significant factor in your retention mind-set. When you invest in learning, you are more likely to value it. Most people equate value with money, time, and effort spent. When you don't pay for learning, you don't appreciate it. When you don't invest your time in it, you don't take it as seriously. When you don't sacrifice, you don't value the effort or the results.

   That's not to say you should waste money and time. If you can get something of quality for less effort and cost, take advantage of it, but be aware that you won't place as much value on it. The more you invest, the greater your motivation to stay with the seminar, coaching, or counseling engagement.

Books are great examples of high-quality content for relatively little investment. For less than the price of a dinner, you can gain the insights of authors, executives, researchers, and scholars that have taken a lifetime to develop. Buy books and reap the rewards of others' experiences, failures, knowledge, and wisdom.

A learning mind-set also requires an investment of your mental and physical energy. A clear mind, free of stress, and surroundings free of distractions, allows you to concentrate on learning. Being fully rested and getting a full night's sleep before any learning event makes your mind sharper and your retention greater. Invest in learning by giving it your best time, energy, and money.

2. **Take Notes**—Take notes on the key points. Writing or typing notes reinforces the information in your mind and helps imprint the points in your memory. I find it helpful to take notes twice. I handwrite them on a notepad while in training, in lectures, or when reading a book; then later, I transcribe them to my computer so I can access and refer to them online. By synchronizing my mobile phone with my computer, I also have my notes with me wherever I go.

3. **Put Notes into Frameworks**—Frameworks can be models, diagrams, flowcharts, clusters, analogies, metaphors, acrostics, acronyms, rhymes, or anything that puts your key learning points into context. *Activating Your Ambition* uses the acronym AMBITION to create a framework for the eight principles to becoming application ready. Consolidate the key points into simple frameworks to give context to what you want to remember.

Frameworks take the load off your short-term memory and help move your learning from short-term to long-term memory.

Harold D. Stolovitch and Erica J. Keeps, specialists in human instruction and performance, suggest in their book *Telling Ain't Training*, "For training and learning purposes, it's important to create meaningful chunks that condense several pieces of information into one. This facilitates perception, learning, and retention. By creating a single chunk, we reduce the short-term memory load." Reduce the information you want to retain to concise points and put them into a diagram, model, acronym, or whatever structure helps you remember.

4. **Discuss It**—Talk about what you learned with someone else. Discussing key points and sharing opinions leave deeper and longer-lasting impressions. Find someone with whom you can have a rigorous exchange of ideas. Talk with others who listen well, probe into your points, and challenge you when they don't understand or when they disagree. The process of discussion and debate creates clarity in your thinking and learning.

5. **Apply It**—Apply what you've learned. Applying it moves you from the intellectual to the practical and gives your knowledge context. Using your knowledge creates experiences, building more permanent neural networks in your brain. Using a newly learned sales tactic or parenting method increases your retention dramatically. This is most effective when you put it into practice immediately. Within a few days, unapplied learning dissipates. If you don't apply what you learn within the first week, the odds are that you won't recall enough of it to use it properly.

Quickly embed your learning in your work, marriage, hobbies, or whatever part of your daily life it applies to. Create experiences so the learning has context. The first day after a seminar, make time to put your new knowledge into practice. Create an environment where you can put key points from a book into action. Have a standing appointment with your staff, boss, spouse, or whoever is appropriate, directly after your coaching or counseling session so you can immediately discuss your learning, if not directly apply it.

6. **Teach It**—Teaching is the most effective way to build and retain knowledge. Teaching uses all the elements of retention—investment, note consolidation, frameworks, discussion, and application. To teach something without deepening your own understanding is almost impossible. Teaching represents your best opportunity to make your new knowledge, skills, behavior, attitude, style, or approach permanent—for you.

   Find opportunities to teach what you have learned. Consider how teaching might be useful in your journey, whether formal or informal, as long as it involves preparation and delivery. You might teach co-workers, friends, family, neighbors, or fellow church members. Teach at professional society meetings, social club outings, or on your own through seminars and workshops. Any opportunities to teach will make your road to normalcy faster.

Consider Your Attention Span

Some people have trouble focusing their attention for more than a minute or two. For them, much of what we've covered in *Activating Your Ambition* will be difficult. Planning, visualizing, reflecting, and discipline require focused concentration. If you can't concentrate, you are at a disadvantage from the start.

If you are easily distracted and feel perpetually restless, you might be experiencing symptoms of Attention Deficit Disorder (ADD). ADD, also known as Attention Deficit Hyperactivity Disorder (ADHD), is diagnosed in about 5 percent of the population, and researchers estimate that up to 10 percent have the disorder but are undiagnosed. Symptoms of ADD are restlessness, impulsivity, hyperactivity, and distractibility. If you experience these symptoms, include in your journey the possible diagnosis and treatment of this disorder. You must be able to concentrate before you can seriously pursue your self-development and maintain your discipline.

Treatments for ADD include medication, nutrition, coaching, and counseling to learn coping skills and adaptive behaviors. With proper treatment, ADD can be controlled, and many very successful people, like actress Whoopi Goldberg and chief executive officer Charles Schwab, have managed their ADD.

Stay Steady through Emotional Highs and Lows

Be aware of the "honeymoon affect" as you move toward normalcy. In the early stages, you can be enamored by the newness, excitement, and large gains of your self-development program. This early excitement is the honeymoon effect. It's a great feeling, but it doesn't last. Once the newness wears off and the honeymoon is over, the excitement dwindles and progress slows. What was once stimulating becomes mundane. You become bored.

To combat the honeymoon effect, plan for it. Lean on your motivation. Stay focused on the incremental steps and milestones that give you a sense of accomplishment. Maintain your discipline. Stay steady.

A cousin of the honeymoon affect is the "plateau affect." Early in your journey, you may believe you've reached normalcy only to discover what you've really experienced is a premature self-development plateau. If this happens, resist the temptation to declare victory. You may feel you've gone as far as you can go and won the battle as best you can, but don't celebrate just yet. Give yourself a little more time if you still have improvement to make. Try other techniques to get yourself back on a growth trajectory. Celebrate a milestone if you've reached one, but withhold your final celebration. Declare victory only when you've achieved unconscious competence.

Success in self-development doesn't feel like a big bang; it feels like normalcy.

Be aware of emotional highs and lows, and of premature notions of success or failure. Success in self-development doesn't feel like a big bang; it feels like normalcy. Stay steady and focused.

Expect Setbacks

No matter how ready you are for your journey, you will experience a few bumps along the way. You will make a mistake, give in to a temptation, be discouraged, or hit an emotional low at some point. Just don't let your setbacks derail you, permanently dampen your enthusiasm, or invalidate your belief in yourself or your goal. Don't confuse a temporary issue with a fatal failure.

Your perceptions become self-fulfilling prophecies. View your obstacles, problems, and setbacks as learning opportunities and essential steps. Link a step backward to two steps forwards—a net gain of a step.

Prepare for and anticipate setbacks. Create plans to deal with them so you can learn and keep moving forward. The more setbacks you encounter, the more you'll learn and the faster you'll reach your end goal. Consider each setback as one more you won't have to contend with again. Thomas Edison considered each of his ten thousand attempts to producing a working lightbulb a step closer to achieving his goal.

Know When to Give Up

What if, after repeated attempts and practice, you make little, if any, progress? What if your desire is to become a great public speaker but after two months of practice and application you still struggle to put two sentences together in front of a group of people? When do you give up? When do you change your course?

I believe that with enough knowledge, motivation, belief, time, and support from others, you can do anything you want. However, at some point, the frustration, costs, energy, and time required can outweigh the benefits. The guideline for knowing when to quit or change course is subjective. My best advice is at least to give yourself a solid chance. Apply all the principles we've mentioned, put together a cogent plan with incremental steps, maintain your focus, practice, be disciplined, and get as far as you can. Then if your progress stalls, you have three choices: 1) keep going, 2) change your course, or 3) quit.

1. **Keep Going**—If you have invested a lot of time and feel you are on the right course, give it more time. Studies of successful people show they keep going at the very end when others quit.

People often unknowingly quit just before they are about to reach their goal.

2. **Change Your Course**—If you can't get around your roadblock or move past your plateau, consider changing your approach or the goal. If the benefits of your goal remain higher than the costs, energy, and frustration you are encountering, maintain the goal but try modifying your approach. Revisit and validate your baseline of awareness. Seek insight from others. Brainstorm new incremental steps. If after a solid retry, you are still stuck, modify your objective to one you can more realistically achieve.

3. **Quit**—If you have exhausted alternative approaches and the costs, energy, and frustrations now outweigh your anticipated benefits, quitting may be your best option. The uniqueness that qualifies you for countless endeavors may be your Achilles' heel for this one. If you have a special gift or strong talent in one area, its double edge may prevent you from achieving in another. My talent for analytical thinking makes getting in touch with my emotions difficult. In some settings, my strength is my weakness. In your case, your natural abilities may make your endeavor all but impossible. If so, relinquish this objective and choose another more suited to your eventual success.

If, for example, you've used all the tools in the eight principles of *Activating Your Ambition* to be more extroverted but find the energy and frustration of being more sociable too high, accept your introverted nature. An introverted nature may limit your career as a sales executive or a travel guide, but there are plenty of other careers for introverts. Think about a new career path as a world-famous poker player, accountant, graphic designer, programmer, or negotiator.

Quitting is an acceptable solution as long as it is not an excuse. If you are quitting so you can satisfy an urge or succumb to a temptation, you are not contending with a natural limitation but a learned one. You may think that you've made some progress, so one weekend of binge drinking, smoking a pack of cigarettes, or treating yourself to a trip to a buffet restaurant will be okay. It won't. Your belief is false confidence reinforcing the illusion that since you've made some progress, you can easily get back to that point again. The reality is that restarting a stopped initiative is even harder than starting it for the first time. For many who try to quit smoking, the failure of each try at quitting weakens their resolve. The only normalcy they reach is a frustrating cycle of starting and stopping.

Consider, too, that if your self-improvement program is critical to your health and well-being, quitting it will have severe consequences. If this is your situation, instead of quitting, change course. If your lack of exercise puts you at high risk of diabetes, instead of giving up, change your exercise routine. If your level of stress puts you at risk for a stroke, instead of quitting your stress-reduction program altogether, try different tactics. If you are so introverted you can't get a job, instead of declaring defeat, hire a coach or read different books on the subject. If your uncontrolled anger prevents you from collaborating with co-workers, instead of quitting your goal, change your surroundings. If you face derailment of your health, marriage, or career, persevere. The downside of failure is too great to ignore.

If at the end of a solid try, you determine that your goal is impossible to achieve, realize that the journey wasn't a waste of time. Knowing you gave your best will prevent any future regrets. Take satisfaction in what you learned in your journey and about yourself.

Benjamin Franklin pursued an overly aggressive self-development program in which he had to admit defeat. Franklin hated wasting time looking for things. His goal was moral perfection, which included putting all his possessions in their proper places, an idea he called "order." In his autobiography, which he wrote at the age of seventy, he said, "In the end, I found ORDER impossible to implement in my life. Now that I'm old and my memory has grown poor, I wish I had practiced more of it in my youth. So now it is clear I never achieved the moral perfection I had been so determined to acquire. I never even got close. Nonetheless, I was definitely a better and happier person for making the effort. I'd like everyone who reads this book to know that this one self-improvement program, with God's blessing, contributed more to the quality and happiness of my life than anything else I tried."

You too can find happiness and contentment in a journey only partially completed.

Reward Yourself

As you make incremental progress, reward yourself. Do it with others as appropriate, and enjoy your progress on your own as well. Your journey to normalcy shouldn't be all work with no fun. Your effort deserves celebration and needs frequent reinforcement. Reward yourself at each completed milestone. Plan a short trip, buy a book, go to a movie, or arrange to do some other activity you enjoy. Just don't deceive yourself. Defer your rewards until you genuinely achieve your milestone. Don't reinforce a lack of progress by rewarding it. And when you do reward yourself, don't use a reward that compromises your journey. If you are on a diet, don't make the reward an ice cream cake. Make it something else you enjoy that doesn't damage your goal.

Hit the Inflection Point

If you're getting into better physical condition, one day you'll look down and notice a flatter stomach. If you're gaining control over anger, one day you'll realize you just kept your cool when you would normally have blown up. If you're developing your coaching skills, one day an employee will leave your office excited from your session with her, and you'll realize you've become a pretty good coach. While these realizations don't signal the end of your journey, they signal an important milestone.

They represent an *inflection point*—a point at which you have developed significantly, and at which the nature of your journey changes. Your change, anxiety, and investment shift from increasing difficulty to decreasing difficulty. It is the point your journey transitions from hard to easy. After coming through many turns and around various obstacles, you'll realize that you've just turned the last corner. The finish line will still be ahead of you, but for the first time, you will see it. Any lingering doubt will vanish, your belief in yourself will be firmly cemented, and your motivation will be centered on a real experience, not merely a mental picture.

Your inflection point represents your entry into the fourth and final phase of the Conscious Competence Learning Model—unconscious competence. The learning, practice, discipline, focus, and dedication have paid off, and the hard part is over. The new behavior you so desired is very close to being a natural part of you. You are still not fully mature in your new competency, but you are competent enough that the remainder of your journey is just a matter of continued execution. You no longer have to navigate past the temptations or the stress of second-guessing yourself.

When you've been focused on executing your plan, your inflection point will sneak up on you. When you hit it, you will be first surprised and then elated. Look forward to it, but don't focus on it. It will come soon enough. Keep your mental energy focused on your plan.

Continue repeating the cycle of consistent application, realizing the benefits of your progress and growing more confident. As this cycle repeats itself, your activities and results become natural. They begin to fade into your subconscious and become part of your comfort zone and the new you.

When you have reached the inflection point of your journey, let your coach, partner, or your support team know. Let me know, too, at ambition@alpinelink.com. I'd appreciate the opportunity to join you in celebrating the accomplishment of this critical milestone.

Activating Your Ambition

Making your new competency, attitude, or behavior normal will take time. It can take many months—even several years—for temptations to go away, habits to become second nature, and competencies to develop fully. Just remember why you're doing it and that it's worth the investment. You have to have habits, so you might as well make them good ones and put time to work for you instead of against you. Goals seem impossible only when you are not heading toward them. Put yourself on the path toward your goal, and what once seemed impossible becomes not only possible, but probable.

Goals seem impossible only when you are not heading toward them.

On the page of your road map titled "Activating Your Ambition Scorecard," score how well you currently do in applying the concepts of *normalcy*. In the section of your road map titled "My Normalcy," list any new actions, incremental steps, and milestones you need to incorporate into your plan. Identify safe opportunities in which to practice. Identify any more situations that are likely to tempt you to fall back on old habits, and plan your responses and actions to them. Establish the measurements you will use to track your progress and the rewards you will enjoy when you achieve your milestones.

12
Ambition Activated

Most people live and die with their music still
unplayed. They never dare to try.

–Mary Kay Ash

The eight principles of *Activating Your Ambition* focus on actions
and activities you control. They are principles you own. Self-awareness,
motivation, belief, a plan of incremental steps, time, initiation, the
engagement of others, and persistence in reaching normalcy are up
to you decide and act upon. *Activating Your Ambition* is a self-directed
learning and development approach. Through the application of these
principles, you and those who apply them with you will progress
toward your peak potential.

When you dig into the roots of success—past the symptoms, lucky
circumstances, doctored-up vendor success stories, and people who try
to steal the limelight—you find people who execute and people who

have a mind-set of continuous improvement. You find an eagerness and discipline to reach higher and higher levels of achievement. You find the eight principles of *Activating Your Ambition*. People who have the mind-set and ability to change their behavior achieve. Declining performance, failing initiatives, and stalled projects result from the defeating attitudes and inabilities of individuals.

This is not to say that factors outside your individual control can't make improving performance easier or more difficult. Systems, processes, incentives, decisions, cultures, budgets, and other people can make your desires much easier or harder to attain than others.

If you live, play, or work in an environment that's at odds with your desire to take action, improve yourself, or improve your organization, there is still action you can take. If you are building a new professional skill that is out of alignment with your employer's incentives, business processes, and culture, your journey will be harder but not impossible. If you are learning a new approach to selling, but your organization's sales-automation system, sales-compensation plan, or resource-allocation model is tied to a different approach, using your new sales approach will be arduous but not impossible. I've worked in a transactional sales environment that valued only short, hard-charging sales pursuits yet developed and followed a consultative selling approach that ended up being good for both me and the company.

Dealing with outside influences comes down to two options. One is to apply the principles of *Activating Your Ambition* as best you can without concern for the uncontrollable variables around you. The principles are robust enough to help you overcome most obstacles, and you can realize a sizable return on your investment regardless of the unsupportive elements around you.

The second option is to change or influence those elements before you begin or in parallel with your journey. If you can influence or control some of the unsupportive people, systems, processes, and incentives, do what you can to align them with the new direction you plan to head. The improved alignment will make your return on investment even greater and more sustainable.

If you're pursuing a healthier diet to increase your energy level but your family regularly stocks the pantry with candy and junk food, ask them to move their junk food to their private areas and eat it when you are not around. Or if you're learning to take initiative but your work environment is purely reactive, ask for an outlet to practice your new ability. See if you can host a suggestion program or initiate quarterly brainstorming sessions.

Aligning your self-development pursuit to your environment makes your journey much easier and more valuable. It also creates value for those around you. Most self-improvement changes that help you also help others.

Most self-improvement changes that help you also help others.

Identify any elements of your environment that are out of alignment with your goals and invite your stakeholders to help put them into better alignment. They might have just been waiting for someone to make the recommendation and take the initiative. Be a leader and lead the way.

Summary

When you apply the eight principles of *Activating Your Ambition*, you are ready to tackle even the most difficult challenges—to learn a new skill, change a behavior, or overcome a bad habit. You can earn a degree, make exercise a normal way of life, change your eating habits, improve your marriage, increase your earnings, become a better leader, or accomplish just about anything you set your mind to. All you need is to apply the eight principles to a clear goal.

Here is a brief summary of how to turn your objective into your achievement:

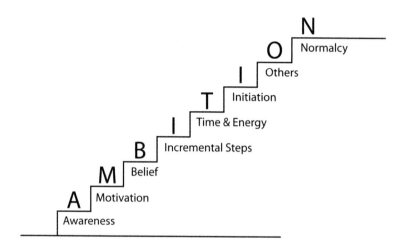

Awareness—Accurate self-awareness is the foundation to your self-development journey. Discover the truth about your strengths and weaknesses. Get past any self-deceptions. Start your journey on reality, not perception. Establish your end goal and decide how best to reach it. Be clear and confident in how you will bridge the gap between where you are and where you're going.

Motivation—Identify what motivates you. Understand the likely benefits of your endeavor. Employ the many sources of motivation available to you. Motivation sustains you when you're tempted to fall back into old habits, fuels your inner drive and willpower, and gets you to the finish line.

Belief—Believe you can succeed and that the benefits to be attained are realistic. Be confident. Have a can-do attitude. Belief reassures you when the going gets tough, reinforces your motivation, and sustains you when you might otherwise question the feasibility of reaching your goal. Plan responses to your anticipated obstacles, risks, and temptations so you know ahead of time you will prevail.

Incremental Steps—Develop a written road map with incremental steps and milestones. By methodically accomplishing small steps toward your goal, you build sustainable competency and confidence. Easily started incremental steps help you avoid getting so far outside your comfort zone that you jump back into old habits to find security and comfort.

Time and Energy—Incorporate actions into your journey that give you the time and energy you need to pursue your goal. Include time-saving and energy-producing practices in your daily routine. Ensuring that adequate time and energy is available ensures your goal gets its necessary focus.

Initiation—Move your ambition from planning to execution. Set a scheduled start date that gives you a solid launch. Anticipate any circumstances or events that you need to schedule around. Identify your opportunity triggers so that when they occur, you engage them. Accommodate your plan to your learning style to make your journey easier. Take responsibility and maintain an internal locus of control.

Others—Engage others in the planning and execution stages of your journey. They give you needed support and encouragement and help hold you accountable. Develop a "fan club" of family, friends, and co-workers to join you in celebrating your achievements. Pursue your journey as part of a community.

Normalcy—Stay on your journey long enough for your desired behavior to become your normal behavior. Measure your progress and make adjustments as you learn and develop. Create a habit of practice and discipline. Anticipate the inflection point where your journey starts the downhill finish.

Give Yourself the Best Odds

For people accustomed to winging it or avoiding self-improvement until it's forced on them, the systematic approach of *Activating Your Ambition* may seem too structured or mechanical. It may look like overkill. I will be the first to agree that it's not warranted for every endeavor. I don't create a written plan for everything I do, but for any important self-development goal that is outside your comfort zone, the few hours or days you spend becoming application ready will be more than offset by the quicker and easier success you will experience.

The eight principles of *Activating Your Ambition* improve your odds of success. If you don't want to gamble with your future, use your new knowledge and ability to put the odds in your favor. Why not make your odds of success as high as possible?

Stay on Track

In pursuing my own ambitions, I sometimes get stuck. It happens to everyone. Circumstances change, we change, and so does everything else in life. When I get stuck, I run through the eight principles in my head and assess how well I'm doing. This structured approach lets me reassess the primary enablers to success and is a great framework through which to check myself. I first gauge my foundation of awareness and knowledge. Do I need to do more research, talk to experts in the field, or revalidate my base assumptions? I check my motivation. Am I still motivated to pursue this endeavor? Do I need to rebuild my motivation? Are the benefits still realistic?

I then check my belief. Do I still believe in this ambition and believe that it's within my reach? Have I dealt with the possible risks to my benefits? I revalidate that the steps I'm pursuing are easy to achieve. Am I trying to do too much too fast? Are the steps in my road map incremental? I look at my schedule and affirm that I'm creating adequate time to participate in actions I have outlined in my road map. I consider my energy level. Am I just too tired to get excited or engaged today?

If all is well, I consider other people. Am I taking advantage of the support of others? Am I making use of those who have gone on similar journeys before me? Am I trying to do too much on my own?

And last, I consider normalcy. Am I experiencing the normal effects of change and its discomfort? Am I closer to becoming comfortable with my change? Do I just need to hang in there a little longer? Am I taking it one day at a time? Am I practicing enough and applying myself?

When you feel stuck, think through the eight principles. You will either find reassurance that you are on the right track or identify what you need to do to get back on track.

Good luck in your self-development endeavor. With proper attention to the eight principles of *Activating Your Ambition*, you can do whatever you set your mind to. These principles work for me, my clients, numerous others, and they will work for you.

Activating Your Ambition

As a final thought, if you've made it to this last chapter and are still unsure how to apply what you've learned here, pick a small endeavor and give it a try. First apply the eight principles of *Activating Your*

Ambition on a small scale. Gain some experience with the approach. The return may be only a small one, but on your first time through, the real value comes in learning the process and gaining the confidence that now you can do anything you put your mind to. On your next endeavor, you'll be ready for a more substantial goal, a more substantial investment, and a more substantial reward.

I truly believe you can accomplish anything you want if you have the necessary tools and resources—the eight principles of *Activating Your Ambition*—in your toolkit. If a deaf man can become the greatest musician in the world and a man without arms and legs can type forty-three words a minute, nothing is impossible. Booker T. Washington, the nineteenth-century American educator and African-American civil rights leader, said, "You measure the size of the accomplishment by the obstacles you had to overcome to reach your goals."

If you have lingering doubts about pursuing your objective, answer one question: Will you regret not giving it a try? If there's a chance you will someday look back and regret not pursuing your objective, you owe it to yourself to try, if only to avoid the nagging thoughts and lingering question, "I wonder what would have happened if…"The biggest regrets people have are not what they did but what they left undone.

If you have lingering doubts about pursuing your objective, answer one question: Will you regret not giving it a try?

Don't let your objectives remain unfulfilled dreams. Don't let *Activating Your Ambition* be an academic exercise. Don't leave yourself with lingering doubts and questions. Instead, put AMBITION into your objective and reach for your peak potential.

Part 3

Tools for Activating Your Ambition

Sample Road Map

This is an example of a simple self-development road map. Note that the actions cover all eight principles of *Activating your Ambition*.

Objective: I am in good physical condition, have increased my energy level, feel better, and have increased mental acuity.			
Obstacles to overcome: Lack of time to dedicate to working out, tendency to overeat.			
Plan Last Updated: Dec 15th			

AMBITION	Action or Milestone Description	Planned Date	Actual Date
A	Evaluate and select an exercise program to follow: • Ask friends about programs they recommend. • Research programs on Internet. • Talk to local fitness store.	Mar 1	Mar 12
	Evaluate and select a diet to follow: • Talk to my doctor about ideal weight and supplements. • Research diet and nutrition programs.	Mar 1	Mar 12
M	Take picture of my overweight self in swim trunks to carry around in wallet.	Mar 15	Mar 10
B	Engage in a confidence-boosting activity that uses my new fitness, e.g., 10K run.	July 1	Dec 15
	Avoid overeating by not becoming famished—eat five small meals a day.	Apr 8	ongoing
I	Plan workouts—Mon–Sat 6-7am, alternate cardio and strength daily.	Feb 1	Apr 5
	Review progress and update plan.	May 15	Oct 17
T	Wake up an hour earlier six days a week to work out.	Apr 1	ongoing
I	Begin workout program.	Apr 2	Apr 2
	Eat according to diet plan.	Apr 2	ongoing
	Look for opportunities to use new conditioning, e.g., mountain bike race.	Aug 30	Aug 30
O	Involve spouse and get her to start same exercise, diet program.	Mar 15	Mar 20
	Tell friends about goal and plans.	Apr 30	Apr 30
N	Stay on the exercise program for 120 days or until it becomes a habit.	Aug 1	Jun 1
	Stay on diet for 120 days until it becomes easy and routine.	Aug 1	Dec 15

Sample Daily Scorecard

Here is an example scorecard to track ongoing actions or progress against life objectives:

	Mon	Tues	Wed	Thurs	Fri	Sat	Sun
Nutrition – Eat fruit, vegetables, whole grains, and protein in limited portions; eat 5–6 times/day; no fried foods, pizza, candy	+	+	-	-	+	-	+
Exercise – One hour of cardio or strength training per day.	A	B	A	A	C	F	n/a
Reading – Thirty minutes of nonfiction per day.	45	30	30	15	0	30	60
Family – Two hours spent with family.	A	A	A	B	B	A	A
Intentional – 40 percent of day spent on proactive activity.	A	B	C	A	C	A	A
Fear – Fear did not limit or restrict me in any way. Used courage.	A	A	A	A	C	A	A
Exhibit EQ – Walked around office twice during the day to meet and talk to people.	+	-	=	+	+	n/a	n/a
Productivity – Little time wasted, followed "do, delegate, delete, or file" principle.	-	+	+	+	+	+	+
Positive Attitude – Attitude of gratitude; remained constructive in all communication.	+	-	+	+	+	-	+
Feedback – When I saw it, I said it. Gave constructive feedback.	+	+	-	-	+	-	+
Listening – Gave people my undivided attention when approached.	A	B	C	A	C	A	A
Community – Reinforced shared values, teamwork.	A	A	A	A	C	A	A
Partnering – Made one call to a partner, gave them something of value.	-	+	+	+	+	n/a	n/a
Conflict – Confronted conflict and engaged in constructive dialog.	-	+	+	+	+	+	n/a

This scorecard employs several scoring methods. Depending on the measure you are tracking, you might use a "+" or a "-"symbol in the box to represent that you achieved your daily goal or did not. You might also use a grading system like A, B, C, D, or F. For metrics needing more detail you might prefer to quantify what you did, e.g. read 30 minutes, ate 2500 calories, trained for 45 minutes. Use whatever system makes the most sense for you. What is important is you record and track your progress.

About the Author

Mike Hawkins

Mike Hawkins is a seasoned executive coach and expert in helping people reach their goals. He is president of Alpine Link Corporation, where he has become a respected practitioner, speaker, and thought-leader on self-improvement, business improvement, and leadership. He has a reputation for consistently leading organizations and individuals to higher levels of achievement.

Prior to founding Alpine Link Corp., he developed his practical perspectives on behavioral change through his own personal victories in self-improvement together with his unique combination of experience in engineering, sales, and senior management. He has worked in many industries, including management consulting, information technology, financial services, manufacturing, construction, energy, telecommunications, utilities, and nonprofits.

Throughout Mike's career, he has accepted the toughest assignments and excelled in overcoming challenging issues. He truly understands not just what to do and why to do it, but how to do it. In his executive coaching experience and in turning around underperforming businesses, he has uncovered recurring root cause issues that limit performance. As a result, Mike has refined several frameworks including Activating Your Ambition™, The SCOPE of Leadership™, and Peak Potential Selling™ to help organizations and individuals break through their limitations and achieve new levels of success.

To contact Mike Hawkins, e-mail ambition@alpinelink.com.